Gay Christians

PETER COLEMAN

Gay Christians

A Moral Dilemma

★

SCM PRESS
London

TRINITY PRESS INTERNATIONAL
Philadelphia

First published 1989

SCM Press   Trinity Press International
26–30 Tottenham Road   3725 Chestnut Street
London N1 4BZ   Philadelphia, Pa. 19104

British Library Cataloguing in Publication Data

Coleman, Peter
   Gay Christians.
   1. Homosexuality. Attitudes of Christian church, history
   I. Title
   261.8′35766′09

   ISBN 0–334–00532–9

Library of Congress Cataloging-in-Publication Data available

Photoset by J&L Composition Ltd, Filey, North Yorkshire
and printed in Great Britain by
Richard Clay Ltd, Bungay, Suffolk

CONTENTS

PREFACE

For more than thirty years the Christian churches have been actively debating the moral problem of homosexual behaviour. This book is intended as a guide to that debate, but set in a wider context, with a good deal of historical information, and an extensive review of the relevant passages from the Bible. But it is also about people, past and present, straight and gay, believers and unbelievers, saints and sinners, about how they have sometimes loved and forgiven each other, and sometimes feared and hated each other.

Moral problems are about people, about how they act, and about how they ought to act. To understand people is the first step towards talking sense about what 'ought' can mean for them, and so, before coming to scripture and history, an attempt has to be made to understanding those people who are different from the majority because they are homosexual. This is not easy for anyone like me who happens to be a heterosexual male; we cannot honestly pretend to get inside the skin of this different kind of person, whose sexuality is so like ours, and yet in crucial ways quite opposite. Fortunately, in our times, they have become free to speak for themselves.

Setting this debate in a wide context is important because Christianity is a religious faith which takes seriously the world and its history as an expression of God's love and activity. The historical background given here begins with a quite long description of the life style of the early Christians in the midst of a pagan culture and how the triumph of the church in the Christendom period meant that from the sixth century CE onwards, the time of Justinian, to the appointment of the Wolfenden Committee in 1954, the official moral teaching of the church and the Criminal Law of England were united in condemning homosexual behaviour.

Some detail is given of legal regulations from Roman times to the present day to show how society has set boundaries round this problem at different times in the Christian era. The change in English Law made by the Sexual Offences Act of 1967 is significant, not only because it broke that unity, a sign of a more general sundering between church and state morality made inevitable in an increasingly secular and pluralist society. It also marked the high point of the success of liberal opinion in post-war Britain, perhaps best described by the expression 'happy to tolerate differences' than by the more popular and misleading slogans of the time such as 'the permissive society' or 'the new morality'.

The Bible is for Christians the primary source of authority in questions of morality as of faith. Much of the debate in the churches about the morality of homosexual acts has focussed on the proper interpretation of biblical texts, and sometimes this has become a kind of test case for the broader issue of how scripture is to be used to yield its proper guidance for the contemporary moral problems of the world. I try to delve into the nowadays technical world of biblical scholarship in a cautious but detailed way to explain why the meanings of words and the situations when the authors of scripture originally wrote them down matters enormously if we are to understand aright how the traditional Christian hostility to homosexual behaviour was first formed.

The sudden arrival of the current AIDS epidemic in all parts of the world may seem to make a book like this totally unnecessary. At the time of writing, there is no definite sign of an antidote to the deadly Human Immunodeficiency Virus (HIV) and unless and until one is found, millions of people who infect each other with contaminated blood are doomed to die. The virus is passed in several ways: through previously used needles for injections, a hazard for drug takers; through the womb of an infected pregnant woman, a threat both to the foetus and to its mother, whose resistence may be lowered during pregnancy; and through any kind of sexual intercourse, vaginal or anal, not protected by a condom. The contraceptive pill gives no protection against HIV.

So far, statistics about the spread of the disease have shown that drug takers and active homosexual people are most at risk, but the scenario is changing. Homosexual people in developed countries are adopting a more cautious life style, while in less well informed societies, unchecked prostitution and casual sex spread the infection among heterosexuals. Education about the danger of AIDS, common sense and prudence are demanded of the human race to defeat this modern plague, and the abandonment of promiscuous unprotected sex will become a 'must' for all, irrespective of any debate about Christian morality.

That said, the fact that homosexual lovers may protect themselves from AIDS by using condoms would only make the debate about the morality of homosexual behaviour unnecessary among Christians if their rule against it was based solely on a prudential principle that one should not pass on a killing disease. A similar argument might be used, and indeed often has been, for justifying any kind of sexual relationship between heterosexual people provided they do not conceive unwanted children. As we shall see, for Christians the similarity of the two cases is not close, and in any case, the virtues of celibacy and chastity do not rest mainly on prudential arguments. Of course, prudence is a virtue, and although AIDS has to be regarded by moral theologians as an accidental genetic mutation, not a punishment from God for promiscuity, that does not mean that if fear of AIDS prompts a person to a more cautious life style, the Christians would object. They would be glad, but not content if fear were the only spur to moral responsibility. Analysing these and related moral problems is the subject of the last part of this book.

This book is intended for general readers, not for scholars, so notes and references to sources are kept to a minimum. In writing it, I have drawn on the extensive researches of many experts in this field, and the notes and bibliography show those books which I have found particularly valuable. Sometimes I have had to reduce a large block of information to its barest outlines; at others I mention minor incidents or facts about people which are strictly unnecessary to the main issue but may flesh out the story acceptably. The views I take on controversial aspects of this subject are my own, but that does not mean I wish to be polemical or press for a particular resolution of the debate.

I have drawn much material in this book from my experience of the English churches, our own theological tradition, and several specialist Working Parties of which I was a member but I hope that has not made for narrowness or lack of ecumenical and international perspective. All the churches have been wrestling equally with this moral problem in recent years, and in particular, there have been close links and cross-influences between the Christians in the United States of America and the United Kingdom. Many significant books have been published simultaneously both sides of the 'pond' as the Americans call the Atlantic, and resolutions of many church bodies in recent years show a family likeness. There has been an inevitable polarization between traditional and liberal views world wide, and although I cannot record the whole range of that, I quote American and Vatican sources sufficiently I hope for a fair balance.

It does not seem to me surprising that after thirty years the debate has not yet reached a definite conclusion. It is a difficult subject, asking Christians to come to terms with a kind of human sexuality which for the vast majority of them is alien to their own disposition and desires, and seeking moral approval for kinds of same sex friendship and love-making which are clearly contrary to a long established teaching of the churches. To the heterosexual person, some homosexual activities seem strange and repugnant, and this tends to complicate our attitudes to what might otherwise appear to be a reasonable request from a minority of the human race to live their own lives as best they can. Unlike many other claims to basic human rights, to which the Christian conscience has freely responded in recent years, the request from homosexual people that they should be left free to express their sexual difference in the particular ways open to them seems disconcerting.

It is not proving at all easy for heterosexual Christians to agree to this change, and this book tries to explain why that is so, and how the limits of tolerance have shifted back and forth in recent years. Those limits are set not by fashion, nor by moral codes and laws, but by loyalties. There is a proper loyalty Christians give to the teaching of the Bible and the tradition of the church. There is also a proper loyalty Christians give to any brother or sister in need, without such loyalty faith is dead. When a gay Christian asks for acceptance, those loyalties appear to clash.

PART ONE

★

1

The Clash of Loyalties

Introduction

The preface suggests that the moral problem about homosexual behaviour Christians have been debating in the past thirty years is best understood as a clash of loyalties between obeying a long established teaching of the church and the basic Christian moral principle 'love your neighbour in need'. I think that is the best short description of the central issue, but it is a judgment I make at the end of the period under review; it did not seem like that thirty years ago.

Human events do not follow clear and tidy patterns. Dividing the substance of this book into four separate parts, Sexuality, Bible, History, and Morality enables me to examine each of these components in the debate systematically, but such a system is somewhat artificial because most of the people involved at the time, church leaders, politicians, lawyers, theologians, ministers and laity were reacting to the pressure of events and asked to give often quick judgments on a difficult problem that had not been studied as a moral question for ages. It was a matter for the psychologists to worry about! Nearly everyone will have known people whom they thought to be homosexual, and had heard about Oscar Wilde, E. M. Forster, T. E. Lawrence and Victoria Sackville-West, to name a few among many whose homosexuality was mentioned in books published in the fifties. Most people were aware that both the law and the Christian attitude were officially opposed to homosexual acts, but many a blind eye was turned. Officially, gay church members were assumed to be celibate, but many pastors knew that was being somewhat economical with the truth.

So it seems worth while first to tell the story from 1950 to 1988, both chronologically to show what happened, and also in terms of the kinds of arguments which began to appear. I hope this fly on the wall approach will be useful preparation for the more detailed and technical discussion that follows and give a general idea of how the debate has taken shape. It may also encourage some freedom of choice, allowing readers to decide for themselves what aspects they are particularly interested in, and what they can happily skip.

A Change in the Law?

The public debate about homosexual behaviour was a consequence of some notable trials of well-known people in the mid-fifties, fully reported in the press. There was also at the time some evidence that people known to be homosexual were particularly susceptible to blackmail, and if they held sensitive positions in the armed forces or Government service, they might be a potential risk to national security. These trials and suspicions alerted public opinion, but not all the anxiety was directed at those who broke the law or might betray secrets; others feared there would be unjustified persecution of people who were of homosexual orientation but in all respects decent citizens.

The churches were drawn into the public debate not only because of their tradition of hostility to homosexual practices, but also because they were already much involved in a re-assessment of their own principles of sexual morality. The post-war world was experiencing a liberalization of attitudes towards sex outside marriage and to divorce. The development of safe and easy-to-use contraceptives and dire warnings about excessive population growth were combined with a new perception of the meaning of sexuality. It was seen to be more about how people express their relationships to each other in depth, less about pro-creation. On the one hand, the Christians felt the demand of loyalty to their traditional stance on all these issues; on the other hand, they wanted to take seriously the new understandings of human sexuality and personal relationships. Since their fundamental principles of morality were generous love and the acceptance of people as they were, perhaps God was asking the churches to respond positively to the new situation and not merely withdraw in judgment. That said, it was not primarily this awareness among Christians of a clash of loyalties between old and new truth about sexuality which moved them to share in the public debate about the morality of homosexual behaviour. They were pushed somewhat reluctantly into it because they were asked to consider a change in the law.

English Criminal Law had long forbidden the act of anal inter-course, or sodomy as it was often called, but from 1885 onwards, to this had been added the lesser offence of gross indecency. The original intention of this law had been the protection of minors, both boys and girls, and had been passed by Parliament at a time when child prostitution was an ugly feature of Victorian London, and other large cities. But it was a loosely-worded statute, and considerably widened the scope for police action against known homosexual people. Oscar Wilde was the first victim of the new law, but as time passed, prosecutions became few and intermittant, for the social problem it was directed at largely vanished with the start of the First World War. The police responded to complaints about homosexual assault or indecency, but did not harry unnecessarily. When Cold War fears of espionage came into conflict with the general mood of liberalization in sexual attitudes, the Government decided it was time to set up a Home Office Committee to review the situation and advise whether or not the existing law was satisfactory.

In the event, the Wolfenden Committee recommended that the 1885 Act should be replaced by a new law which removed homosexual behaviour in private between adults over twenty-one years old from prohibition by the Criminal Law. Ten years passed between that Report and its implementation by the Sexual Offences Act of 1967, and this period allowed a very wide-ranging debate about the new principle. The Church of England had been asked to submit evidence to the Wolfenden Committee, and did so through its Moral Welfare Committee, arguing in favour of a change in the law on the ground that sexual offenders were more likely to be helped by medical and psychological treatment than by prison.

The cautious approval of the Moral Welfare Committee came as a surprise to some members of Parliament, and it was not at first clear if the Church of England would officially support the Wolfenden Committee proposal. That it would was made plain by the Archbishop of Canterbury in a House of Lords debate in 1965, when he stated that homosexual acts were wrong, but the plea of the Wolfenden Report had cogency in that not all sins are properly given the status of crimes. The Archbishop's carefully worded opinion was based on the important distinction in moral philosophy between crime and sin, but as was to be expected, it was interpreted in various ways. It reassured the Government that they could implement the new law without a protest from the established church, and in fact the other major churches expressed the same view. The Church of England Assembly gave its approval to the main recommendations by a narrow margin of seventeen votes in a debate on 14 November 1957 introduced by the Bishop of Exeter, a leading moral theologian. But in the minds of ordinary people, the distinction between crime and sin was easily misunderstood, and led some to assume that the church had adopted the new morality and gone soft on sexual sin.

The churches' cautious approval of the change in the law was in reality one sign among many that the old close partnership between church and state morality could be no longer sustained in the pattern that had been appropriate for a nation whose citizens were for the most part practising Christians. England, like most other developed countries in the world, had been influenced by the philosophy of the Enlightenment from the eighteenth century onwards, and had become pluralist and secular. No doubt the vast majority of the population still gave some kind of assent to the existence of God, but it was a folk religion rather than an active discipleship, and the church could no longer expect the Government to base all its legislation on specifically Christian principles. As with divorce, so with homosexuality, the churches could hope to teach and influence society; less than in the past could they press their morality in all respects on a country which now included both confident atheists and adherants to other religions. In any case, it was obvious in the sixties that the churches were uncertain among themselves about many moral issues, and it soon became clear that the problem of homosexuality was to become a test case of the wider dispute between those who held traditional views and the liberals.

An Old Problem Reconsidered

In one sense, for Christians, the debate about the morality of homosexual behaviour can be seen as the re-working of an old problem, for it is clear from the pages of the New Testament, and other writings from the first century onwards, that the subject was considered by the earliest Christian thinkers. Although the evidence is sparse, documents surviving from that period usually express un-deviating hostility, and show that the leaders of the early church were aware of homosexual activities and firmly opposed to what they considered an immoral aspect of the pagan society in which they lived.

As the church gained dominance in Europe, that hostility was incorporated in both its Canon Law and the State Laws throughout Christendom. These laws were in many respects basically similar to those of the old Roman system, but reviewed and revised to reflect the precepts of Christian morality. Thus, for marriage, the Christian influence led to the establishment of a matrimonial law which stressed life-long commitment to a monogamous relationship. This had in fact been required by the old Patrician law, but had been gradually eroded as the Empire decayed. The Christian view was of course equally consonant with the teaching of Judaism. Similarly, for homosexual acts, the long-standing prohibitions in Athenian and Roman law, frequently disregarded though they were, found new and strong expression in the rules of Christendom. This, again, matched what was taught in the Old Testament and in the Epistles of St Paul.

In questioning this long-established tradition, many Christians in the sixties argued on one or more of four main grounds that that modification of the old rule was necessary. These grounds were the changed perception of sexuality, the realization that there was a credibility gap between the official line of church and state and the actual way homosexual people were treated, the need to come to terms with changed views about the authority of the Bible, and the emergence of the movement for Gay Liberation.

The first argument claims that the new perception of human sexuality has to be accepted, but it belongs to a pattern of social life and culture fundamentally different from the ancient one into which Christianity was born, and out of which the New Testament was written. St Paul's strictures on homosexual behaviour, the main texts on which the Christian hostility is based, are a continuation of a tradition firmly embedded in the Old Testament and its time. Attempts to read off a solution for our day from what happened in Sodom three thousand years ago are mistaken, the argument goes. Instead of a strong sense of an extended family, and strict regulations for association between the sexes, we have got rid of sexual discrimination in many respects, learnt the lessons of the feminist movement, and socially and at work relate in open ways which would have horrified the moral susceptibilities of the Jews. Not only in our freedom of contact between the sexes socially, but also in our recognition of private choice rather than public rule as a guide to relationships is our life style totally different from theirs. We can add to that difference all the knowledge of ourselves as persons which comes to us from the discoveries of the behavioural sciences, notably psychology, and related aspects of medical and genetic research. The two cultures cannot be matched.

Secondly, history shows there is a credibility gap between the official teaching against homosexual behaviour and what actually happened throughout Christian history. As we have already noticed, for the greater part of Christian history, State Law punished those who committed homosexual acts, and while the Law maintained the same rule as the church, the church had little need to question it. To be more precise, for European countries from the days of the Roman Emperor Justinian in the sixth century until the development of new and less restrictive legislation in Napoleonic times, the prohibition against sodomy was fixed in the Canon and State Laws of Christendom. It remained the same in Britain until 1967, and continues in Islamic countries who base their laws on the Koran. As the eminent Jurist Sir William Blackstone had expressed it in his commentary on the Laws of England in 1753, sodomy was: 'the infamous crime against nature not fit to be named among Christians.'

That was the official view, but a little digging into church history soon showed that the offence was by no means as absent in the life of the church and the nation as this dictum suggested. Sodomy was fiercely condemned in many early Christian writings, and church synods and councils passed resolutions forbidding it, obviously because they needed to. The regulations of the medieval religious and monastic orders included detailed regulations concerning the penitential discipline of those who committed homosexual sins. The Reformation theologians maintained the condemnation in their Bible commentaries, and Christian social reformers in Victorian times attacked the vice of homosexual prostitution. In the manuals of pastoral theology provided for clergy in guiding those who asked their counsel, cautious advice was given. The standard work of moral and pastoral theology for Roman Catholic priests, published in English in 1935, discussed homosexual sin in Latin to protect the laity from knowledge that would have harmed them. From Victorian times onwards, a number of novels discussed homosexual relationships as a major or minor theme. These were sometimes printed privately, or suppressed by the police as obscene, but the Lady Chatterley case demonstrated that the law was relaxing its attempts at censorship, and serious literature about gay life began to appear in print.

In sum, although the churches officially took a firm line, in counselling and pastoral care this was not always followed. There was of course a private system of discipline for those clergy who were found guilty in court, but public trial was avoided if possible and bishops preferred to use their own discretionary powers. As more of this history became known, it began to look as if the churches had been officially maintaining a strict moral stance while practising in private a much more flexible and merciful situation ethic. It was time for this dichotomy to be openly faced.

Thirdly, attitudes to the Bible and its authority on moral questions had changed. Biblical scholarship over the past two hundred years has shown that each and every book in the Bible has a literary history of its own. It was written out of a particular situation and context, and the truth it contains, and the meaning to be given to any particular passage is to be assessed in a careful way, recognizing this history. We cannot use the Bible as a lawyer might look up a Statute or case as a precedent, nor as a professional man or woman might refer to a code of practice. As we shall see, searching and interpreting scripture relevant to homosexual behaviour has proved in the past thirty years to be a complex and sometimes disputed process.

In the sixties, the emergence of an open and articulate movement among homosexual people for what is usually called Gay Liberation became possible because it was anticipated that the Wolfenden Committee recommendations would become law, and therefore the risk of 'coming out' was lessened. Organizations like the Albany Trust pioneered calm and informative publications about the difficulties gay people faced, and they ran a helpful counselling service. Several Christian leaders supported the Trust. The word gay was used as a generic term for men and women who came out, not because they were happy in the normal English sense of that word, but because it was somewhat self affirming. The homosexual association of the word derived from the name of a Greek youth, Gannymede, who in classical Greek legend had fascinated Zeus, the father of the Gods. There is little evidence to suggest that the homosexual orientation as such is more frequently found in our world than in the past.

The size of the gay minority, for so long hidden, now became apparent. Most civilizations of which we have records, both sophisticated and primitive, seem to have between five and ten per cent of their populations of homosexual orientation. What changes is the degree of recognition any form of society gives to this significant minority of their citizens. The Gay Liberation movement, and the related political movement for Gay Rights made certain that was recognized. That is not to say that it has won easy approval, and sometimes it appears that the social discrimination against gay people has become more severe than it used to be when there was scant public awareness of homosexuality at all. Some Christians reacted to Gay Lib with strong sympathy, for others it was frankly a shock, and reaction set in.

Back to the Bible

The emergence of the Gay Lib movement added a new focus to the long-standing debate about the authority of the Bible, and probably because they were on the whole unsympathetic to any supposed challenge to its unique authority, it was among the Evangelical section of the churches that most alarm was felt. Whatever some styles of biblical scholarship might say, if the Bible gave clear teaching on the subject, there was no need to look beyond it. Searching the scriptures for guidance about homosexuality, however, proved to be no easy matter.

To anticipate a problem which will be dealt with more thoroughly later, there is as it happens no word in the original languages of the Bible, neither in the Hebrew of the Old Testament nor in the Greek of the New Testament, which can be precisely translated as homosexual. Although the word is actually a compound of Greek and Latin nouns, it was not used in that combination as an English word until late Victorian times, and then only at first in technical journals. The more familiar word, sodomy, which for much longer has been used in legal language to mean, precisely, anal intercourse, is not used in that sense in any of the standard English translations of the Bible. As the proper name for a long ago destroyed town in Palestine, Sodom occurs frequently, and the people who lived there are often described as particularly wicked, but it would be quite misleading to suppose that every time the word sodom appeared in the Bible, a reference to homosexual sin was intended. It sometimes does, but it depends on the context.

The first serious attempt to review the texts was made by the scholarly Dr Sherwin Bailey, who as secretary of the working party which produced evidence for the Wolfenden Committee, did much of the ground work himself. He published a fuller assessment soon after, notable not only for its detailed scrutiny of all biblical texts which could possibly be relevant, but also for a long historical section which brought together much information previously largely unknown. Bailey was cautious, already well-known for his teaching in defence of Christian marriage, but his interpretation of the biblical references to homosexuality tended to ameliorate their severity. It would be unfair to call him a liberal but he clearly thought the traditional view was unjust, and hoped to show that the Bible did not support it.

In particular, Bailey took the meaning of the Sodom story to be a rebuke for inhospitality, and Paul's condemnation as limited to those heterosexual people who perverted their own nature in homosexual acts. The hostility of the Christian tradition, he argued, was set more by the antagonism between the Jews and the Greeks in the inter-testamental period than by proper understanding of the canonical scriptures. Bailey worked as a pioneer, at great speed, and not all his views have stood the test of time, but he is rightly respected for showing all those who have since worked on this material where they have to search.

If Bailey's argument was controversial, his mastery of texts and ancient languages was difficult for the ordinary Christian to criticize. Most Christians learn the contents of the Bible selectively, at church or in private reading. Lectionaries and systems of Bible reading notes concentrate on the major themes of faith, the history of salvation. This means churchgoers are more familiar with some parts of the Pentateuch and the major prophets than with, for example, key passages in Leviticus which are crucial for discovering biblical teaching about homosexuality. The New Testament Gospels are better known than the Epistles, and they do not mention the subject. For moral questions, the Ten Commandments and the Sermon on the Mount are the basic teaching blocks, though St Paul's description of the Christian graces set out in the simple form of a household code in Galatians is an obvious addition. In other words, searching the pages of the Bible for guidance on minor topics, as homosexuality clearly was for the biblical authors, is no easy task for the non-specialist.

To put the matter another way, the churches have through the centuries paid close attention to scripture on major issues of faith, and indeed the Reformation sprang from just this kind of attention to questions like forgiveness and justification by faith, the authority of Popes, bishops, and the meaning of sacraments. But we are not used to handling scripture as a text book for solving moral problems. I stress this now in a preliminary way because some of the difficulty contemporary Christians have found in coming to any consensus about the biblical texts on this subject lies in the disparate and not always suitable methods of approach to the Bible they have used. It is understandable that a Christian puzzled by what he hears on the media or reads of a controversial church report will turn to scripture in the hope that he will find there some clear guidance, a text which puts the matter beyond doubt. And if he finds that other Christians, and particularly Bible scholars, take different and often tentative views, he will feel irritated, and inclined to adopt whatever solution seems to be most simple, even if that means being selective in the texts he follows.

It is an old preacher's wisdom that a text without a context is a pretext, and therefore the search for biblical guidance about homosexuality has required a substantial amount of digging into the context of biblical references to make sure we understand aright what we are reading. Contextual study of course includes not only some awareness of the historical and social situation which existed when the texts were first written or gathered together, but also some grasp of the linguistic significance; what did these words mean at that time?

Bailey's ameliorating interpretation of the biblical texts in the fifties was at first widely accepted, especially by those who shared his view that they were unfairly used to condemn all homosexuals, but when the question 'what did these words mean to those who wrote them down like this?' was further pondered, it seemed clear that the prohibition was intended to apply to all homosexual acts, and not to perverted heterosexuals. Those Christians who were convinced that the church had rightly understood the biblical basis of the traditional teaching were reassured, and as we shall see, the latest translations of the Bible have well-nigh universally adopted modern explicit language to remove any doubt of what the original meant to say. For some Christians, these arguments about words have probably seemed tedious, and perhaps reminiscent of the methods of the Jewish scribes rebuked in the Gospels, but nearly two thousand years separates us from the situation which gave birth to the New Testament. We have had to be sure we know what its authors meant, though that is not necessarily the same as knowing what it ought to mean for us.

Assessing the Tradition

In this debate, we have had to learn to handle scripture properly, and at the same time face the fact that the Christian moral tradition, while not inconsistent with scripture, and indeed based on it and checked by it, also develops a proper life and history of its own. What began as a judgment of the Apostles and Fathers is repeated in preaching and instruction to catechumens, written down and declared in Council decisions, and by these means becomes entrenched in the moral consciousness of God's people. Once there, it sticks, defended as a Roman Catholic might say, by the Magisterium of the church which does not err.

One can demonstrate this ability of Christian moral principles to develop an enduring life of their own by the obvious example of marriage. Our tradition says that this human institution is provided by and approved of by God himself, as part of his creative order for mankind. The still much loved preface to the *Book of Common Prayer* marriage service simply states:

> it is an honourable estate, instituted by God in the time of man's innocency, ... which holy estate, Christ adorned and beautified with his presence, and first miracle that he wrought, in Cana of Galilee.

Later in the service, there is a direct quotation from a saying of Jesus (Those whom God has joined together, let no man put asunder (Matt. 19.6; Mark. 10.9)) but it was assumed by the compilers of the Prayer Book, (and by those of the ASB in our day) that the people present in church were familiar with the Old Testament texts from Genesis which point to this doctrine, and with the Gospels where it is re-affirmed. One has to say that not only is the Prayer Book Preface in fact a construction, perfectly properly of course, from several texts scattered in scripture, but also that the major teaching St John enshrines in the story of the wedding at Cana is not about marriage. No doubt he and his readers knew Jesus approved of it, but John wants to tell us that the miracle of the water turned into wine shows the superiority of Christ's sacrifice on the cross to the now redundant Jewish system of atonement by animal sacrifices oft repeated. St John wishes us to understand that the water of purification becomes the wine of Christ's blood. In fact the ASB marriage service limits the reference to Cana to make clear Jesus was a guest at it, and in effect shifts the emphasis – Christ, through his spirit is with us now.

Realizing from this example that deriving Christian moral teaching from the pages of the Bible is not always as straightforward as it seems, though none the less a proper and necessary task, is a salutary warning. In a similar way, repugnance to homosexual practices was without question so long entrenched within Christian morality that when in our day its scriptural basis had to be re-worked, it is almost true to say that at the beginning no one was very sure where to look. All the books of moral theology had always said it was wrong; not many people knew why, at least in terms of a biblical basis.

The function of Christian tradition is to clarify and preserve God's revelation, not to replace it, but this will mean, as the proper exegesis of scripture also requires, a continual re-making in language and thought forms which enable it to be received by contemporary people. Perhaps an example at this stage will help.

Traditional Jewish religious teaching distinguishes between the status of men and women, and some sections of modern Judaism will regard that distinction as God given and unchangeable. In present day Israel, as in most other Western States, the Feminist Movement is challenging this tradition as immoral, contrary to human rights and dignities, and in effect demanding that this attitude be abandoned as a left-over perspective from more primitive times. Even if the legal system accepts such a change, it remains the case that orthodox Jews have to decide whether or not to agree, or to maintain their own tradition in matters where the rule of law does not apply. Thus, in some synagogues, (as in mosques, for Islam maintains the same rule) a distinction is preserved at worship and in ministry between men and women.

Now it is simple enough to imagine a dialogue among the Jews of a particular congregation about what should happen in their own synagogue. Should they stick to the tradition, modify it, or change it directly? Much will depend, as the dialogue continues, on such factors as the importance the congregation puts on the notion of loyalty to a common tradition and inheritance; asking perhaps how free they are to decide the matter for themselves, how far they must await a corporate and united decision among their fellow orthodox Jews. Then they will have to evaluate how secure and certain the old tradition really is. Was it very clearly expressed in the old documents? Are those documents actually from the date supposed, or in fact later copies which may reflect a partisan or local view? Then, they can ask was there originally a variety of views? In the days when the tradition was settled, did a respectable minority accept the equality of women, even if the decision of the majority went the other way? Was the tradition as then settled based on factual information which has since proved to be mistaken? (It is, for example, a discovery of our century that the sex of a child is determined by its father's chromosomes, so any moral rule of past times based on the assumption that the mother was responsible has to be jettisoned. One wonders how King Henry VIII would have reacted to this discovery had he known it!)

This must seem a very complicated set of questions to work through, and yet a catechism of a similar kind has to be addressed to the Christian tradition. The law has changed, but that does not settle whether or not practising homosexual people should be welcome in church. How loyal to our tradition ought we to be if we perceive it leads to rejection of some of our fellow Christians? Is it a matter that each congregation can settle for itself, or does it require an ecumenical and universal agreement among the denominations? What do we know of the formation of the traditional attitude?. Was it an accurate reflection of the teaching of Jesus, or was it like slavery, a problem that could not be dealt with in the circumstances of the time but would be changed later. Was it based on inaccurate information – the assumption that sexual orientation was a matter of choice not nature? And so the debate has gone on.

Having to question its moral tradition like this has not been an easy task for the churches, especially in these days of instant mass media attention. Members of Synods and similar bodies have had to accept that however difficult the subject under discussion, there is an expectation that the guts of it can be reduced to a few lines for a television news report. If that is not forthcoming, the church faces the humiliation of seeing a serious discussion distorted to match the reporters' views of what it ought to do or say. Thus, in 1987, the debate on homosexual behaviour introduced to the Synod by the Rev. Tony Higton through the private member's motion procedure led to the passing of an amended resolution containing the phrase 'falling short of God's design'.

The amendment was probably the best form of words to find general agreement in such a situation, but they sounded like a fudge to the media. 'Pulpit poofs can stay' one newspaper proclaimed. As some people knew, but not apparently the press, a special working party had already been set up to report privately to the House of Bishops, but that group needed further time to complete its work, and it was uncertain when or if its report would be published. It helped neither the church nor gay people to have such an uneasy debate with what looked like a panic solution to meet media demands.

The signs of disarray shown by the General Synod debate in 1987 was not for lack of previous work on the problem of homosexual behaviour; it was because the membership of the Synod remained divided in their convictions, and had found little to agree about in the sequence of reports and studies prepared by the Board of Social

Responsibility and similar bodies in other denominations. There had been three previous Anglican reports, in 1956, 1970, and 1979 and these are discussed in detail in the historical review in Part 4. The 1979 Report, prepared by a working party chaired by the Bishop of Gloucester, was *received* by the General Synod after debate in 1981, a guarded non-committed recognition. A Methodist report of the same year was treated much the same. Vatican statements remained firmly traditional, though American Catholic Bishops indicated a fresh approach was called for. It was clear that however much the liberals piped, authoratative church bodies, no doubt accurately reflecting the opinion in most pews, were not prepared to dance to the new tune.

This survey has described in outline how the debate in the churches about the sinfulness of homosexual behaviour has developed, since it ceased to be a criminal offence. The rest of the book fills in the substance. I end it with a re-iteration of the central problem to be solved. The moral dilemma about homosexuality presents itself to some Christians in the form: How dare I feel sympathy for gay people and their sexual behaviour if my basic commitment is to Christ, and to the truth of God's will as revealed in the teaching of scripture and the tradition of the church through the ages? In hard cases, loyalty to Christ has to override human sympathy. Other Christians can and do sense the dilemma in a directly opposite way. Since loyalty to Christ and scripture requires the acceptance of all people in love not judgment and that has to include not only inadequate, unfortunate and handicapped people but also those who are simply different, therefore I must accept homosexuals and allow them to express their sexuality in the only ways open to them. I cannot order them to be celibate because that is a vocation, not a rule, even if traditional Christianity tried to make it one.

Some ten years ago, in a more comprehensive review of the situation up to that time, I concluded that the trend in discussion had been towards more tolerance and understanding, though no representative body of any major Christian church had actually decided that the old traditional hostility was wrong. That is still the position. In terms of tolerance, I now suspect that the Christian world is more divided than it was. The clash of loyalties has sharpened and progress in the debate seems stalled. It would be good if we could reconcile our differences, and begin to be more positive.

PART TWO

2

Understanding Homosexuality

Introduction

The publicity given to Gay Liberation movements in recent years, and the freedom to 'come out', mean that few people can be unaware that a substantial minority of the human race, usually estimated as between five and ten per cent of adult men and women in the developed countries of the world are of homosexual orientation. The open presence of this gay minority has been associated in many minds with the emergence of 'permissiveness' to which the churches and conservatively minded people have been on the whole unsympathetic, and the beginning of the AIDS epidemic has added to the mood of disquiet and anxiety which surrounds gay people in the community. Against a mistaken belief that homosexuality is a new phenomenon, or at least one that has grown enormously since the 1967 Act was passed, we need to set the fact that some recognition of homosexual people and of various aspects of their behaviour is to be found in most forms of human society, ancient and modern, the Pacific Islands and the ranches of Arizona as well as Soho and the Bronx, Oxford and Cambridge as well as Athens and Rome.

Anthropological and sociological studies show the universal presence of a minority of people with a homosexual orientation in the nations of the world. Similarly, in law, in literature and especially in the teaching about it found in all the major religions, there is the clearest possible evidence that homosexual behaviour has been approved, tolerated, laughed at and rebuked throughout human history. In Indian and Chinese religion it has been tolerated, in Islam it has not. There was nothing unique about the contrast between Jewish and Canaanite attitudes to sodomy, some ancient Greeks called it the disease from the East; the English once called it the French vice, and vice versa. In the debate about it at the 1988 Lambeth Conference, one African Bishop said it was a corruption brought to his country by the Arabs. The only sure truth is that homosexual people are part of the human race, everywhere.

The brief description of homosexuality given here is limited to a summary of medical opinion about its nature and causes. The inadequacy of what follows in terms of personal feeling and even more in terms of affection and love will be readily apparent. But equally, reticence and embarrassment have long been powerful influences in the Christian tradition concerning homosexuality, and if that tradition is now confronted with an excess of explicitness and pornographic polemic, then the common-place facts are worth setting down even if they can do little more than challenge some misunderstandings.

After a century of medical and psychological study, the generally agreed facts about homosexuality are few. It is clear that as research proceeds, no easy solution to the question of aetiology has been found, nor is there at present much confidence in the probability of successful treatment and cure. Indeed, medical opinion seems to have moved on to the view that the homosexual orientation in itself is not pathological, and therefore, as such, calls for no interference by doctors. Homosexual people are not ill. It remains true, of course, that some people who are homosexual do need treatment, and their sexual anxiety may be part of a more complex problem which does call for help, though that can equally be said of heterosexual people.

Words and Meanings

In modern English, medical terminology usually makes use of Latin and Greek words, and the related sciences psychology and psychiatry thus refer to reasoning (logy) about 'the soul' and its healing (iatry). Some confusion may be caused when roots of both the ancient languages are combined. The Greek prefix *homo-* has been added to the Latin noun *sexus* to indicate an attraction or sexual preference for the same sex, in distinction from the more usual 'hetero-sexual' attraction, where the prefix means 'other' or 'different'. The confusion occurs where the Greek *homo-* is mistakenly read as the identical Latin word for 'man', thereby apparently implying that the homosexual choice is concerned with males, whereas in fact, it equally applies to females. Female homosexuality is also described as *'lesbianism'*, taking its name from the Island of Lesbos, where the Greek poet Sappho once lived in a female community and wrote erotic poetry which is often, though need not be, interpreted as predominantly homosexual in tone. The term *'homophobia'* has recently emerged to describe the reaction of fear and dislike which the heterosexual majority tend to express to homosexual culture and people.

The terms 'homosexual' and 'heterosexual' can be used in a range of meanings. Narrowly, they indicate the direction of the sexual drive, that is, the sexual gender to which a person will be attracted in terms of eroticism or sexual behaviour. Whether or not any action ensues depends, of course, on circumstances and intentions, and therefore to designate a person as being homosexual need not imply actual sexual activity with the same sex any more than it does with heterosexual people. But in popular and more pejorative use identifying a person as having a homosexual character is often taken to mean that he or she is sexually active as one.

One way of avoiding this mistake is to distinguish the homosexual *condition* from homosexual *behaviour*, but this distinction is in some ways unsatisfactory, for it suggests a clearer separation between disposition and action than the nature of human sexuality warrants. A person's awareness of another's sexuality does not operate in sharply distinct categories, and the components of interest, attraction, friendship, love and physical expression present in relationships are influenced by moral and practical considerations as they develop or fade rather than by simple switching from 'condition' to 'behaviour'. That said, it is useful to be able to indicate when actual physical 'lovemaking' is being referred to, and in this book, '*homosexual behaviour*' or '*homosexual genital acts*' are used to describe this.

Such terms as 'sexual behaviour' and 'love-making' are, of course, ambiguous and are not necessarily limited to descriptions of vaginal or anal intercourse among heterosexual and homosexual couples respectively. Although *anal intercourse*, also known as sodomy or buggery, is still technically illegal, even within marriage, it may be used by heterosexual couples as a means of contraception or as a variant form of sexual pleasure. Some male homosexuals, but probably a minority, prefer it, but the majority of them seem to find mutual masturbation and other forms of erotic contact more satisfactory. Aesthetic and hygienic considerations also may be relevant. Among Lesbians similar behaviour is found. The Latin words '*fellatio*' and '*cunnilingus*', found chiefly in the ascetic theology of ancient and mediaeval times, refer to the oral stimulation of male or female genitalia, between both hetero- and homosexual couples. The modern expression is usually '*oral sex*' and is quite widely recommended in some magazines and manuals concerned with sexual techniques.

Before the present day terminology emerged, other expressions to describe homosexuality were used, mostly implying explicit physical contact. Among such expressions were '*pederasty*', '*unnatural vice*', '*sodomy*' (from the biblical tradition) and '*buggery*', which is now an archaic legalism, but originated as a term of abuse for a group of Christian heretics in Bulgaria, who were supposed to match their false beliefs with perverted sexuality. Among slang terms, '*gay*' has become a popular description among homosexual people themselves, etymologically based on the legend of Ganymede, and *'fairy'*, *'pansy'* and *'queer'* are slang homophobic expressions. Of more importance are the terms 'inversion' and 'perversion', used by the early psychologists and Freud to distinguish between those whose condition was exclusively homosexual and those whose sexual drive could be directed either way. The expressions *'bi-sexual'*, *'ambi-sexual'* or *'inter-sexual'* mean, according to context, either those whose physical structure is hermaphrodite, or those whose sexual orientation is neither exclusively hetero- or homo-sexual.

Paedophilia is the modern term for all kinds of sexual relationships between adults and young children of the same or opposite sex. *Pederasty* is sometimes still used for this, but originally among the Greeks referred only to homosexual relationships between adult males and post-pubertal male youths. Paedophilia describes both heterosexual and homosexual relationships, where an ante-pubertal child is involved. By the Sexual Offences Act of 1967, adults over twenty-one may consent to homosexual behaviour in private, but the general law concerning heterosexual intercourse places the age of consent at sixteen years. Current medical opinion suggests that *paedophilia* is best regarded as a sexual abnormality and, like *voyeurism* and *fetichism*, may require treatment or restraint where others are at risk or affronted. Since such problems occur for heterosexual people as well as homosexuals, they are not further considered in this book.

Physical and Genetic Factors

Human sexuality can be described in a number of ways. The most obvious is physical appearance. At birth, the baby is designated male or female from observation of its external genitalia, though it is now possible to discover the gender of a foetus by examination of the amniotic fluid that surrounds it in the womb. Body shape, appearance, voice and styles of dress usually conform to the genetic distinction in broad terms, though the wide range of human physical types, as well as changes in fashion, can deceive a casual observer.

The physical distinction between male and female results genetically from the chromosomal pattern established at conception. Human cells normally contain twenty-three pairs of chromosomes, of which one pair, usually called XX or XY, determines the sex of the person, as female or male respectively. Women produce in the ovary eggs having X chromosomes, and male spermatozoa develop in the testes having either an X or a Y chromosome. At the moment of conception the fusion of the male X with the female X establishes a female, while that of a male Y with a female X establishes a male. Since a man produces equal numbers of X and Y spermatozoa, the sex of the child is random and should be statistically approximately equal. In fact, some six per cent more boys are conceived, especially among younger parents, but men are slightly less robust so that by the age of thirty-three the numbers of men and women living have evened out.

Chromosomal abnormalities occur in a small number of conceptions where an extra or missing chromosome leads to untypical development. Thus an additional chromosome on the twenty-first pair leads to Down's syndrome or mongolism, present in perhaps one in seven hundred viable babies, and rarer additions to other pairs of chromosomes are known. Such variation has also been found in the sex chromosomes, notably XO and XXX in females, and XXY and XYY in males. XO females, suffering from Turners syndrome may not develop properly at puberty, and similar effects may be found where the XXX pattern is present. Among males, the XXY pattern (Klinefelter's syndrome) may result in reduced sexual drive and poor genital development, while the XYY pattern produces men who can be unusually tall, but not thereby exceptionally masculine. Some evidence suggests this category includes a higher than expected proportion of men who suffer from psychiatric conditions and perhaps criminal tendencies.

Research into these chromosomal variations is relatively recent. The sex determination factor itself was not firmly demonstrated until 1959 although the chromosomal differences between males and females were observed earlier in this century. While progress has been rapid, greatly assisted by new microscopic techniques in conjunction with cell staining, no clear evidence has yet been found of a direct chromosomic origin for homosexuality.

After conception, the basic physical pattern of the developing foetus is female, but from the seventh week onwards the sex glands or gonads follow the already established genetic 'instructions' and begin to secrete hormones, androgens for males, and oestrogens for females. Both hormones are, in fact, produced in every foetus, oestrogens being a development from androgens and the balance of each is important. Provided this is normal, male or female internal and external genital organs develop in the familiar anatomical pattern, while certain brain cells act as receptors for these hormones and build up patterns which eventually form the male and female characteristics.

After birth, but probably within the first five years of life, the child learns its gender type and behaves accordingly. This process, sometimes called 'imprinting' is complex, partly a response to external infuences – learning to correspond with being a boy or a girl as society and the family demonstrate the two roles, and partly an expression of all that has been 'laid down' by genetic distinction and hormonal influence. When the hormonal chemistry is not balanced in the normal way, variations in development of the internal and external sex organs takes place, and this leads to various kinds of inter-sexual characteristics. A person may grow up with apparently male or female external genitalia, but in fact have the opposite chromosomal pattern. If detected early in childhood, injection of the correct hormone may assist the formation of the correct physical organs, genetically speaking, and in later life, so-called 'sex-change' operations can sometimes remedy the chemical mistake by anatomical adjustments. These inter-sexual problems are rare and do not, in themselves, explain homosexuality, though they may cause some people uncertainty about their sexual role and homosexual behaviour may result.

The normal process of sexual development is completed at puberty, when the pituitary gland stimulates the sexual glands to produce more of the appropriate hormones, the secondary sexual characteristics develop and the various components of the reproductive systems become fertile. It is often through the medical investigation of infertility or incapacity for satisfactory intercourse, that the underlying genetic and hormonal imbalance comes to light and steps can be taken to alleviate its consequences.

Reports of research in progress on rats and other small mammals suggest that artificially introduced alterations in the hormonal balance at early stages of development can lead to homosexual characteristics being demonstrated later. Workers in this field have found that the neurophysiology of humans is much more complex, and probably includes other as yet unidentified transmitters as well as the sex hormones, so it would be precipitate to claim at this stage that the causes of homosexuality are hormonal, or could be corrected at the foetal stage by appropriate injections.

Hormonal injections have been found to affect the intensity of the sexual drive in humans, but the effect is to strengthen or diminish the drive in the already established direction, not to alter its direction. Since the technology required to measure the minute quantities of the hormonal fluids in the body has only recently been developed, it is probable that further experiment will help our understanding of the importance or otherwise of this body chemistry as a physical factor in the aetiology of the homosexual condition. There is some evidence to suggest that such a genetic factor may dispose towards certain personality traits which, in turn, increase the likelihood of homosexuality emerging. Similarly, some recent research indicates that if pregnant women are subjected to unusual stress, their testosterone level drops, and a factor like this could affect the foetus and predispose the future child towards a more homosexual orientation. No clear results are assured of any of these theories, but, at present, it seems that hormonal factors are at least as important as environmental ones in the aetiology of homosexuality. The best guess is that it is caused by a combination of both factors, perhaps of equal significance.

Sexual Orientation

Although necessary for clarity, the simple division of people as either homo- or heterosexual is misleading; most of us are more complex than that. The recognition that the drive of human sexuality is not consistently and exclusively directed towards the same or opposite sex, but is better represented as in varying degrees flexible in aim, was demonstrated in a convincing way by Dr Albert Kinsey and has been confirmed by subsequent research. He suggested a seven point scale, reflecting his findings that the majority of the men and women interviewed could recall some interest in sexual activity other than that which now predominated. His statistics showed that among a large and carefully checked group of white Americans, thirty-seven per cent of the males had at least some overt homosexual experience between adolescence and old age, and that eight per cent of the males were exclusively homosexual for a period of three years between the ages of sixteen and fifty-five. The study of women, published five years later and based on a smaller sample, showed that thirteen per cent of women had overt homosexual experience by the age of forty-five years. These findings can not, of course, tell us precisely how many men and women in present day society are predominantly homosexual, but there seem good grounds for concluding that the oft-quoted figure of five per cent is a reliable minimum estimate.

Kinsey was the Professor of Zoology at Indiana University when he was asked in 1938 by the Association of Women Students there to initiate a course on marriage, and found very little research had been done in terms of factual information about human sexuality. By the time he died in 1956, he and his associates had interviewed over 17000 people about their sexual experience. The data originally collected by Kinsey had been checked and tested with subsequent groups, and in 1978 Alan Bell and Martin Weinburg published on behalf of the Kinsey Institute a substantial review which confirmed and elaborated the flexible orientation model. They emphasized the danger of stereotyping homosexual people as irresponsible in their sexual conduct, contributing to social decay, and suffering from psychological pain and maladjustment. In fact, they suggest that objectionable sexual advances are far more apt to be made by a heterosexual than a homosexual, and rape and sexual violence occur more frequently in a heterosexual context. The relatively rare violence among homosexuals is usually the result of male youths 'hunting queers'. They conclude:

> The least ambiguous finding of our investigation is that homosexuality is not necessarily related to pathology. Thus, decisions about homosexual men and women, whether they have to do with employment or child custody or counselling should never be made on the basis of sexual orientation alone.[1]

The Kinsey Institute for research in Sex, Gender and Reproduction, as it is now called, is still linked with Indiana University and the present Director is Dr June Reinisch. In recent reports (1988) evidence of interaction between nominally distinct Sexual Orientation groups is further discussed. Thus about a quarter of self-identified gay men have been married, and three quarters of lesbian women over eighteen years old have had sex with a man at least once. (For comparison, among married men thirty-seven per cent are said to have had an extramarital female partner, and the estimate of extramarital relationships among wives is said to be twenty-nine per cent.) The Institute also reports evidence from doctors in California and New York that, as a result of the AIDS epidemic, anal intercourse and other high risk activities among gay men have decreased dramatically since 1984, and no new infection from this source has been seen in recent months (1988).[2]

The consequences of recognizing this flexibility involve several adjustments to traditional thinking. First, it provides a ready explanation for the transient emergence of homosexual interests among those who have previously been predominantly heterosexual but find themselves confined to one-sex institutions such as prisons or the Armed Forces. On release, the heterosexual orientation revives. Secondly, bisexuality can be understood as arising from the lack of a marked exclusive disposition either way, and it may well be that the proportion of human beings who occupy the middle ground of the scale, and are therefore capable under the appropriate stimulus to relate temporarily or for a long period, to either their own or the opposite sex in behavioural terms, may prove to be much higher than those classified as exclusively homosexual or heterosexual. The strength of the sexual drive of these 'middle' people may not be, of course, so strong as that of those at the ends of the scale, and a distinction needs to be made between capacity for sexual arousal by a member of the same sex in some circumstances, and a real sexual preference. The evidence that more gay women have experience of heterosexual intercourse than gay men do probably reflects the social fact of masculine initiative in sexual activities.

The evidence that many people have a measure of flexibility in the direction of their sexual drive is of considerable importance in understanding homosexuality, particularly for those who are involved in counselling. It helps to explain, for example, the story of those who like Oscar Wilde find their preference changing in their mature years. Wilde was clearly heterosexual as a student, married Constance and had children, and then found his sexual interests shifting towards male friends, and occasionally to younger men. During his youth he contracted a venereal disease and for some time feared to be sexually active, entering marriage after he was told he was cured. Presumably, he would be somewhat centrally placed on the Kinsey scale, able to move either way. Later anxiety about a recurrance of the disease may have pushed him away from heterosexual expression.

Many young people have a variety of reasons for not being heterosexually active, and some will claim a homosexual orientation as a means of escaping from a prospect for which they are not ready. Similarly, older people can appear to change, claiming their real nature has always been homosexual – information that can sound almost unbelieveable to their husband, wife or children after many years. Some women will escape from an emotionally unsatisfactory marriage to, as they sense, a less demanding or less threatening lesbian relationship, not because of a long standing same sex orientation, but as a rationalization for a move pressed on them by other non-sexual factors. Flexibility of this kind, or some history of it should not lead to the assumption that the claimed orientation is false, or can be easily altered, but it serves as a warning that any instant or superficial judgment about fixed orientation should be avoided, especially by or for young people under thirty years old. There are often what are called push-pull factors involved, such as anxiety, disgust, fear and resentment which push people away from a basic heterosexual drive, and pull factors such as the remaining sexual drive, the need for human contact warmth, and friendship, and the opportunity to set up some kind of non-demanding domestic base which encourage homosexual relationships. Bell and Weinberg found some similarities between the causes of change to homosexual relationships and causes for divorce among married heterosexual people – in effect unhappy and unfulfilling relationships.

It may be that some claims that religious faith can cause a change in orientation by conversion indicate in fact not so much as is claimed for the strength of a different morality, but more about the power of an accepting community or relationship which provides what was previously lacking for a troubled person. A rough and ready test of an orientation that is securely fixed at the homosexual end of the Kinsey scale is the answer a person gives to the question: how does sexual intercourse with a person of the other sex seem to you? If the answer is a definite rejection, a sense of repulsion, that is prima facie evidence of a firmly fixed homosexual orientation. If the answer is 'maybe', or 'if only', there may be some flexibility, but any further counselling should be the proper work of a professionally qualified person, and not to be meddled with by untrained advisers. It is not surprising that many 'middle' people find themselves admitting that same or other gender relationships are possible for them, though usually being clear which is their preference. Equally, those of fixed orientation often say that they have always known themselves to be gay, as in fact most heterosexual people say they have always been so, an indication perhaps that sexual orientation for some people is often settled long before puberty.

Psychological Factors

Apart from the necessary caveats about simplistic type-casting, and exaggerated claims about the effectiveness of 'permanent' cures, the fact of flexibility does offer a genuine possibility of change for some homosexual people, with proper professional help, if they wish it. Then, by implication, flexibility makes the moral argument more complicated. What it may be right to ask of some people in transition, actually or potentially, might be thought to be different from what may be asked of those whose orientation seems to be fixed. (This is the old argument about perverts and inverts in a modern guise.) But flexibility also raises a further and important issue by asking what factors in a person's previous life beyond everyday 'push and pull' circumstances may have set them in a homosexual direction. These factors are often assumed to be psychological, and in practice, that means the emotional experiences of early life.

Although Sigmund Freud is rightly regarded as the father of modern psychological studies, and his researches into the causes of homosexuality opened the way to our modern understanding of it, his pioneering studies have inevitably been modified by later work. Freud investigated the theory that a child's sexual orientation would normally develop through same sex attraction to heterosexual attraction through relationships with mother and father, unless some inadequacy or dominance inhibited this growth. It is not possible here to review Freud's work in detail, nor describe properly the various later systems based on it. While it is generally agreed that childhood conflicts in the nuclear family may increase the likelihood of a homosexual orientation, not all homosexual adults have such a history of conflict. The idea that hostile or remote fathers, or possessive mothers predispose their children towards homosexuality by slowing down or inhibiting the transfer of affection to the other parent is now expressed in a different form.

Among contemporary psychologists, Dr Elizabeth Moberly describes the emotional progress of a child as having to pass through a same sex period, girls to mother, boys to father, and this is a normal development for everyone. If the same sex relationship is unsatisfactory, a child can in varying degree get stuck there, and not move on to the heterosexual goal. Moberly finds that although the phenomenon of homosexuality is complex and many-faceted, one constant principle suggests itself: that the homosexual – whether man or woman – has suffered from some deficit in the relationship with the parent of the same sex, and that there is a corresponding drive to make good this deficit – through the medium of same sex relationships. Deficit does not always imply wilful maltreatment by the parent, but something of a traumatic nature, perhaps neglect or absence which has led to disruption in the normal attachment.

The consequence of this deficit is that the person suffering from it attempts to restore the disrupted attachment and make up for the missing growth by same sex love, so that homosexual relationships are properly to be understood as not pathological in themselves, but as attempts to restore the deficit. It follows that same sex love should be a healing process though Moberly does not think it needs to be acted out in sexual behaviour. (Heterosexual relationships are simply irrelevant at this stage) Homosexual relationships should therefore be a means of living through a mourning process for the earlier deficit in order eventually to move on to a more secure heterosexuality. The difficulty of this position, Moberly recognizes, is that it does not always seem to work out in this way. But, she argues, we will not always be told about it if it does, and in any case where two same sex people have a similar deficit they may not be able to overcome sufficiently their own original defensive detachment to help each other. Here lies a cause for the transitory nature of many gay relationships. Professional help may be needed to deal with radical cases of detachment.[3]

The Other Love

So far, in this chapter, we have considered the homosexual orientation as a problem which calls for scientific investigation and explanation. A century of research by the behavioural and medical sciences has helped our understanding, but it is clear we still know only a little about causes, and even less about cures. No longer regarded as an illness, homosexuality as such is not now high on the priority list for further urgent study, in comparison with major health problems in the world. AIDS is, because it is a killer, and because in the longer term it chiefly threatens both the heterosexual majority and the unborn child.

Homosexual people, however, are human beings, who live in relationship with each other and with a heterosexual majority who sometimes surround them with hostility, not least at present, when recent tolerance seems to be ebbing away. As some gay people put it, there is a problem, but not among us. The problem is among heterosexual people who cannot cope with their own need to reject us. From a heterosexual viewpoint, homosexuality is a departure from a perceived norm. But from the viewpoint of a homosexual person whose same sex orientation is firmly established, and who therefore has only known himself or herself like that, their self-awareness is as clearly a 'natural' part of their character as a heterosexual person's different awareness is. They notice gay people in a room, become friends, feel affection for each other, become infatuated, fall in love, are driven to act in lust or love by the pain in their loins, just as heterosexual people do. The fact that their choice of who to relate to is of the same gender and not the different one makes, they claim, no difference to how they feel, and how they have to act out or restrain their sexual drives.

Such a claim comes strangely to modern society because of its unfamiliarity, and that has been largely the result of the traditionally hostile attitudes of Judaism, Christianity and Islam, so deeply embedded in our culture. It is of course also in part a simple reaction to difference, made fiercer by its challenge to one of the most crucial parts of our being, our sexuality. If it is true, as most psychological theories about sexual development suggest, that heterosexual people have passed through a homosexual phase, and homosexual people have stalled there, meeting each other will involve not just intellectual acceptance, but learning to cope with instinctive apprehension. Simply put, the encounter between a straight and a gay person may trigger emotional attitudes based on hidden residues of past experiences in either or both of them. Unresolved conflicts or painful memories of a personal odyssey in the sub-conscious set up anxiety, and therefore all too easily antipathy.

Disarming that antipathy has proved difficult for gay people, and one way of trying to explain what this other love is like is to refer to the classical Greek experience and justification of it. Looking back to that articulate culture, deeply sensitive to love and beauty, has the advantage of some detachment from our times and personal experiences, but it takes us to a society where homosexual love was thought, by some writers, to be morally preferable to heterosexual love.

In one of his earlier writings on homosexuality, Freud recalled the Greek myth which described the splitting in half of human persons into male and female genders, who thereafter spent much energy seeking their other half. Freud puts it this way:

The popular view of the sexual instinct is beautifully reflected in the poetic fable which tells how the original human beings were cut up into two halves – men and women – and how these are always striving to unite again in love. It comes as a great suprise therefore to learn that there are men whose sexual object is a man and not a woman, and women whose sexual object is a woman and not a man ... The number of such people is very considerable, though there are difficulties in describing it very precisely.[4]

Freud could expect a greater familiarity with Greek mythology among his original readers than would be sensible today. So it may help to set out here a fuller account of the fable. The best known source is Plato's *Symposium*, where the story appears in a more elaborate form than Freud gives. Plato's *Symposium* is a literary device for discussing the nature of love by setting it as a dialogue during the course of a dinner party. The supposed guests are famous people, but the place of honour is reserved for Socrates whose philosophy is being thus presented as a refinement and corrective of what the others have already suggested.

The conversation progresses from rather crude ideas, which are gently mocked, to the affirmation of the highest form of divine love which transcends all merely human relationships. In the middle of the dialogue, the androgynous myth is presented by the playwright Aristophanes. He reminds the party that there were originally three kinds of creatures, males, females and also hermaphrodites, who as a third species combined some characteristics of the other two. To cope with the unexpected ability and hubris of these three creatures, Zeus split each in half with the result that the creatures became happily occupied with the search for their other halves. Half males searched for male lovers, female halves found each other and became lesbian couples, the hermaphrodite halves found different gender herm-aphrodite halves and did the breeding. The myth is not of course meant to be taken too seriously, (the real Aristophanes was a brilliant comedian and satirist), but it prepared the way for the argument that homosexual love was a higher form than heterosexual love, provided it was between a mature man and a grown youth, not with a boy.

No woman is present at the party, but Plato includes a feminine view by allowing Socrates to reminisce about what he was taught some ten years previously by Dotima, his 'instructress in the art of love'. She argues that the desire to procreate seizes people as the only way of replacing the human race and becoming themselves immortal. Dotima was presumably a respectable courtesan, it being the Greek custom for young men to be thus introduced to sexual intercourse, and there is a touch of irony here because Socrates had married a lady called Xanthippe, reputedly a shrew. Plato, himself unmarried, thus represents procreation as a kind of animal necessity by which humanity mistakenly seek immortality. Physical procreation is dismissed as one of the lowest forms love (eros) can take. Plato commends instead the search for spiritual procreation, the activity of the soul in loving pursuit of the truth. This is the higher spiritual form of eros, and Plato really believes this; he is not writing *The Symposium* entirely tongue in cheek, as we might cynically think. Since the male gender is much more highly regarded than the female, the search of the male halves for each other is not being described as some form of justification for an abnormality, but as the reason for pursuing idealized homosexual devotion – this is the best of vocations for a real man.[5]

It is fair to add that Plato in later writings abandoned his conviction that gay love was best, coming to realize that all forms of sexual activity outside marriage were less than ideal. In his last work, *The Laws* he argues that sodomy should be suppressed entirely, 'sowing seed in defiance of nature', he calls it, and if a man has intercourse with any woman, hired or procured in some other way, he must do so without any other man or woman getting to know about it![6]

As we shall see in the next part of this book, St Paul and other early Christian writers, express their opposition to homosexual behaviour in terms similar to those finally used by Plato, as contrary to nature. They do not bother with the view of it Plato argues for in the final part of his *Symposium*. In any case, the perversion of sexuality the church repudiated was a crude form of homosexuality inescapably associated with pagan religion, child abuse and prostitution. Plato's Fable survives of course in the commonplace of our day that we are still seeking or have found our other half, but the concept of re-uniting the sundered Adam is in any case fully expressed in Genesis and the Christian doctrine of marriage. The biblical concept of Genesis 2.22 has been described as healing the original wound of creation, because woman was taken out of man and is re-united to make one flesh, whereas the alternative account of Genesis 1.27, suggests man and woman are created together as separate but complementary persons. The sense of heterosexual marriage as the ideal, emphasized in the *Laws* of Plato, but not in either of the Genesis accounts nor in the Fable, figures prominently in the 1987 General Synod debate (see pp. 164ff. below).

The study of Greek literature was never of course lost in European history, but because of the Christian teaching, much was bowdlerized for popular consumption, and the institution of pederasty ignored as an aberration now best forgotten. That kind of censorship and reticence began to drop away in Victorian times, and the initial studies of sexual inversion, as it was called, by Havelock Ellis in his vast review *Studies in the Psychology of Sex* were matched by essays on homosexuality in classical literature, of which the privately printed *A Problem in Greek Ethics*, by J. A. Symonds was an important example. Oscar Wilde gave a discreet but ill-received insight into his own perception in his novel *The Picture of Dorian Gray*, published in 1890. His public plea that 'the other love' be taken seriously, happened in a dramatic and probably unpremeditated way during his trial for gross indecency at the Old Bailey under the then recently passed Act of 1885. As evidence of his guilt, counsel asked him about the meaning of a poem by his lover, Lord Alfred Douglas, entitled 'The Two Loves'. In reply to the question: 'Is it not clear that the love described in the poem related to natural love and unnatural love?', Wilde replied:

> What is the 'Love that dare not speak its name'? – 'The Love that dare not speak its name' in this century is such a great affection of an elder for a younger man as there was between David and Jonathan, such as Plato made the very basis of his philosophy, and such as you find in the sonnets of Michelangelo and Shakespeare. It is that deep, spiritual affection that is as pure as it is perfect. It dictates and pervades great works of art like those of Shakespeare and Michelangelo, and those two letters of mine, such as they are. It is in this century misunderstood, so much misunderstood that it may be described as the 'Love that dare not speak its name', and on account of it I am placed where I am now. It is beautiful, it is fine, it is the noblest form of affection. There is nothing unnatural about it. It is intellectual, and it repeatedly exists between an elder and a younger man, when the elder man has intellect, and the younger man has all the joy, hope and glamour of life before him. That it should be so the world does not understand. The world mocks at it and sometimes puts one in the pillory for it.[7]

To the jury this speech must have been moving, for they disagreed on their verdict and he was released, only to be recharged and found guilty at a later trial. But Wilde's rhetoric was actually better than his history, and he is not alone in being selective about thoughts and people in his own cause. That said, Wilde's speech in court that day remains a clear statement of the homosexual case, and it is not easy to find modern equivalents that match its force.

We Speak for Ourselves

Oscar Wilde's plea for the recognition of the 'other love', apparently an unprepared declaration forced out of him by the strain of the court proceedings, remains a fine example of how a homosexual person's interior feelings may be expressed. The literature of this is now vast and impossible to quote adequately here. The freedom homosexual people have found to describe their situations and feelings has been progressive in this century and vary from a shy and apologetic tone to a greater self-confidence, both in expression and in description of life-styles which, as they become lived out more openly in the community, are felt to be the appropriate and morally respectable alternative for those whom heterosexual marriage would be a sham. I select from the abundant material three sources which show this variation and growth of confidence.

In 1976, Jack Bubuscio provided a well-balanced collection of gay people's accounts of themselves in *We Speak for Ourselves*, and the three quotations which follow are taken from this book (names are altered).

Consider, for example, the story of Claude, thirty-eight, who, as a young man consulted the literature of homosexuality – 'analytical, fictional, and confessional' – in the hope of finding some acceptable sense of self-as-homosexual:

You can't name a book that I didn't consult. And in each of them the message rang out loud and clear: you're a criminal, and your crime is against God, nature, society, yourself. As I talk to you I wonder what on earth made me persevere. I think, perhaps, because one *must* know *who* one is, and *why* one is different. And as homosexuality was not, in those days, something you dared discuss in polite conversation, one consulted the 'experts'. And this is what I did. I read everything I could get my hands on. But the literature was uniformly negative. How well I remember those *thousands* of case studies shrouded in gloom and doom, all written in plaintive tones of guilt and self-hatred. I wanted to cry aloud after reading them. The unhappy homosexual! Sentenced to 'life' for the crime of being gay. How ironic that word, 'gay', seemed to me then . . . . I began to look upon the straight world with envy and sorrow. The heterosexual inhabited a kind of golden world from which I was for ever excluded.[8]

Babuscio continues: 'It is very difficult to feel good about oneself when so little of a positive nature is said about one's own kind.' Since the sense of self is in large part determined by an individual's perception of his or her social role, popular stereotypes and social expectations are liable to count for a great deal in the development of the gay person's self-concept. This can be seen in the story of Martin, twenty-four:

The problem I was faced with years ago, when I first realized I was gay, was learning to like myself. This isn't easy when people think of you as sick or immature. Before I even knew I was homosexual, I remember my school friends talking about the 'pooves'. When finally I realized I was '*one of them*', you can imagine how I felt .... I fought my homosexuality for a long time. I'd persuade myself that I couldn't be *entirely* gay since I didn't behave like the stereotyped gays they joke about on telly, or that you see in films. Eventually, though, I couldn't deny it any longer. That is, I couldn't deny it *to myself*. I still laughed along with the others when 'queer jokes' were told. I hated myself afterwards, and also felt disloyal. And, of course, all this only aggravated my feelings of guilt. And yet, I felt it was wiser to say nothing because if all the others felt this way about homosexuals, there must be some good reason. And I *didn't* want to lose my friends .... There were *so many* risks in being open. So I kept my homosexuality a secret for as long as I could.[9]

Babuscio then tells the story of a church-going girl: 'Tina, for example, is a young, recently divorced mother of a seven-year-old son who once lived "in constant fear of succumbing, some day, to the temptation of loving another woman"':

Mother would always speak of my future in terms of a home and family. 'Now, when you're married, dear', and 'Your husband' – It made me think of the family as part of some grand design and I felt, who am I to upset everyone's plans for me? Yet I couldn't generate even the slightest enthusiasm for the prospect of one day being a wife, mother, homemaker .... I was very confused by my attitude. I seemed, to myself unique.

When I was about fifteen I began to experience 'feelings' for other girls. I felt very guilty about this. It was quite bad enough thinking about *boys* in that way. It was positively *evil* to have these feelings for girls. Still, two and two didn't yet add up to 'lesbian'. I was learning, though, what it means to be different, and to feel isolated.

One night I remember I couldn't sleep because a close friend, someone towards whom I felt very close, for whom I had very warm feelings (and who, I think, felt the same way about me), suddenly moved up north. I was despondent! I wanted to die, I felt so suddenly alone. At about two o'clock in the morning, I was still awake. I put my robe on and started down to the kitchen. But when I came into the hall I saw the light was on in my parents' room. I could hear them talking in hushed voices. It was something to do with this girl who had 'disgraced' herself with a woman who was lodging in her parents' home. I heard my mother say, in the voice she generally reserved for sinners, 'There's a special place in hell for *those* women . . . .' Our parish priest apparently agreed, because on the following Sunday his sermon was full of oblique references to the affair, and these were 'spiced' with quotations from the Scriptures. Leviticus, I think . . . .

I suppose the more sophisticated knew precisely what the old fellow was on about, but I was much too naive. A friend later explained it to me: '*Lesbians*', she said. And that was all. The next day I went to the library and checked the dictionaries. After reading the entry for 'lesbian', I was in a panic. I imagined all of hell's devils pointing at me. I was in no doubt now. My feelings had branded me a sinner.[10]

In later chapters, Babuscio continues his series of quotations and comments, to give a broad description of the gay scene, what it means to come out, and how gay people come together in a variety of relationships. In the new revised edition, he adds an immensely sad analysis of the consequences of AIDS for the conditions under which gay life has now to be lived, and gives some examples of the backlash of intolerance with which they are now threatened. This includes a reported statement by a South Staffordshire District Councillor in 1986 that 'ninety per cent of Queers should be gassed'. This backlash has also been reflected in Government action through its Department of Education guidelines on Sex Education in schools and the Local Government Act of 1987, Clause 28. (See Part 4, p. 172.) Such violent expressions of homophobia suggest perhaps the kind of triggering mechanism described above. The present author was surprised to receive, some years ago, a letter from a member of the House of Lords, active at the time in church affairs but now dead, who wrote to me 'all buggers should be castrated, and lesbians should be put into state brothels where they will learn the proper use of their sex organs'! What seemed then a relic from past prejudice appears now to be once again an attitude thought proper to express in public. If that is the case, it becomes a Christian duty to ensure that the citizens rights of homosexual people be respected.

Very different in mood, and facing in particular the possibility that the ordination of openly homosexual people into the ministry requires church congregations to work through uncomfortable matters in human sexuality and relationships is the very recent *Dear God, I'm Gay*.[11] This book is in the form of an exchange of letters – imaginary but credible – between straight and gay people, and resulted from the work of a study group called together by the Rev. Donald Eadie, who is Chairman of the Birmingham District of the Methodist Church. (It

is not an official publication of that Church, which has a new Working
Party in action on the subject. See p. 151.)

Here are extracts from correspondence between a gay man applying
for a post as minister in a Methodist Mission, and the Senior Circuit
Steward. After describing his general qualifications, the applicant
continues:

> I must explain the entry on the form relating to family. You will
> probably have read in the Church Press my statement at the last
> Methodist Conference that I am a homosexual, and that I believe
> God accepts me as I am, to serve him and his people as a Christian
> minister. I have a life partner, a man of my age, who is a keen
> Christian, with whom I have been living since our partnership was
> blessed at one of our Churches in a service led by my super-
> intendant minister. I am asking that, if I am appointed, my life-
> partner may be permitted to live at the manse. He would be willing
> to pay a suitable rent if required.

The Steward replies that he and his colleagues are unanimous in not
recommending him to the appointment, and gives three reasons:

> Firstly, we believe that our church members would not accept your
> domestic situation. To save embarrassment we will not put your
> application to the circuit meeting. The subject of sexuality has
> never, to our knowledge, been openly discussed at any of our
> churches. Secondly, the young people in our Church clubs are
> aware of the danger of AIDS, and it would be a very bad example
> to them if we had a homosexual minister in charge of youth work.
> Finally, there could be some scandalous publicity if the local press
> found out you were homosexual and that you and your friend lived
> together in the manse.

The applicant replies expressing his disappointment, and makes *inter
alia* these points:

> I wonder how it is possible for your folk to achieve a well-
> thought-out and mature attitude to sexuality if they never talk
> openly about it. Your youth club people will feel let down if
> the subject is completely 'taboo'. About ten per cent of the popula-
> tion are homosexually orientated, including many Christians. If
> people who come to your Churches are made to feel their deepest
> problems are ignored or not regarded sympathetically they will
> feel rejected. Yet surely Jesus welcomes everybody as they are?
> The avoidance of AIDS has been much discussed among homo-
> sexuals over five years and probably heterosexuals are now more
> at risk.[12]

Perhaps enough has been said already of the plight homosexual people find themselves in, surrounded by this resurgent hostility. The moral problem is discussed further in Part 5, but it is appropriate here to re-iterate the primary claim homosexual people make to be allowed to relate to each other according to their sexual orientation and not to be further oppressed by a heterosexual demand they cannot meet. The Genesis narratives about the creation of Adam and Eve who cleave together to make one flesh and heal the original wound of creation is the standard biblical text on which the theology of Christian marriage is based. That is fair enough, but the narratives also describe the same yearning to find the other half as the Androgynous myth suggests in Plato's symposium, albeit from a very different culture and with religious premises unlike those of the Greeks. The myth of re-union is universal, because the human experience of the yearning for it is.

Obviously the search of each human person to relate particularly to another person is as powerful as the instinctive drive to procreate, and in some ways the whole notion of sexuality is too limited and indeed marred by its association with genital acts to serve as an adequate description of this yearning. Realizing this gives strength to the new theology of sexuality which makes relationship primary, and this leaves space for those who do not find any genital activity necessary. In the words of a current pop song, 'I don't want a lover, I just need a friend.' The need is to affirm oneself in and by one's contacts with other people, and the richness and variety of friendship and companionship need not involve genital intimacy, indeed it may be a hindrance to it, because negatively it tends to concentrate overmuch on one aspect of human expression.

One of the most poignant sections of *Dear God, I'm Gay* gives a putative discussion between a husband and wife, Bob and Mary, when Bob decides to tell her he is bi-sexual:

Dear Mary,

When I first 'came out' to you I was so uncertain, so fearful. Many women would have rejected their male partners because they turned out to be other than heterosexual. Now panic has turned to relief and joy. I am so glad you have accepted me.

It was painful and difficult for me to discover the truth about myself. I am married to a woman but attracted to men. I am bi-sexual. I have suppressed an important part of myself. But I recognize there is pain in this for you, too. Perhaps you feel that you have been deceived, that you have been made to look a fool. There is a crucial difference between an intellectual acceptance of gays and lesbians, and an emotional acceptance that one's own partner is not what you thought he was. I can only plead that I still love you and want to be married to you. I pray that you will learn to love me as I am.

Dear Bob,

Thank you for your note on the kitchen table this morning. I was shocked, but not entirely surprised. Bisexuality. It is taking me time to come to terms with that word, that concept. Before we were married I sometimes wondered if you were gay, but you were so obviously attracted to me that I put the thought aside. It never occurred to me that you might be bi-sexual.

I have done some thinking and reading, but there are still areas which frighten me. Sometimes I feel very lost and alone. But at other times it is as though nothing has changed. We continue our normal lives. I love you very very much.

But all this has changed my thinking about God. I no longer believe in a God who condemns a large proportion of the population because they love in a different way. God who is love must surely be at the heart of all true loving. Jesus stood with those who were condemned by society. So must I, otherwise I am denying you, my beloved.

But what about you. And how do you propose to express the homosexual side of your nature, given that you are married and a practising Christian? For you must express it somehow if you are to be at peace with yourself at last.[13]

As the exchange of letters continues, Bob says that he is not going to take a lover, no one else will take Mary's place, but he wishes to form a deep friendship with a man. They agree they need to be open with each other, not possessive, and work out new boundaries for what belongs to their marriage and what belongs to friendship, neither being totally excluded from contact with the other's 'friend'. This imaginary correspondence points the way towards solving what must be in reality for many couples a very difficult problem, more likely to end in despair and divorce. Bob and Mary are a little too good to be true, but in actual situations of this kind, honesty, and the ability of the 'friend' to accept a limited role will be crucial factors.

There have always been long term stable affectionate and close same gender friendships where much of domestic life is shared for convenience and economy, but where no sexual activity occurs. Such companionship among professional people like teachers has often led to shared homes and holidays, and such arrangements used to be accepted as a genuine alternative life-style. The present anxiety about sex tends to assume wrongly that genital activity must be involved, and this assumption can become an unfair form of oppression, and interference with private life. Conversely where sexual activity complements and develops from a broadly based relationship, as in marriage, it is rightly claimed to be a fulfilling expression of all else. This is the commonplace of modern understandings of relationships, and describes a situation in which the ability to have children is not an essential element, nor is a permanent commitment. Thus described, homosexual people will wish to say that such a pattern of sexuality is appropriate and meaningful for them as much as for heterosexual people. If society now accepts without question, as it seems to, heterosexual people living together, within which everything including genital intimacy is shared without long-term commitment, or any thought of marriage, is it not hypocritical, gay people will say, to condemn us for claiming the same freedom, and for much the same reasons.

A final word must be said about homosexual 'marriage'. This is obviously not possible, in a legally recognized sense, and what is meant is some sort of private commitment to permanency, with the possible addition among religious people of a prayer or blessing provided by a sympathetic minister. It seems to happen occasionally, mostly in America, where for example the Metropolitan Community Church is especially constituted for gay people. It is often said by gay people that because the institution of marriage is so closely linked culturally and socially with heterosexuality, it is not a helpful model for them. But the theoretical question, 'Can prayer be made to God that these persons should find with each other a loving and long-lasting relationship of mutual help and comfort?' is not too easily answered by an absolute negative. Nor, since it is a private and personal decision, can a rider be realistically imposed such as 'provided you have separate beds'. Sufficient perhaps to say that at present only very few ministers of the major Christian denominations feel able in good conscience to share in such blessing services, and it can hardly be expected that their authorities would encourage them officially to do so.

To round off this set of quotations in which gay people speak for themselves about their relationships, I draw on a research project undertaken by two American doctors about long-lasting relationships between adult male couples. David McWhirter and Andrew Mattison work at the School of Medicine at California University; they are gay, and have been together now for some sixteen years. Their research method, by interviewing 156 gay couples over a period of five years, has some similarity to that of Kinsey, though they recognize that their study could only have been undertaken in the seventies and eighties, when the social climate permitted such an enquiry.

Their report, entitled *The Male Couple*,[14] is valuable not only for its findings and statistical tables, but for the frequent and sometimes light-hearted quotations they record from their interviewees. The average age of all participants was thirty-seven years, the youngest twenty and the oldest sixty-nine. Although some had courted at length, the majority tended to move into shared accommodation within a month of first meeting. Love at first sight was not an uncommon experience, and physical attraction and behaviour were well-nigh universal. As with heterosexual couples, the longer-lasting relationships become less dependent on love-making as the uniting factor.

Their main conclusion is that such partnerships pass through up to six stages, from 'blending' in the first year through 'nesting' and 'maintaining' by the fifth year, 'building' between six and ten years, and on to 'releasing' and 'renewing' as the twentieth year approaches. In some respects, these stages seem similar to those of a heterosexual married couple, particularly in building a common establishment, managing joint incomes, and finding a mutually acceptable life pattern, while learning to leave freedom to each other for external interests, without jealousy. In other respects the differences are marked, notably about initial expectations of permanency and sexual fidelity which are not assumed, and of course the presence of children, though in fact some fifty children were sharing in these partnerships. Presumably, these children came from previous heterosexual marriages rather than adoption. It seems likely that successful partnerships of this kind are mostly achieved by those of long-settled homosexual orientation, and eighty per cent of the participants placed themselves at the end of the Kinsey scale as exclusively homosexual. Some of the most durable relationships were between younger and older men, with an age difference of perhaps ten to fifteen years. This factor is not to be understood as a form of pederasty in the classical pattern but as perhaps a matching of those with complementary needs – fathers and sons.

As a cameo of one of these relationships at the fourth stage after nine years and collaborating, *Walt*, aged forty, a barber with his own shop, and *Manny*, aged thirty-seven, the local postman speak of their life together:

Walt: 'Sometimes we look at each other and just shake our heads. I think I know what he's thinking, and he knows what I'm thinking too often.'

Manny: 'We haven't always been such good friends. But the roughest days are behind us now. They'd better be. I know he's reliable because he's been hanging in there even when I used to get so drunk nobody else could handle me.'

Walt: 'We each have our separate ways. Manny plays golf on Saturdays, and you couldn't drag me out there with a team of wild horses. I go off to the beach to muscle watch.'

Manny: 'I suppose even if we are together another nine years, there will be some things to get used to with each other. But the truth is, when Walt had his appendix out last summer I thought it was me that wasn't going to make it.'[15]

There is obviously a vast difference between the calm domesticity of Walt and Manny in San Diego, and some of the traumas reported by London-based Babuscio. And it would be naive to end this chapter with a supposition that the self-confidence now shown by some gay couples in a tolerant community could be quickly universalized by education and argument. What reports like those of McWhirter and Mattison may achieve is the repudiation of incorrect stereotyping in the old negative fashion.

★

3

The Old Testament

Preliminary Information

When the Christian churches are faced with a moral problem which seems to be new, the primary authority of scripture requires that a careful check must be made to find any texts relevant to it, and of the historical and literary context in which they were written down. Not all apparently new moral issues can be directly referred to scripture, of course, but in the case of homosexual behaviour, which has existed in all times and places in human history, it would be surprising if the biblical authors never mentioned it at all. In fact they did occasionally refer to it, and in the long history of the Bible, the translators did their best to reflect the meaning of the original texts, using the vocabulary of their time, quite clear to them, but sometimes seeming vague to us. Our newest translations use modern language which restores for us the clarity of the original Hebrew or Greek text. But accurate translation is essential, and in commenting on the biblical references to homosexual behaviour, I have examined in some detail those words and passages which have been most scrutinized and caused difficulty or controversy. Most modern books about homosexuality by Christian scholars discuss these controversies at length, but in the space available to me it is not possible to refer to them by name. I can only hope that those who are expert in this field of study will think that I give a fair summary, though the views I stress are my own.

References to homosexuality in the Bible are infrequent and difficult to identify, especially in older English translations, such as the King James and the Revised Version. Indeed, although the actual word has come into common use since the publication of the Wolfenden Committee Report of 1957, it occurs only once in the New English Bible of 1970, not at all in the Jerusalem Bible of 1966, nor in the Common Bible, an ecumenical edition of the Revised Standard Version published in 1973. It is found in the Good News Bible of 1976; in the New International Version of 1979 the equivalent phrase is 'to have sex with', the homosexual meaning being made clear from the context.

The diversity of translations now available to the churches can be seen as a strength or a weakness. The strength is partly one of freshness. Replacing familiar old words with new vernacular expressions can awaken attention, and there are passages which are obscure in the old translations. The weakness is uncertainty, as any Bible study group using a mixture of translations will discover. One might say we need a single modern authorized version. For references to homosexuality, the modern translations tend to be explicit where the older versions appear to us imprecise or open to several interpretations. The vocabulary has changed, and we do not always immediately sense what is meant; the same difficulty can be found in reading Shakespeare. However, our growing knowledge of the social and moral situation of biblical times has helped clear up some ambiguities. That said, clarity about the meaning of texts is not the end of the matter; applying their meaning to our very different world is a task of interpretation, not merely translation.

Homosexual behaviour is not a matter of any great importance to the biblical writers; they only mention it peripherally as an example of the kind of sin which offends against God's plan for human sexuality. That plan, as it is expressed in scripture in general terms, places strong emphasis on marriage and family life, and on fidelity and chastity in personal relations. These emphases, though clear, were not easily obeyed, as several comments in the Gospels about the hardness of men's hearts make clear. But with this teaching in mind, such failures as adultery, divorce, and prostitution are regarded by the biblical writers as the major faults, and homosexuality is likewise condemned. We should note that the word Sodom, originally the name of a town in Southern Palestine which is now associated with the legal term for anal intercourse, is often used in the Bible as a synonym of general wickedness, particularly among those who are not God's people in an Old Testament Covenant sense, or within the New Testament community of the redeemed; in the Bible the word does not always imply sexual sin.

Alongside the stress on marriage as the primary relationship God plans between men and women, there is also in scripture a steadily increasing emphasis on love and friendship, and in the New Testament the *agape* of God is perceived as both the explanation of the incarnation itself and the root principle of all Christian morality. But love, in biblical perspective is not in opposition to rules of conduct. As St Augustine was to express it later, 'Love God, and then what you will, do.' In principle, therefore, there can be no conflict between the demands of love and any moral precept pleasing to God, but in practice the connection is not always readily seen. The teaching of Jesus needs balanced scrutiny at this point.

Resolving the conflict between the ethics of Judaism and the new way of love is a preoccupation of the early church, easily demonstrable for example in the writings attributed to St Paul. In one sense it can be said that there is an obvious continuity between Old Testament and New Testament moral teaching; nothing important commended by Paul would be abhorrent to his one-time rabbinic teachers, except where it involved ritual and ceremonial Jewish practices now made redundant in Christ.

But in another sense, the new religion, freeing itself from much which was ethnically and culturally Jewish as it sought to claim for Christ the pluralist gentile world of the Mediterranean found itself confronted with the powerful long-existing systems of law and ethics of the Roman and Greek civilizations. If, as was believed, God had not left himself without witness among them, it became necessary to begin a sifting process. Given the primacy of the revelation of God known in the Jewish Torah, and no Christian leader felt himself totally distanced from that inheritance any more than Christ himself had been, what similarities and what differences in the other moralities of the time could the Christians baptize into their own system, and what had to be rejected. These were difficult questions, and the Christians were still wrestling with them at the end of the period of composition of the books that now comprise our New Testament.

The first Christians lived in a changing world, just as the Jews of that time did. The Dispersion of the Jews, the continual invasion of their homeland, and the inevitable passing of time had led to marked changes in their outlook since the days when the latest books of the Old Testament had been written. The middle section of this chapter covers the inter-testamental period, that is the space between the composition of the Old and New Testaments. Study of this period shows how in the Jewish communities the relatively muted hostility to homosexuality in the earlier times became more strident as a result of their clash with Greek culture. Despite their willingness to re-work their inherited Jewish traditions, it will be seen that the early Christians did not deviate from the Rabbinic teaching about homosexual behaviour. Although only a small part of the extant documents from the inter-testamental period are included in our Bibles, as the Apocrypha, some quotations from them help us to understand better both the similarities and distinctiveness of the New Testament references, particularly those in St Paul's epistles.

Old Testament Introduction

Before considering the particular Old Testament texts which are clearly relevant to homosexual behaviour, it is useful to describe the general character of Old Testament morality. In some ways, scholars think, the emergence of a distinctive Israelite morality was a process of fits and starts, new insights understood and remembered, then abandoned and recovered, but in other ways it can be said that there is a more or less straightforward development in the Old Testament from common Semitic customary law in the countries of the fertile crescent to a distinctive religious ethic of Israel. That distinctiveness is not always seen in difference from the morality of other countries, of which Egypt and Babylon are predominant at the time, so much as in the deliberate assessment of them by the biblical authors, accepting and replacing precepts to fit in with the overview and perspective particular to the faith of Israel.

In the Old Testament, a clear condemnation of homosexual behaviour is found twice in the Book of Leviticus. Other relevant passages are the story of the destruction of Sodom in Genesis, and a somewhat similar event at Gibeah described in the Book of Judges. The practice of Temple prostitution in the Canaanite religion which is denounced in Deuteronomy and in the Books of the Kings very probably included the sexual exploitation of both sexes, some of it homosexual, but the whole situation was obviously repugnant to Israel, and needs no elucidation here. Some authors have found in the friendship between David and Jonathan an implied homosexual component, or some kind of bi-sexual disposition in David. Although he has been married to Michal and then Abigail, he is still able to say of Jonathan that 'your love for me was wonderful, surpassing the love of women' (II Samuel 1.26). From the scant details given in the Book of Samuel, this can only be conjecture, and it is not further discussed in this chapter.

The work of biblical scholars over the past two centuries in identifying the sources and complex history which lie behind the Old Testament books as we know them provides a good deal of contextual information to assist our understanding of these texts. I hope that the generally agreed views about the four source elements in the composition of the Pentateuch are sufficiently familiar to need no re-iteration here. Quotations from the Bible are taken from the New English Bible, and significant differences in other translations available to the general reader are noted.

The Destruction of Sodom and Gomorrah (Genesis 19)

(a) The narrative

The catastrophe that overtook these two cities of the plain at the base of the Dead Sea is described in Genesis 18.16–19.29, and the sequence of events set out there has been traditionally interpreted by Jewish, Islamic, and Christian commentators as a clear demonstration of God's wrath at those who attempt anal intercourse. But the destruction of Sodom is part of a much longer narrative, the story of Abraham, which continues from chapters 12–24 of Genesis, and a consideration of the whole story helps towards the interpretation of the events at Sodom. The lives of the patriarchs in these chapters have been called sagas, by which is meant not merely records in a factual sense, but the expression in literary form of how people 'think of their history'. These patriarchal traditions, therefore, though they contain history, are for belief, not just for information about the origins of the Israelites.

Abraham is the first Old Testament 'personality', the pioneer of Israel's faith, and the saga records the development of his special relationship with God. Lot, Abraham's nephew, appears in the saga as a relatively less satisfactory character. Originally a settler in Sodom, preferring the comforts of urban life to the spartan style of Abraham, Lot is captured in a tribal raid but he is rescued by his uncle and returns home. Abraham is visited by the Lord and two companions and is promised an heir. Then the Lord says he must visit Sodom and Gomorrah to see for himself whether or not the outcry against them justifies their destruction.

Abraham intercedes for Sodom, and the Lord agrees that he will not destroy it if ten good men are found there. The Lord then departs and his two companions, now identified as angels, travel at great speed to Sodom and meet Lot at the gates of the city. Lot appears to recognize the true identity of his visitors, and offers them the appropriate eastern hospitality to distinguished guests. They agree to come home with him, but after supper the townspeople surround the house and an ugly situation develops:

> They called to Lot and asked him where the men were who had entered the house that night. 'Bring them out' they shouted, 'so that we can have intercourse with them.' Lot went out into the doorway to them, closed the door behind him and said, 'No, my friends, do not be so wicked. Look, I have two daughters, both virgins; let me bring them out to you, and you can do what you

like with them, but do not touch these men, because they have
come under the shelter of my roof.'

(New English Bible, Genesis 19.5–8)

Lot's offer of his daughters is rejected and he is threatened as an
alien in the city with worse than they have in mind for his visitors.
Once the immediate danger from the mob is averted by striking
them blind, the total destruction of Sodom is deferred long enough
for Lot and his family to escape.

(b) Comment

The investigation of the oral and written sources of the books of
the Pentateuch by Old Testament scholars provide a sufficient
basis for reckoning the Sodom narrative to be the earliest indication of hostility to homosexual behaviour in the Old Testament.
The supposition that Moses was the author of the whole Pentateuch,
despite the difficulty that his own death is described within it, is
seldom accepted today. Instead, the basic formation of the text as
we now know it seems to have resulted from a process of
collection, reflection, and editing over a period of some five
centuries. The process began early after the setting up of the monarchy around 1000 years BCE, and ended with the re-establishment
of Israel after the exile in the sixth century BCE. The existing
Hebrew texts we have come mostly from copies made after the
time of Christ, though the material in the Dead Sea Scrolls
encourages us to think they are accurate.

The precise sites of the five cities of the plain, including Sodom
and Gomorrah, have proved difficult to identify, though they are
usually placed at the southern end of the Dead Sea, and possibly
are now submerged. The region has been subject to earthquake
and subsidence, and is, of course, within the northern part of the
great Rift Valley running down from Syria to the African Lakes.
The presence of sulphurous springs, oil, and bitumen at the east
bank of the sea have led some commentators to suggest a natural
explanation for the destruction of the cities, especially when this
geological information is associated with archaeological evidence
of the abandonment of a possible site around 1400 BCE.

To the questions 'How, when and why was Sodom destroyed?',
there can be few confident answers apart from those suggested in
the saga itself, and those who press beyond the Yahwist's explanation of divine intervention suggest that the actual natural disaster
was still remembered at the time of Abraham, and a theological or
aetiological explanation was attached to the memory as the tale
was told. Alternatively, later than Abraham, but before the

conquest of Canaan, observation of the destroyed sites during the patriarchal period and the migration northwards was used as a didactic opportunity. In either case, the description of Sodom as a place of wickedness worthy of divine indignation and judgment became entrenched in the saga of Abraham.

As the Yahwist presents the story of Sodom, however, the chief focus of interest lies not in the wickedness of the city itself, but in the development of the relationship between God and Abraham, so that Abraham becomes, *inter alia*, convinced of God's justice. Sodom is, from the beginning, a city destined for destruction and this is made plain in chapter 13, verses 11 and 13: 'The men of Sodom were wicked, great sinners against the Lord.' But before God acts, he decides to take Abraham into his confidence and explain the action he feels bound to take. The ensuing discussion (18.17–38) develops several major themes. Among them is the universality of the just judgment of God, who hears and responds to the cry of the oppressed from the cities of the plain, in no sense places belonging to Israel. Then there is the theme of communal responsibility, and its contrast, drawn out by Abraham's plea, of communal merit, for it is not suggested that the ten righteous, if such be found, should save only themselves. There is further, in the whole narrative, an underlying motif of great significance in the Bible, that the just shall live by faith. Abraham does, profoundly, and Lot attempts to, but the inadequacy of his commitment is shown by the difficulty the angels have in persuading him to leave the city in time. With all these themes introduced into the discussion that precedes the events that precipitate the city's destruction, it is clear that the wickedness of the men of Sodom is generalized and established in advance. What happens when the angelic visitors accept Lot's hospitality is an illustration of that wickedness, further evidence of an abominable state of affairs which requires God's justice to be expressed in punishment, and not in itself the cause of that judgment.[1]

That the wickedness of Sodom was understood in broad terms within the Israelite tradition can be demonstrated from the other references to Sodom in the Old Testament. In later writings, various sins are suggested within the general conviction that Sodom represents in an archetypal way the alienation from Yahweh that provokes his destructive wrath. Thus in Isaiah chapter 1 insincere sacrifice, injustice, and oppression are considered the major sins of Sodom: in Ezekiel chapter 16 they are pride and neglect of the poor, and in Jeremiah chapter 12, adultery and hypocrisy are mentioned. It seems then that both in the introduction to the events at Sodom and in subsequent reference to it in the Old Testament, no special emphasis is placed on homosexual sin, but it is nevertheless clear that the narrative itself suggests an attempt at homosexual assault which Lot attempts to defeat by appealing to the code of hospitality and the offer of a heterosexual alternative.

The theme of hospitality has been introduced into the narrative at the beginning of chapter 18 when Abraham entertains the three visitors and in a similar way Lot insists on receiving the angelic visitors to Sodom, who were prepared at first to spend the night in the streets. The townspeople invade their privacy, and the communal responsibility for this offence is stressed. What they demand, according to the New English Bible translation, is intercourse with the visitors, and this makes explicit that sodomy was intended, conforming to the traditional interpretation of the text, of which the older translation, from the King James version onwards was 'that we might know them'.

The Hebrew word here translated as intercourse is '*yadha*', which is very commonly used in the Old Testament and usually means 'to know' in the ordinary sense of 'being acquainted with'. Apart from this usual meaning, *yadha* is also occasionally used to imply sexual intercourse or coital knowledge, and this special use is familiar from the King James and subsequent English Bibles, and in the legal term 'carnal knowledge', now somewhat archaic. *Yadha* occurs ten times in the Old Testament with this meaning of sexual intercourse, and in each case apart from the Sodom narrative (and Judges chapter 19 see below) heterosexual intercourse is clearly intended and a child results. Thus in Genesis 4, where the conception of Cain (v. 1), Enoch (v. 17) and Seth (v. 25) are described by *yadha*, the older translations use 'knew' and the New English Bible uses 'lay with'.

The possibility of ambiguity in the use of *yadha* in the Sodom story and thence of the exclusion of any reference to homosexual assault has attracted a good deal of attention among commentators in this century, though it was also noted by Calvin who thought the ambiguity was deliberate and meant to deceive. Sherwin Bailey, at the time of the Wolfenden Committee, argued that the assumption that *yadha* has the untypical sexual connotation in the Sodom narrative is mistaken. In his view the story makes better sense if the ordinary meaning of *yadha* is understood, for then the townspeople of Sodom simply exercise their civic right to enquire who the strangers are. They wish to establish for themselves the harmlessness of the foreigners, for after all, Lot himself is an alien, the times are dangerous, and the visitors may be spies. It would be a sensible precaution to check the credentials of strangers within the walls. If this view is accepted, the wickedness of the townspeople can be said to be adequately shown by their refusal to allow Lot to exercise hospitality and their attempt to break into his house.[2]

Although Bailey's argument has found a ready acceptance among some subsequent writers on the biblical attitude to homosexuality, and does, if it stands, cast serious doubts on the traditional interpretation, there are stronger arguments for continuing to hold that the Yahwist intended to preserve the tradition that the men of Sodom were so wicked that they did not even hesitate to attempt buggery with strangers. The practice of inflicting this indecency on defeated enemies in the Middle East countries in ancient times has been clearly established, and homosexual assault on the young and on other vulnerable people was forbidden in the laws of other nations in the Fertile Crescent during the period of the Patriarchs. It is not, therefore intrinsically unlikely that the Israelite tradition would contain such a derogatory tale.

Further, there seems to be a macabre symmetry about the tale as it is traditionally interpreted. Modern readers will find the offer of the daughters as a substitute distasteful, but it has to be remembered that the place of women was inferior and it would have been regarded as moral for Lot to preserve his angelic visitors and protect the honour of the Lord whom they represented by making such an offer. Presumably the townspeople were not aware of the status of the visitors, and Lot's offer of his daughters would seem something of an over-reaction if all that was being asked was a check on the *bona fides* of the visitors. The Yahwist uses the word *yadha* again in verse 7, for the daughters 'have not yet known a man' ('both virgins' in the New English Bible translation), so a rather extraordinary subtlety is inferred in the narrative if the word changes its meaning from 'acquaintance' to 'intercourse' as the dialogue proceeds.

The story of Sodom's destruction is, therefore, one of Israel's ancient traditions, taken into the Pentateuch unchanged, woven into the saga of Abraham and Lot, and establishing primarily the universal justice of God. Among the various wickednesses attributed to this foreign city inhospitality and homosexual assault are included. While this study shows that the Sodom narrative should not be taken, by itself, as the definitive text in the Bible for condemning homosexual practice, it remains the case that the Pentateuchal editors from first to last evidently thought such condemnation appropriate.

The Rape of the Levite Concubine at Gibeah (Judges 19)

(a) Introductory note

Although this narrative is found in the Hebrew Old Testament after the Pentateuch, in the group of books known as the former prophets, and may have reached its final form as late as the fifth century BCE, it refers to the period of the Israelite settlement in Canaan, and has some obvious similarities to the Sodom story. It is therefore convenient to consider it now before the prohibitions of the Holiness Code in Leviticus.

(b) The narrative

The story begins with a Levite from the hill country of Ephraim taking as wife a concubine from Bethlehem. In a fit of anger she returns to her father's home, but the Levite follows her, and after a family reconciliation, he sets out with her and a servant to return north to Ephraim. They pass by Jerusalem, not at this time occupied by the tribes of Israel, and arrive at Gibeah in Benjamite territory. They are offered hospitality for the night by an old man who lives in the town but who is himself a stranger (*ger*) to the townspeople, and also an Ephraimite. As they settle down to supper, they are interrupted:

> While they were enjoying themselves, some of the worst scoundrels in the town surrounded the house, hurling themselves against the door and shouting to the old man who owned the house, 'Bring out the man who has gone into your house, for us to have intercourse with him'. The owner of the house went to them and said 'No, my friends, do nothing so wicked. This man is my guest; do not commit this outrage. Here is my daughter, a virgin; let me bring her out to you. Rape her and do to her what you please; but you shall not commit such an outrage against this man.' But the men refused to listen to him, so the Levite took hold of his concubine and thrust her outside for them. They assaulted her and abused her all night till the morning, and when dawn broke, they let her go. (*New English Bible*, Judges 19.22–25)

The concubine dies as a result of this outrage, and the Levite dissects her body and sends a portion of it to each of the other eleven tribes, blaming the Benjamites for their refusal to deal with the offenders themselves. The consequence is a punitive 'Holy War' between the eleven tribes and the Benjamites, which ends after a good deal of killing, with a reconciliation.

(c) Comment

The Book of the Judges covers the early period of the Israelites' settlement in Canaan in the thirteenth and twelfth centuries BCE, and points towards the need for the establishment of the monarchy – when everyone did that which was right in his own eyes, there was no King in Israel (21.25). The original compilation of these traditional stories about local heroes and rulers during the settlement period may have been made by a pre-deuteronomic editor, and his work is thought to have been several times revised, so that the version we now have is probably post-exilic. The twelve tribes are described as settling into their allotted areas, knowing themselves bound together in principle by their committal to or covenant with Yahweh, and in practice struggling to form an institutional relationship with each other, while at the same time maintaining an uneasy peace both with the previous inhabitants of their territories, and with powerful surrounding nations.

The final five chapters of Judges are additions to the main part of the book, and chiefly describe the tribe of Dan's migration north, and then the war between Benjamin and the remaining tribes, for which the cause, or as some scholars suggest, the pretext, is the rape of the Levite's concubine. Gibeah was a town just east of the main road north from Jerusalem, and is now called Tel-el-Ful. Recent excavations there indicate that a violent destruction of the site took place in the twelfth century BCE.

Although no reference to Sodom is made in the Judges story, the apparent similarities between the townspeople's assault at Sodom and the scoundrels' rape at Gibeah are marked, and it has often been suggested that the Judges version is the old tale reworked for a new didactic purpose. In both stories there is a serious breach of hospitality, the Levite is entitled to respect as the angels were, and the demand to bring out the man (men) that we may have intercourse with them is identical, though only a few men are involved at Gibeah, and the corporate responsibility there is applied to the Benjamites as a tribe, not to the actual attackers. The Hebrew word *yadha* is used for the demand, and in reference to the virgin daughter who has not 'known' men. Like Lot, the old man offers his daughter as a substitute, but at this point the stories diverge. Instead of the intervention of the angels, the Levite surrenders his concubine, and the assault follows, the Hebrew words making clear its brutality.

The main didactic purpose of the Gibeah narrative seems to be to draw out from the memory of the feuds among the tribes a warning that the lack of a central ruler was a serious disadvantage for the emerging notionally united tribal league. It is unlikely that there existed among the tribes in the twelfth century BCE any common codified system of criminal law, but there may well have been some consensus that breach of hospitality to the Levite and sexual violence to his woman were serious crimes. Such precepts would not have been unique to Israel in the twelfth century BCE. A post-exilic editor, adding these chapters as an appendix might, however, be glad to imply ancient witness to such structure and law.

Biblical translators from the Septuagint onwards have noted the possible ambiguity in the word '*yadha*' in this narrative. As with the Sodom text, modern Bibles either use 'know' or follow the NEB and the Good News Bible which describes the men of Gibeah as sexual perverts who want to have sex with the Levite. It seems that there is here again in the original Jahwist source the deliberate choice of an ambiguous word, while making clear from the context that homosexual behaviour was intended and condemned.

This conclusion, clear as it is, must not, however, obscure the fact that, like the Sodom narrative, the attribution of homosexual behaviour to the scoundrels of Gibeah is not the chief emphasis. As with the story of Lot in Genesis, which acts as a counterpoint to the obedience of Abraham, so in this appendix to Judges, the insignificant and inferior tribe of Benjamin is denigrated in comparison with the high calling of the whole tribal league. Sodom had been an alien place, inhabited by foreigners, and long known in ruins. The quarrels between the tribes were much more recent history, and the Gibeathites a disgrace to the family who were punished and reformed. The tale may have been sharpened in the telling, but then King Saul's birthplace had been Gibeah, as a later Jewish reader might have recalled with a wry smile.[3]

The Holiness Code (Leviticus 18 and 20)

(a) Introduction

While many of the exiles from Jerusalem sat down and wept by the waters of Babylon, some of them were busy writing. They had brought with them the priestly traditions associated with the Temple, now in ruins, and also the great epic story of Israel, already composed from the original works of the Yahwist, Elohist and Deuteronomist. Into this epic, they inserted the material from the Jerusalem Priestly tradition at appropriate points, notably in Exodus and Numbers, but chiefly in the Book of Leviticus, as it is called in the Septuagint. These insertions completed the Pentateuch as we now know it, though in its final form it probably dates from after the return of Ezra to Jerusalem, and the rebuilding of the Temple after 458 BCE.

At the time of Jesus, these regulations still set the pattern for the cultic and ritual life associated with the re-built Temple, its worship, and the priests who served it. But the Temple was destroyed again, finally, by the Romans, and Judaism has never since had a central sanctuary; only the wailing wall remains to bear witness to an institution that has gone for ever. It is not therefore

surprising that the Book of Leviticus has never been of major interest
to Christians, and few perhaps realize that the 'Love your neighbour'
command so much emphasized by Jesus appears twice in Leviticus 19.
In verse 18, it refers to fellow countrymen of the Jews, and in verse 35
it refers to aliens who have settled among them.

This 'Neighbour Command' belongs to a special section of Leviticus,
originally an independent collection of precepts which come from
earlier sources than the rest of the book. This section (chapters 17–26)
includes rules for personal and family morality, and is called 'The
Holiness Code', so named because the key injunction from which all
else flows is the command:

> You shall be holy, because I, the Lord your God, am holy
> (Lev. 19.2).

Although the Code begins with injunctions about slaughtering animals,
its main concern is with the life style of the community of the
Israelites, and family matters and sexual offences are major topics. In
chapter 18 and again in chapter 20 there are direct prohibitions of
male homosexual behaviour.

(b) The texts

> You shall not lie with a man as with a woman: that is an
> abomination. You shall not have sexual intercourse with any beast
> to make yourself unclean with it, nor shall a woman submit herself
> to intercourse with a beast; that is a violation of nature (Lev.
> 18.22–23).

> If a man has intercourse with a man as with a woman, they both
> commit an abomination. They shall both be put to death; their
> blood shall be on their own heads (Lev. 20.13).

(c) Comment

The narrative setting of the Holiness Code shows that it consists of
speeches made by Moses to the Israelites gathered at Sinai; a study of
its precepts suggests an association with the teaching of Jeremiah and
Ezekiel at the end of the sixth century BCE, but it may have passed
through several stages of editing, and contain substance and phrasing
much older. Both ch. 18 and ch. 20 probably once existed separately
as legal codes, dealing with the same sexual offences, but with marked
differences in style and order. After the exile, they were eventually
used in services at the second Temple, set out in a liturgical style,
somewhat akin to the recital of the Decalogue in Cranmer's prayer
book, the phrase 'I am the Lord' being the congregational responses.

The second chapter of the Code, Leviticus 18 in the modern

numbering, begins with a brief narrative section. The Israelites waiting at Sinai, are not to follow the institutions of the Egyptians 'where you once dwelt' not those of the land of Canaan 'to which I am bringing you'. They must keep God's ways and institutions – He is the Lord. There follows in verses 6–18 a list of prohibitions of sexual intercourse by a man with his female blood relations. Its scope is wider than a list of prohibited degrees for marriage, extending to all those living in the camp or group of tents. The New English Bible rendering 'intercourse' is more satisfactory than 'uncover the nakedness' of the Jerusalem translation, which is also retained by the Common Bible and its antecedents. Although this is an alternative meaning in the Hebrew it is euphemistic and perhaps misleading in the context here.

The following verses (19–23) contain a miscellaneous list of sexual malpractices, not necessarily concerned with family life, and this list may have been originally a separate code which in pre-exilic times incurred the death penalty. Intercourse during menstruation, or with a neighbour's wife, offering children for temple prostitution, male homosexual behaviour, and bestiality are all forbidden. The chapter concludes with an explanation that the land of Canaan became unclean because the inhabitants behaved like this, and God has driven them out in punishment. If the Israelites do the same things they will be cut off from worship – our word would be excommunicated – but they will not be sent into exile.

The next section of the Holiness Code (ch. 19) is more general and marked by a strong humane sense of care for the underprivileged and aliens, and 20.1–9 reverts to the issue of child prostitution and child sacrifice. This horrible practice, repudiated in Genesis and by Jeremiah and Ezekiel, took place at a shrine in the valley of Ben-hinnom near Jerusalem until suppressed by Josiah.

The second list of sexual offences, in 20.10–21, covers most of the same matters as ch. 18, but set out in a different order, with some new clauses and significantly, adding a range of appropriate punishments to each prohibition. Whereas the wording in the first list is cast in the apodeictic style, that is direct command, the second list of offences is expressed conditionally – *if* men behave homosexually together, they commit an abomination and shall be put to death, a sentence that the community would have to implement, at least in theory. In fact, the political situation of Judaism often prevented this, and in any case there is later evidence that the Rabbis regarded the death penalty as a shame and failure and were often adept in discovering extenuating circumstances. The frequent mention of capital punishment in these verses is probably intended to remind post-exilic Jews that they are fortunate to escape the severity of earlier times.

That is all the more reason for living holy lives on their return from Babylon.

There are no serious difficulties in translation of these texts. The New English Bible expression, 'lie with a man as with a woman' (ch. 18), seems less specific than 'intercourse with a man as with a woman' (ch. 20), but the Hebrew phrase is identical. It does not mean 'lie down' in a sense of getting off one's feet, but 'adopting the position for intercourse' or most literally, 'crouching in a coital position'. The Common Bible and its antecedents from the King James version onwards, and the Jerusalem, preserve the expression 'lie with' for both verses and use the same for the preceding verses prohibiting intercourse with blood relations. More recent translations tend to use a variety of expressions including intercourse, and sexual relations. The most precise equivalent to the Hebrew in modern English is sexual intercourse, vaginally, anally, or with animals as the case may be. It is not clear if seminal emission was required for the commission of these offences, or whether a wider range of sexual contact or juxtaposition, including some degree of nakedness, would have been sufficient as the euphemistic language suggests. Legal precision concerning actions of such a private and personal kind is notoriously difficult to achieve. A comparison may be made with the ambiguity of the English expression 'to sleep with someone'. The essential point being made of course is that sexual activity must be limited to those who are married to each other.

The word 'abomination' (Hebrew – *to'ebah*) needs some explanation. In English the word expresses disgust or disapproval, but in the Bible its predominant meaning is concerned with religious truth rather than morality or aesthetics. Among the range of meanings in the Old Testament it is used, for example, in the closing chapters of Genesis to describe the Egyptians' dislike of foreigners and their eating habits. The prophets see the worship of idols and the cult of Canaan as abominable to the Lord and deceit in business is an abomination – false scales – in Proverbs 11.1. In Deuteronomy and Kings, 'abomination' is used as in Jeremiah and Ezekiel, to describe the Canaanite idolatory, focussed on the hill shrines, their ritual and their prostitutes.

In the Holiness Code *to'ebah* is used only in regard to homosexual behaviour (18.22 and 20.13), and in the summary (18.26–30). In the 'cleanness regulations' referring to animals in Leviticus ch. 11, most English translations use 'abomination' for those thought unclean, but the New English Bible draws out the difference in the Hebrew text by using 'vermin'. The distinction between clean and unclean animals in the Jewish tradition may have begun by the recognition that the so-called unclean animals were used in alien religious rites, so the attribution may have deeper significance than mere dietary or health considerations. It seems, however, in the Holiness Code that the association of homosexual intercourse with the Canaanites' temple prostitution and child sacrifice is firm.

These texts from the Holiness Code show that by 400 BCE the Jewish people were being warned in their Torah that male homosexual behaviour was an abomination to the Lord. It had once been a capital crime, but now it is thought to make them unclean and therefore must imply excommunication from the worship and also from the fellowship of Israel. The concluding verses of Leviticus 18 make this clear. Declaring such behaviour abominable placed it in a well-recognized category of sin, somewhat equivalent perhaps to mortal sin in traditional Catholic spiritual discipline.

Scholars have scrutinized these texts from Leviticus in recent years to elicit if possible the reason or reasons for the prohibition of homosexual behaviour. A distinction is made in 18.22–24, (NEB) between homosexual behaviour between males, which is called an abomination, and bestiality, which for a man makes him unclean, but when a woman submits to it, is described as a violation of nature. This distinction is not made so clearly in other translations. In contemporary English, the word 'violation' can be used to indicate sexual assault, but in this verse the Hebrew word can also be translated as perversion, or more literally as confusion. The distinction made here in the New English Bible may be intended to indicate degrees of outrage, the man acting, the woman being forced to submit, but other modern translations are content to use a range of words such as detestable, perverted and defile, and it may be that for these particular four offences, it was sufficient to show as a reason that God was outraged by such behaviour and required the death penalty.[4]

In the light of subsequent attitudes to homosexual behaviour, it is also worth considering a wider significance of the notion of nature being violated or confused. In the account of creation, described in the Priestly narrative at the beginning of Genesis, God names his creatures 'according to their kind', so sexual activity with an animal could be understood as a confusion, an attempted breach of the natural division of species from the creation. The expression 'violation of nature' also occurs in the NEB rendering of ch. 20. where it refers to intercourse between a man and his daughter-in-law. For this, the older versions use 'confusion' and recent translations have 'incest' which is legally correct.

Other possible or additional reasons for these prohibitions include the suggestion that they involve the misuse of semen, provided by God for the continuation of each kind in its order, and so this sub-code has a unifying theme – the misuse or waste of human seed. Although abandoning children to pagan worship is primarily an insult to God, obliquely this is a waste. As a separate matter, the bestiality prohibition may have reference to the cultic ritual of intercourse between humans and sacred animals, a form of imitative magic practised at the Canaanite shrines, and offensive to the Israelites for that reason as well.

All that noted, the addition of these four offences to the rules concerning the extended family in ch. 18 does suggest that in the minds of the original compilers or the later editors, some form of association or a common theme was perceived. All these acts crossed the boundary between natural and unnatural behaviour. Bestiality was the worst breach, but the others shared in the same basic flaw; they were contrary to the fixed order of creation. Although this notion is not made articulate in these verses, by inference, the concept of what is abominable to God takes on a further meaning; there is here an embryonic sense of natural law. This sense is entirely personalized in the will of God; it is not yet seen as part of the framework of the universe, as it is later understood in Greek and scholastic Christian thought. For the Hebrew mind, neither natural aversion nor the sense of the good are thought of in separate categories from the will of God, and Jewish theocratic and theonomic perceptions make no distinction between sound religion and good morals.[5]

The choice of words any team of translators uses will reflect inevitably the style and convictions of their times, and it may not be unfair to suggest that the long Christian tradition of describing some sexual offences as unnatural led the NEB team to use this expression. Others since have hesitated, unaware that any sense of natural law can be no more than tentatively attributed to these Jewish writers at work on the Leviticus codes long before the birth of Plato. All that noted, the central reason for the condemnation in the codes must be that confusion in sexual behaviour disturbs the extensive but close-knit family structure which the Holiness Code is commending. Adultery, homosexual behaviour and bestiality are all logically linked as threats to family harmony and as a potential denial of the natural order God has provided. This link is taken seriously by St Paul in the Epistle to the Romans, but by then, as we shall see the doctrine of Natural Law is far more clearly defined.[6]

Summary of the Old Testament Evidence

The study of these three Old Testament passages clearly referring to homosexual behaviour, when taken in historical and literary context, shows a continuing tradition of disapproval. The story of Sodom's destruction, and the somewhat similar tale of outrage at Gibeah established a traditional explanation for this disapproval, and it was also expressed legally in one of the minor codes of capital offences dating originally from the same early period. The fierce confrontation with all that was involved in the temple rituals of the Canaanite religion re-inforced the tradition and found its clearest expression in the final forms of the Holiness Code. It is used there with other precepts to define the life of a 'clean' Israelite, fit to worship God and be a member of his community in the restored nation.

From the variety of words used in the Holiness Code to show why God hates sexual irregularities and malpractices, the notions of confusion between species created as distinct, the misuse of semen, and the violation of the natural order can be distinguished, but any sophisticated arguments based on such distinction are precarious. Old Testament morality concerning sexual relationships is in basic principle committed to the defence of family and married life, and everything outside it is seen as a threat and an outrage, an abomination not to be permitted in Israel.

The declaration and protection of this principle was one of the continuing tasks of the Old Testament authors. Of course, condemning homosexuality was never an important aspect of this task, hence the paucity of references to it, but where it is mentioned, the hostility is consistent. It is sometimes suggested that this hostility may be little more than the usual homophobic reactions of ordinary men, and in any case part of the general negative attitude taken in legal and moral codes of the Middle East during the centuries when Israel's traditions were forming. But the final Canon of the Torah was not merely the work of scissors and paste sub-editors tidying up other people's material. The Priestly editors were religious men, pondering the story of Israel's faith and failure. Confronted with this teaching about homosexuality, they retained it in their revisions and offered a mixture of reasons for it. Maybe distaste for buggery played a part in their considerations, but they moved on towards a theology of sexuality which necessarily excluded such activity.

4

The Inter-testamental Period

Introduction

There was an interval of some three hundred years between the completion of the Old Testament books eventually included in the Hebrew canon and the composition of the major writings of the New Testament. This interval was of great significance in Palestine, both for political changes and religious developments, and it is of crucial importance to an understanding of Christianity. Within this inter-testamental period, as it is called, Judaism was forced to take the decisive step of becoming a religion based on a book rather than a building, for the Temple was desecrated and later destroyed. Jesus himself lived through some of its most disturbed years, and by its end, the essential characteristics of Christine doctrine and ethics were being settled.

By the time Jesus was born, the Jewish people had long ceased to be a close-knit group living in central Palestine. Some stayed behind in Babylon after the exile, and a prosperous Jewish community developed there. It was later to be an influential centre for Rabbinic learning. Both commerce and captivity had taken other Jews to the west, notably to Alexandria, and other places around the Mediterranean which were part of the extensive Greek or Roman Empire. Their departure was called the exile (*golah* in Hebrew) or the scattering (*diaspora* in Greek). Jerusalem itself was internationalized by trade and by occupation forces, Greek, Egyptian, Syrian, and Roman. Added to these foreigners was a steadily increasing flow of pilgrims to the Holy City.

The Threat from Hellenism

From the seventh century onwards, Palestine had known Greek trading and increasing seaborne contact, and this increased after the exile. Following the destruction of the Persian Empire by Alexander

the Great and his early death in 323 BCE, the Egyptian Ptolemies
ruled in Palestine and southern Syria for a hundred years until the
Syrian Antiochus III wrested Palestine from them. Like the Persians,
these Egyptian rulers of the Hellenistic empire allowed religious
affairs in Jerusalem to remain under Jewish authority, represented
by the new office of High Priest and the council of influential
families called the Sanhedrin. In terms of culture, commerce, and
intellectual pursuits, the urban Jews were much impressed by Greek
thought, and became accustomed to Greek settlers who renamed
their towns in the Greek language. Even rural Jews had to come to
terms with immigrants in their homeland. As they lost their knowledge of Hebrew, Palestinian Jews became bilingual, learning their
scriptures in Aramaic translations (Targums), but often using Greek
in everyday life.

Jewish nationalism had reacted vigorously to Syrian aggression in
the Maccabaean revolt from 166 BCE onwards, but after an uneasy
truce, their orthodoxy had to contend with the unsatisfactory rule of
the Hasmoneans, combining religious and secular authority until the
Roman Pompeii made Judaea a province of that empire from 63 BCE
onwards. From 37–4 BCE, most of Palestine was ruled for the Romans
by Herod the Great, under the patronage of the Emperor Octavian,
later known as Augustus. Herod was a firm ruler, and a great builder.
He founded the Gymnasium in Jerusalem, and also the vast buildings
of the Temple Mount, of which parts of the Western Wall can still be
seen by tourists. He abolished the Sanhedrin, but in other ways won a
limited religious freedom for the Jews. On his death, his kingdom was
divided between three of his sons. Archaleus, Ethnarch of Judaea
died in 6 CE, and his area came under the jurisdiction of a series of
Roman Prefects. The fourth of these was Pontius Pilate, who with
the other two sons of Herod, Antipas and Philip, are mentioned in the
Gospels. Pilate restored the Sanhedrin, temporarily, but The Temple
was finally destroyed by Titus in 70 CE.

Inter-testamental Jewish Writings

The Jewish religious writings of the inter-testamental period can be
conveniently treated in three somewhat loosely classified groups:
apocryphal, pseudepigraphical, and rabbinic. The apocryphal writings
were known and used by the Christian church in its early period, being
part of the Septuagint and familiar to the Diaspora. These works were
attractive to the Christians, in part because of their emphasis on a
future hope, now seen to be fulfilled in Christ. Written in Greek, and
having assimilated Greek ideas, their language and conceptual framework were perhaps easier for non-Palestinian Christians than orthodox

Rabbinic writings, and they formed a useful bridge for evangelism among the liberal Jews.

The Pseudepigraphical books have been traditionally disregarded in the Christian tradition, not only as non-canonical, but also because until recently they were often known only in Ethiopic or Slavonic translations. The discovery of the Dead Sea Scrolls and the Qumran Library in 1947 has made available fragments of these works which must be dated not later than 68 CE, and it has been increasingly recognized in the past twenty years that the pseudepigrapha were widely read and influential in the inter-testamental period. The programme of translation and publication of these books continues, and as they become available, they provide much new evidence of the life and thought of the time.

The Rabbinic writings are, in principle, the investigation and exegesis of the Torah, protecting it by interpretation, as the development of the literature has been described. There are two forms. The first *Midrash*, meaning deduction, originated with the appointment of a group of authorized leaders after the time of Ezra. It continued in the synagogue practice of reading a section of the Pentateuch and adding narration and explanation, and it developed finally into written commentaries compiled at the Rabbinic academies or by later respected teachers. The second form, *Mishnah*, is a codification of the teaching of the Rabbis on the Torah, but arranged by subject matter in a series of tractates, the biblical texts themselves being omitted. Further codification of Mishnah and other teachings led to the Talmuds, dating from the fifth century CE, and produced in authoritative versions in Palestine and Babylon.

The reaction of orthodox Judaism to the Hellenization of Palestine was to resist syncretism, to see the new situation as a renewal of the old battle with the Canaanites over idolatry and the behaviour which sprang from it, and to abide by the old tradition to which the ancient scrolls bore witness. The Jews of the Diaspora, however, regarded the new apocryphal writings as part of the Wisdom literature of their religion, a supplement to the Torah and the Prophets. The latest works in the Apocrypha may well have been written just before or during the life of Jesus, and both the writers of the New Testament and the early church Fathers were familiar with these books and quoted from them. Although the early church accepted them as part of scripture, they were distinguished from the Hebrew canon, at least in principle if not so clearly in practice, and eventually in the fourth century CE, St Jerome named them *libri ecclesiastici* not *libri canonici*.

It would be misleading to suggest, however, that the canon of the Hebrew Old Testament was finally settled before the Apocryphal books were written. It was a gradual process of adding to the basic

Torah of the Pentateuch and the books of the major prophets an expanding collection of minor historical, poetic and casuistic works as these found general acceptance among the Rabbis. Indeed, only at the Council of Jamnia, around 90 CE, were Ecclesiastes and the Song of Songs accepted. Regular use in the synagogues was probably an important factor in final acceptance, as the Jewish religion became more centred on 'The Book' after the destruction of the second Temple.

To represent the many and diffuse writings of the inter-testamental period concerning homosexuality, it seems best to offer short direct quotation from a wide range of them. Space does not allow much detail about authorship context, or meanings of words, and in any case such details are far less agreed among scholars for these relatively recently discovered works compared with what is securely known about the canonical scriptures. Despite these uncertainties, these writings are from the world in which Christianity was born, show that homosexuality was far more of an issue then than in earlier Israelite times, and help us to understand the climate of thought into which St Paul and others had to enter. Selections are taken from, first, the Apocryphal books of Ecclesiasticus and Wisdom, familiar to Christians, and then from some of the Pseudepigraphal books. The continuing tradition among Jewish people of interpreting the Holiness Code and the Sodom story is represented by Mishnah, Midrash, and the later commentary of Rashi, and the survey is completed by brief references to the two most important Jewish writers of the period, Josephus and Philo.

Reference to Homosexual Behaviour in the Apocrypha

It has already become clear from study of Leviticus that references to homosexual behaviour in the Bible are often elusive, but can be detected with some certainty in association with other offences which the Law of Israel condemned. The same clustering together of references to the sin of Sodom, Temple prostitution, unnatural intercourse and bestiality is found in the Apocrypha. Their context is usually best understood as denunciation of the alien culture in familiar and oft repeated terms, by a nation in crisis, committed to the belief that only by obedience to the Law will they escape the Lord's judgment and survive under his protection.

In *Ecclesiasticus*, originally written in Hebrew about 190 BCE, 16.17 refers to the doom God assigns to the heathen by turning a watered plain into a salt desert, and this is very similar to Psalm 107.34 'He turns fruitful land into a salt desert because the men who dwell there are so wicked'. This seems a clear reference to Sodom, especially to

anyone looking across to the Salt Flats at the end of the Dead Sea
from the heights of Masada. In 16.7 Sodom is referred to as 'Lot's
adopted home, abhorrent in its arrogance'.

The Book of Wisdom has been dated between 100 BCE and 40 CE
and is a composite work from Jewish sources in Alexandria, written in
Greek. The early parts deal with righteousness and wisdom, but in
chapter 10 there begins a history of Israel from Adam to the Exodus.
The survival of Noah and Lot is attributed to the saving power of
Wisdom, and the destruction of Sodom is described:

> She (Wisdom) saved a good man from the destruction of the
> godless, and he escaped the fire that came down on the five cities,
> cities whose wickedness is still attested by a smoking waste ...
> Wisdom they ignored, losing the power to recognize what is good
> and leaving by their lives a monument of folly, such that their
> enormities can never be forgotten (Wisdom of Solomon 10.6–8,
> New English Bible).

The activity of God is here expressed in terms of the divine Wisdom,
and suggests that the author has been influenced by Platonism.
The second reference is similar, but concentrates on the hatred of
strangers and foreigners, presumably with reference to the Egyptian
treatment of the Israelites after Joseph, and then in parenthesis
includes the men of Sodom among those who, with the Egyptians,
were struck blind:

> They were struck with blindness also, like the men at the door of
> the one good man, when yawning darkness fell upon them, and
> each went groping for his own doorway (Wisdom of Solomon 19.17,
> New English Bible).

The context of this verse is a contrast between the 'others' who had
refused to welcome strangers, and the Egyptians who had made slaves
of guests and benefactors. The Revised Version and Jerusalem
Versions by italicization or footnote make clear the reference to
Sodom, though the New English Bible and the Common Bible leave
the literal translation 'others' unexplained, presumably because the
reference to Sodom is clear enough already.

There is one reference to sexual perversion in Wisdom. This occurs
in the interpolation on idolatry, chapters 13–15, a beautifully written
and sharply derisive description of its origins and futile consequences.
With fierce irony, the writer sets out how bereavement or political
obsequiousness leads to the setting up of images and their subsequent
deification. Once this fundamental error is made, then every kind of
moral evil flows from it. The passage is typical of the period, and since

it has some similarity to that in the Epistle to the Romans, chapter 1, it is quoted at length:

> Then, not content with gross error in their knowledge of God, men live in the constant warfare of ignorance and call this monstrous evil, peace. They perform ritual murders of children and secret ceremonies and the frenzied orgies of unnatural cults; the purity of life and marriage is abandoned; and a man treacherously murders his neighbour or corrupts his wife and breaks his heart. All is chaos – bloody murder, theft and fraud, corruption, treachery, riot, perjury, honest men driven to distraction; ingratitude, moral corruption, sexual perversion, breakdown of marriage, adultery, debauchery. For the worship of idols, whose names it is wrong even to mention, it is the beginning, cause and end of every evil (Wisdom 14.22–27, New English Bible).

How far, in fact, child sacrifice was still practised in the mystery cults of the Near East at this time is uncertain, and the whole tone of the denunciation is polemical, perhaps to the point of exaggeration. In every age, some observers see decadence all around, but allowing for that, the list of offences mentioned is reminiscent of those found in the final form of the Holiness Code, and four kinds of sexual sin are enumerated in verse 26.

The first of these, 'sexual perversion' in the NEB translation, implies homosexual behaviour, but the best literal meaning seems to be 'changing of Kind', though the Greek expression (*geneseos enallage*) is unusual. The Jerusalem Bible has 'sins against nature' which has a consistent homosexual meaning in that translation. Some older translations have 'confusion of kind or sex' and the Common Bible has sex perversion.

Since 'kind' meaning 'species' (Hebrew: *mishpachah*) is rendered in the Septuagint as *genesis* and hence reflects the creation of the different species and perhaps of male and female nature, the notion of confusion, contrary to God's order, may be present here. It was noted earlier, in connection with the prohibition of bestiality in the Holiness Code, that confusion of the natural order was the basis of that offence, and child sacrifice and homosexual behaviour were prohibited in the same section. There is no mention of bestiality in this passage in Wisdom, but the whole tenor of it suggests a reiteration of the traditional code and its precepts. The reference to homosexual behaviour would be retained since this was a notorious feature of Hellenism.

To sum up, in the apocryphal books of Ecclesiasticus and Wisdom the traditional attitude to Sodom as the synonym of general wickedness, folly, and inhospitality, is thrice repeated, and in the Wisdom interpolation about idolatry, the prohibition of homosexual behaviour seems probably to be reiterated.

Reference to Homosexual Behaviour in the Jewish Pseudepigrapha

These tracts for the times by Jewish thinkers have historical value, though their ascriptions to well-known Old Testament characters are usually fictitious. For the most part originally written in Hebrew or Aramaic by Palestinian authors, the Pseudepigrapha circulated widely among the dispersed Jews in Greek translations and were as familiar as the Apocrypha to the early Christian Apologists and New Testament writers who refer to them. The discoveries at Qumran show that the community there valued these writings as scripture, and fragments of them were found in the caves.

A new collection of Pseudepigrapha translated into English was edited by Professor James Charlesworth in 1983,[1] and this includes some material from Qumran, but it remains true that much is still dependent on later manuscripts, even translations of translations. The discovery of more early material would help us to be sure of the dating and accuracy of the original texts.

A number of these tracts contain references to the sins of Sodom, often linked with a denunciation of homosexual behaviour more fierce and more explicit than in the canonical books of the Old Testament. The usual explanation for this stronger repudiation is that the Jews of this time, not only in Palestine but everywhere in the Dispersion were confronted with a much more open and commercially exploited tolerance of homosexual behaviour than they had seen before, and they registered their protest. That acknowledged, the prohibitions in the Leviticus Law of Holiness were taught in the Jewish Diaspora communities, and they must have been aware in fact that such practices were not unknown among Jews past and present.

However, as in the Old Testament proper, homosexual behaviour is only mentioned in passing in the Pseudepigraphal writings. In some of them, notably, I Enoch, Jubilees, the Genesis Apocryphon, and the Testament of the Twelve Patriarchs, the 'Confusion of Species' theme is held to apply to the attempted rape on the Angels at Sodom.

In one version of the Second Book of Enoch, known to us only later Slavonic translation, but based quite probably on a pre-Christian Jewish original, a clear link is made of Sodom with pederasty:

> This place, Enoch, has been prepared for those who do not glorify God, who practice on the earth the sin which is against nature, which is child corruption in the anus in the manner of Sodom. (Enoch 10.4).[2]

This sharp description is of those in Hell (the Northern Heaven), and a contrast is made between their situation and the happiness of the Righteous (in Paradise) who are said, among other things *'to give bread to the hungry and cover the naked with clothing'* – (9.3). These phrases are much akin to judgment themes in Isaiah and Matthew 25. It is typical of the character of these tracts that one can readily recognize in them statements and situation which clearly reflect knowledge of the canonical scriptures, but also glosses and additional material which, whether or not familiar to the early church, have not survived as part of the authentic tradition. Allowance must be made for re-editing of the texts in Christian times, not easily now distinguished. There are many similar passages in the pseudepigraphal material from Palestine, but this is too specialized for further quotation here.

As an example of a Diaspora source, the following quotations come from Jewish Communities in Alexandria, and seem certainly pre-Christian. The third Book of Maccabees, despite its misleading name, records Ptolemy's persecution of the Jews and was written in Greek 100 BCE. A precis is given of Jewish history, including:

> Thou who created all things, and governest the whole world . . . and judgest those who do aught in violence and arrogance . . . did burn up with fire and brimstone the men of Sodom, workers of arrogance, who had become known of all for their crimes, and didst make them an example for those who should come after (III Macc. 2.3–5).

This is the somewhat standard reference to Sodom. The contrast, typical of these writings, made between pagans under judgment and believers who will be justified can be found again in the Sibylline Oracles, Book 3. These were also written in Alexandria, some forty years before III Maccabees:

> Those men will have a great fall when they launch on a course of unjust haughtiness. Immediately compulsion to impiety will come upon these men. Male will have intercourse with male and they will set up boys in houses of ill-fame, and in those days there will be a great affliction among men and it will throw everything into confusion (Sibylline Oracles Book 3, lines 183–7).[3]

There will also appear a new God-fearing people:

> . . . at dawn they lift up holy arms towards heaven, from their beds, always sanctifying their flesh with water, . . . they are mindful of holy wedlock, and they do not engage in impious intercourse with male children, as do Phoenicians, Egyptians, Greeks and Romans,

Persians and Galations, transgressing the Holy Law of immortal God (Oracles book 3, lines 590–600).[4]

The eschatological flavour of these Sibylline Oracles helped to make them acceptable to the early Christian fathers, and so it is to be noted that in these quotations, immorality or holiness are thought to flow from an initial choice to reject or believe in God. This perception fits well with the Wisdom literature sense of things, considered earlier in the third chapter, and indicates a general pattern of thought common in this intertestamental period. Given the wide circulation of these Pseudepigrapha among those Jews who would be eventually converted to Christ, it is not surprising that St Paul should use similar language in his condemnation of homosexual behaviour in his Epistles. It is all part of the familiar contrast usually being drawn between pagan and godly life-styles.

Continuation of the Jewish Tradition

Although it is impossible to cover this subject properly, and strict chronology would require the insertion of references to Jewish thought at the appropriate points in the historical section of this book, it is convenient here, as an excursus, to give a very brief record of some of the Jewish thinkers and teaching as it continued after the formation and development of the Christian church. Although for much of Christian history there was antagonism between the churches and the Jewish religion, it often proved valuable for Christian scholars of the Bible, who seldom knew Hebrew, to consult Jewish scholars about questions of interpretation of the Old Testament texts. Beyond that particular need for contact, there was also the more intangible but no less important continual contribution Judaism made to European culture, law and philosophy, and above all to its religious consciousness. Much more indeed than the somewhat grudging Tridentine decree suggests: Judaism is the one heresy God allows.

(a) The Mishnah

This codification of Rabbinic teaching by Rabbi Judah dates from the second century CE, and ranks second only to Hebrew scripture in authority. In its fourth division it lists the jurisdiction of the Sanhedrin for capital offences. Homosexual behaviour is to be punished by stoning:

> These are they that are to be stoned: he that has connection with his mother, his father's wife, his daughter-in-law, a male, or a beast, and the blasphemer and the idolator and he that offers any of his seed to Moloch ... (Quoted from the Mishnah, Sanhedrin 7.4).[5]

This list of offences and punishments shows obvious similarities with the Holiness Code, and it has been noted earlier that in fact the Sanhedrin was seldom free to carry out the death penalty, and was in any case disposed to delay, hear appeals, and avoid rigour when possible. Sodom is only twice mentioned in the Misnah, insignificantly.

(b) Midrash Rabbah-Genesis

This commentary on Genesis comes from Palestine and in the form quoted from is dated in the sixth century CE, though its origins are early in the inter-testamental period. On Genesis 19.5 it says:

> the Sodomites demanded BRING THEM OUT UNTO US, THAT WE MAY KNOW THEM – for sexual purposes (Midrash Rabbah L. 5).

A footnote to this comment adds 'i.e. pederasty, "know being understood as in Genesis 4. v. 1."' In a further comment, on Genesis 19.9, it observes that:

> The Sodomites made an agreement among themselves that whenever a stranger visited them, they should force him to sodomy and rob him of his money (Midrash Rabbah LVII).

This Midrash represents the considered opinion of Rabbis over several centuries and therefore shows how the authentic interpretation of the Sodom story has been shaped. It was part of ancient custom among Semitic people to inflict this indignity on prisoners, and the inhabitants of Sodom were particularly noxious in treating visitors in this way, when they should have offered them hospitality. Even worse, their visitors were actually, the Midrash suggests, the angel Gabriel, sent to overturn Sodom, and Raphael who is to rescue Lot. Pederasty here implies homosexual behaviour generally, not only attacks on young children.

Although this Midrash view of Sodom was long regarded among Jews as authoritative, a later commentary on the Books of the Pentateuch, written by Rashi about 1000 BCE became widely respected. Rashi, actually an abbreviation of his full name, Rabbi Solomon ben Isaac, was a French biblical scholar, whose works were eventually printed in many languages from the seventeenth century onwards. Luther and other Reformers knew his work well.

Rashi's understanding of Genesis 19 is restrained, emphasizing the breach of hospitality and God's patience in delaying the destruction, but he makes the sexual meaning of v. 5 explicit:

> That we may have unnatural connection with them.

(c) Other Early Jewish Authors: Josephus and Philo

(i) *Josephus*. Josephus was a Palestinian Jew, trained in the Law and a Pharisee. Born in 37 CE, he wrote a history of the Jewish War, and followed this with a long account of his nation's history entitled *Jewish Antiquities*. In the first of these books, he describes the southern end of the Dead Sea:

> Once so rich in crops and the wealth of its cities, but now dust and ashes. They say that owing to the impiety of its inhabitants it was burnt up by lightning; indeed there are still marks from the fire from heaven ... To this extent, the stories about the land of Sodom are confirmed by the evidence of our eyes.[6]

In the *Antiquities*, Book 1, Josephus describes the saga of Abraham and Lot in an urbane style for his Roman readers, suggesting these patriarchs were wholly respectable characters. The final stages of the destruction of Sodom are recorded as a sad story of progressive moral decay against which God reluctantly has to act in punishment, despite Abraham's grief and pleading:

> The angels came to the city of the Sodomites and Lot invited them to be his guests, for he was very kind to strangers ... But the Sodomites, on seeing these men of remarkable fair appearance whom Lot had taken under his roof, were bent only on violence and outrage of their youthful beauty. God, indignant at their atrocities, blinded the criminals so that they could not find the entrance to the house, and condemned the whole people of the Sodomites to destruction.

When he comes to the story of the rape at Gibeah, Josephus omits from it any suggestion of homosexual offence, perhaps because he judges it impolitic to stress this subject in a work intended for first-century Romans, to whom his main purpose is to defend Jewish propriety in morals. In any case, the Gibeah story is hardly ever mentioned in other inter-testamental writings, being not from the Pentateuch, and this lack of interest among Jewish writers may also explain why it is ignored or eclipsed by the Sodom narrative in the Christian tradition.

(ii) *Philo*. Living between 20 BCE and 50 CE in Alexandria, a rival city to Rome, with a large Jewish population, Philo was the most influential Hellenistic Jew of his time. He wrote on philosophy and history, and extensively on the Pentateuch and the laws it contained. Under the general heading of marital infidelity, he deals with the sexual offences of the Holiness Code, incest pederasty, bestiality, and intercourse with a woman during the menstrual period which he describes as contrary to nature because generative seeds must not be wasted *'for the sake of a gross and untimely pleasure'*. Philo takes a harsh view of pederasty, and it is clear from the long paragraph he writes about this that he has chiefly in mind the association of mature men with youthful lovers, that is the Greek custom rather than cult prostitution:

> He pursues an unnatural pleasure and does his best to render cities desolate and uninhabited by destroying (or wasting) the means of creation.[7]

This comment tightly links unnatural behaviour, the waste of seed, and the destruction of Sodom, and in his commentary on the Genesis story, Philo lets his imagination run away on the vices of that city and its people. Broadly, he sees the sequence of their downfall, as starting with excessive wealth, then drink, and forbidden forms of sex, adultery being followed by homosexual behaviour, and then sterility. While having no doubt that 'unseemly pederasty' was offered to Sodom's angelic visitors, Philo develops from this an allegorical meaning about the choice between the ways of the flesh and heavenly ascetic wisdom. In contrast with the cool style of Josephus, Philo's allegory seems almost bizarre, but in fact it set a style of biblical interpretation which was often followed among the Christian fathers. Clement, Origen and Ambrose used Philo's ideas freely, and they re-appear constantly in later Christian assessments of the moral problem of homosexual behaviour.

5

The New Testament

Introduction

No references to homosexual behaviour are found in the four Gospels. In the Epistles attributed to St Paul, there are direct references in Romans, I Corinthians, and I Timothy, and in the Catholic Epistles of Jude and II Peter the subject is mentioned in a diffused way.

From the review of the inter-testamentary period already given, it is clear that the Jewish religion at the time of Christ was fiercely opposed to the Greek life-style, regarding homosexuality as one among many aspects of a culture they hated and felt to be contrary to God's will. Given that climate of opposition, it is not surprising that the first Christian leaders, who were all converts from Judaism, took the same view, and for much the same reasons. Only if Jesus himself had challenged the tradition, and we have no evidence that he did, would they have seriously re-assessed what they understood to be a long-established teaching of the Old Testament.

Some caution is necessary, because the references are sparse, of a style similar to those in the Apocrypha, and there is nothing to compare with the Old Testament Sodom and Gibeah narratives or the precise regulation of the Holiness Code. It is clear that the immorality of homosexual behaviour was not an important issue for the early church, but there seems to have been little or no doubt what the rule was. The other Christian writings we have from this period, and the soon to follow teaching from the early church fathers take the same view, and that evidence is surveyed at the beginning of the history section.

The reticence or disinterest is easily explained. For the first Christians, the great question was how to explain the significance of Christ and his gospel to those who had not met him. Then for those who believed and were baptized, the task was to teach the fundamentals of Christian faith and morality. For their morality, the Christians placed great emphasis on the teaching of Jesus about the primacy of the Love Commandments. To be sure, what Jesus had to say about loving your neighbour was not only in fact a quotation from the Book of Leviticus, which all his Jewish hearers had known about from childhood as part of the Mosaic Law read in the synagogue; it was also a text which some of the Rabbinnic teachers of the time stressed as a key to all other rules for living peaceably together in community. But, law-keeping, that is all the precepts of the Torah, had become for many Jews a detailed and onerous burden which was either discouraging to ordinary people or became an end in itself, obscuring the basic principles of love and mercy as Jesus constantly emphasized. His great parable of the Good Samaritan set this old principle in a new context unforgettably, there is no limit to the demands of loving care.

If Christian morality could be summed up by the over-riding principle of love – *agape* – a new disposition in the heart of the believer made possible by the grace of the Holy Spirit, it was nevertheless important for the New Testament writers to stress that Christ had not come to destroy the law but to fulfill it, as he himself taught. He did not abrogate the principles of the Torah, and there is a clear sense of continuity from the moral teaching of Judaism to that of the Christian church, not only as that was found in the Ten Commandments, but also in the insights of the prophets. Although Jewish opponents of the Christians often accused them of lawlessness and immorality, the continuity between Old and New Testament morality is so strong that it is in fact hard to find substantial disagreement between them about what it is good to do. That is actually not surprising if we accept that God is the source of both revelations.

This continuity is of great importance in understanding why the rule about homosexual behaviour was not disputed among the Christians – they simply followed the Jewish teaching on the matter as they did about marriage and much else. They did so of course not so much because they thought of themselves as Jews who had added belief in Jesus to their original faith, though for some perhaps that was true, but because they shared with the Jews their deep disapproval of the pagan morality on sexual matters in the lands where they lived. Not only in Palestine, but in all the countries around the Mediterranean where Christian communities were quickly established by the missionery apostles, they were coming to self-consciousness in their own faith in the midst of morally uncertain and confused societies.

The Social Context

(a) Palestine

Our thoughts about the social situation in Israel at the time of Christ are usually much influenced by the particular events of the passion narratives in the Gospels, which concentrate on the conflicts with the Jewish leaders and the military occupation of the Roman legions. During Passover, the Roman Governor Pilate surveyed the temple area from his Antonia Fortress at the north west corner of the precinct, but his headquarters were at Caesarea, a Greek city on the coast. Equally, the Gospels give us virtually no hint that the civil administration of the whole country was still organized on a basically Greek pattern. It was standard Roman policy for Israel not to interfere with local administration and customs provided political stability and military security were assured. Palestine was in any case largely owned and farmed by rich foreigners, the Jews for the most part being peasants and artisans, apart from a few Sadduccean families with vassal type agreements with Rome.

Among the features of the Hellenistic culture which affronted the religious convictions of the Jerusalem Jews were the brothels and the Gymnasium. It has been suggested that even Jesus and his disciples on their infrequent visits to the city of Jerusalem could not have failed to notice the brothels, where not only women but also boys and young men offered their service to tourists. Pederasty in its commercial form was part of what Hellenistic cultures brought to Jerusalem.[1]

Gymnasia were important features of the Greek style of life, and Herod had built one in Jerusalem. It was not just a sports arena near the Temple area, it was the club, leisure centre and education resource where those who wished to associate themselves with the foreign culture met the expatriates. All sport was played naked, and this disturbed Jewish modesty. (It also meant that Jewish men taking part in the sports could be identified by their circumcision, and some of them had cosmetic operations in an attempt to conceal their nationality. Orthodox Jews regarded this as a form of apostasy.)[2]

(b) Greece and Rome

Outside Israel, many Christians were converted from the colonies of Jewish diaspora. These were long accustomed to the struggle to preserve a racial and religious distinctiveness among often ethnically mixed populations who, over the past three centuries had been incorporated unwillingly into the Greek and Roman Empires. The Hellenism they experienced bore little resemblance to the classical teaching of Aristotle and Plato. In the debased form spread by Alexander's soldiers, it could hardly be regarded as a system of enlightenment, and although in many places it remained true that to accept Greek patterns of life was the assured path to social and commercial success for subject people, for Judaism abroad, as much as at home this was clearly impossible.

Not all Greek and Roman culture was of course repugnant to Jews and Christians. In many ways their patterns of domestic life were much as we might expect: marriage, children, and slaves when they could be afforded, but the position of women in society was different from ours, and in some ways similar to what we see in parts of Islam. Women were secluded from public life, seldom went out alone, only in rich families were they educated and that usually by slaves, and they lacked full rights of citizenship. They entertained guests at home, gave dinner parties and socialized in that limited way. An insight to how Greeks regarded gender difference is given by their statues. Women are depicted in a feminine way, flowing graceful robes marvellously carved, or when nude, idealized in the form of the young Venus, slim by mediterranean standards for normal women. Men are depicted either as the serene philosopher or as the young naked athlete or warrior; Apollo matches Venus but all is idealized, there is nothing of Michaelangelo's sense of skin texture and actual muscle structure.

For men, most leisure time was spent outside the home with other men, at the gymnasium, in the acadamies and theatres, at dining and drinking parties from which married women were excluded. This separation of the sexes made one-sex companionship, affection, love and physical sexuality a normal pattern which is remote from our experience. It was no disgrace to be in love, man with man, woman with woman, and it was normal for there to be a difference of age. The senior partner was in a tutorial role preparing the younger for life in the world, and some aspects of such a relationship could obviously have value, but it was also liable to exploitation and misuse.[4]

As a social institution and custom in Greek life, pederasty included a range of relationships from an honourable teaching and guardianship role to wretched forms of depravity. In its most respectable form, approved by Plato and others, it was a kind of tutorial system for educating and training young men from rich families to take an adult place in society, through a relationship of affection, respect and loyalty. The older man's love for his pupil was expressed in similar terms to those used between a man and a woman and was in theory often declared to be a higher and more noble form of love. But the custom of pederasty assumed sexual contact, and this was regarded as normal and praiseworthy, though a temporary stage for the pupil, from which he was expected to mature into heterosexual marriage.

Despite the famous (or notorious) reputation of the community of women who lived on the island of Lesbos for affectionate same-sex relationships, clear evidence of homosexual behaviour between Greek women is not easy to find. It is depicted in wall paintings and decorated pottery, especially as a form of mutual masturbation using an artificial penis, but otherwise it is only referred to in satirical writings. That Greek men were aware that some women shared in homosexual affection and behaviour is certain, but it was not a matter of importance in the way the institution of pederasty was among males. An unpleasant feature of Greek society was the use of slaves for sexual exploitation and abuse, both heterosexually and homosexually, and in domestic situations as well as in commercial prostitution.

Greek religion took many forms, and at its best could win the not entirely mocking approval of Plato and his friends. But in some of its earliest rituals and celebrations, notably those associated with Dionysius and Bacchus it could include cult prostitution at temples, and behaviour in public processions at festivals which to our culture seem pornographic and obscene. Both men and women adopted costumes which included such excess as monstrous fake phallic symbols, and public nakedness was not unusual. Such behaviour was greeted by spectators with ribaldry, as a form of vulgar display, though it also led on occasion to hostility between the sexes, understandably enough.

Various initiatory ceremonies were linked with Greek religion, and one of these, known in Crete and probably at Corinth, was a re-enaction of the original rape of Gannymede. This legend described how Zeus had seized the handsome youth and made him his cup-bearer. Following this pattern, young men reaching puberty were assembled at a religious party, and the older men present selected one lad each and took him away to be his companion for two months. This ceremony need not have been much more than a rite of passage arranged by the family, a holiday with uncle or a kind of god-father, but also it could be and apparently sometimes was an excuse for a crude and cruel act of violation. The Romans banned the practice officially in 186 BCE, and by the time of the Christian era, public opinion tended to ridicule any adult known to adopt the passive role in sodomy.[5]

Traces of these ancient customs lingered on, in both Hellenistic and roman cities, and Julius Caesar was alleged, at least in the coarse songs of his troops, to have been in his youth catemite to King Nicomedes of Bithynia. The Roman historian Tacitus records that in 64 CE, the Emperor Nero went through a wedding ceremony with a perverted youth called Pythagoras, adding the comment 'everything was public which even at a natural union is veiled by night', and he hints that this crime led to the fire which devastated the city of Rome.[6]

(c) The Christian reaction

Setting out at some length the social context in which the early Christian morality was formed shows why the first Christians often seem to later generations to have produced a brand new morality. There was no point in putting new wine into old bottles. The exuberance of the new faith made a strong appeal particularly to those who were oppressed and wearied of the prevailing decadence. In the mixed communities around the Mediterranean, the Hellenistic life style, much debased from the original Athenian precepts, coalesced with a colonial form of Roman civilization which had abandoned the strict codes of its earlier Patrician period, not least concerning marriage. First-century civilization was ready for reform, and the Christians found themselves with the opportunity to offer a new way.

As a faith, the gospel of forgiveness and acceptance, irrespective of class, race, wealth or ability, was brand new. But in terms of sexual morality, the reform was actually largely a revival of the old way of the Covenant, a re-establishment of the principles of monogamy, chastity and fidelity embedded in Israel's ancient tradition, but which the Jews themselves no longer firmly followed. Given the history and context of their situation, it could hardly have been otherwise. The first Christian leaders were all Jews, trained, more or less, in the precepts of the Torah. And Jesus said he had come to fulfill the law. Thus, in his teaching about divorce and adultery, Jesus was inviting his nation to recall the convictions of their founding fathers, set out in the Laws of Moses.

But the Christian moralists were not merely seeking to impose uniquely Jewish rules on their gentile converts. They respected the Torah, if not all its teachers, but more important they knew that it had long been held in Judaism that some parts of their Law were equally applicable to Gentiles, for God had not left himself without witness among them. Thus, in a form abridged from the Ten Commandments, there also existed the so-called Noachic Code, based supposedly on the covenant with Noah, pre-dating Abraham, and relevant to all nations of the world who necessarily descended from him. These universal precepts included reference to marriage, regarded as the only proper form of sexual expression. As we shall see, when St Paul, writing to Gentile Christians, refers to homosexual behaviour as 'contrary to nature', he bases his argument on the Noachic precepts, which he understands as general rules for all people. (Those Christians who lay stress on the unvarying principles of Natural Law echo this thinking, common in the first century to Judaism, Greece and Rome. It may be borne in mind when considering the later Christian tradition, in Part 4, p. 106).

This combination of Covenant tradition with Noachic precept enabled the Christian apologists to broaden their appeal in a universalistic way. The Jews, Greeks, Romans and everyone else were all under the one set of rules. So we can demonstrate the continuity between Jewish and Christian morality on sexual matters by saying that there is nothing in the writings of St Paul from which an orthodox Rabbi of his time living in Jerusalem would seriously dissent, though he might want to qualify it in detail. This can easily be seen by reading the relevant parts of the Mishnah, a Jewish handbook on disputed moral questions dating from this period. Secondly, in the Apologias of the early Christians, as in the New Testament books, where pagans of Greek or Roman origin are being addressed, it is not entirely fanciful to imagine an old citizen saying: 'Ah yes, I remember my grandparents used to teach something like that.'[7]

The Gospels are silent on the question of homosexual behaviour. This is not surprising, since the four evangelists seem to confine their records of the teaching of Jesus on issues of sexual morality to those that were controversial among the Jews of his time, marriage and divorce, adultery and lust. What he did say about these issues, however, illustrates his general appeal to integrity in personal relationships, and some contemporary Christians assign more importance to this underlying principle than to the specific texts from the Pauline Epistles. References to Sodom in the Gospels treat it as a symbol of wickedness and inhospitability, a warning to self-righteous Jews.

Homosexual behaviour is repudiated in lists of pagan vices in Paul's letters to Romans, I Corinthians and I Timothy. (In the Catholic Epistles, II Peter and Jude, Sodom and the fallen angels legends reappear in the style of the Pseudepigrapha.) From the Pauline texts, two converging convictions can be identified, and although they were strongly expressed, they seem to be treated as obvious, and are not much argued for. First, homosexual behaviour is forbidden in the Jewish and therefore Christian morality. Second, it used to be so among pagans, as contrary to the natural order of things which they respect, as we Christians do, and the pagans should revive their old prohibition of it. But these *en passant* references give the impression that homosexuality is not a central problem for the early church. Indeed, before long the Christian Fathers are reckoning that sexual mores have so much deteriorated that it may be better to abstain altogether, and opt for celibacy.

Pauline Texts

In his Epistle to the Romans, St Paul denounces homosexual behaviour among men and women as a feature of paganism, and in the First Epistle to the Corinthians, he warns Christians that such activity would prevent them entering the Kingdom of God. In the First Epistle to Timothy 'perversion' is said to flout the moral law and the teaching of the gospel, and this probably refers to homosexual behaviour. In the New Testament, Romans is usually printed before Corinthians, to mark its theological pre-eminence, though there seems little doubt that Corinthians was written earlier. Since they were composed within a short period of, perhaps, three years, and their arguments are closely related, the three references are set out here together in the familiar order, and then each is examined in its context:

> In consequence, I say God has given them up to shameful passions. Their women have exchanged natural intercourse for unnatural, and their men in turn, giving up natural relations with women, burn with lust for one another; males behave indecently with males, and are paid in their own persons the fitting wage of such perversions (Romans 1.26–7).

> Surely you know that the unjust will never come into possession of the kingdom of God. Make no mistake: no fornicator or idolater, none who are guilty either of adultery or of homosexual perversion, no thieves or grabbers or drunkards or slanderers or swindlers, will possess the kingdom of God (I Corinthians 6.9–10).

> We all know that the law is an excellent thing, provided we treat it as law, recognizing that it is not aimed at good citizens, but at the lawless and unruly, the impious and sinful, the irreligious and worldly; at patricides and matricides, murderers and fornicators, perverts, kidnappers, liars, perjurers – in fact all whose behaviour flouts the wholesome teaching which conforms with the gospel entrusted to me, the gospel which tells of the glory of God in His etrnal felicity (Timothy 1.8–11).

The Epistle to the Romans

St Paul's Epistle to the Romans is his major theological contribution to the New Testament. He wrote it from Corinth between 56 and 58 CE, towards the end of his final stay in that city, and with his plans already settled to visit Rome after he had been to Jerusalem. His obvious interest in the increasingly important church of the Empire's capital city is matched by his awareness that the Roman Christians may not take the authenticity of his apostleship for granted. The congregation in Rome was probably mostly non-Jewish, and so he writes courteously, perhaps to make a good impression on people he has not met and for a church he has not founded. The difference in style is quite noticeable between this Epistle and the correspondence with the Corinthians. With the Corinthians he is personal and passionate; with the Romans polemic is reserved for the unbelievers.

Most of Romans 1–11 is a vindication of Paul's own understanding of the gospel as God's response to the universal human predicament. For Jews and Gentiles alike, the acceptance by faith of Jesus as Lord is the way to reconciliation with God and to membership of his Kingdom. But for this reconciliation to be received, it is first necessary to understand that the advent of the gospel makes clear that all men, Jews and Gentiles alike, rightly stand under the judgment of God.

In 1.18–32 Paul argues that non-Jews 'have made fools of themselves by exchanging the splendour of immortal God for an image shaped like mortal man'. As T. W. Manson puts it, 'the two counts in the indictment are idolatry and immorality, idolatry being the tap-root of evil'. Paul sees such idolatry as disastrous, for all men are subject to God's laws and the divine wrath falls inescapably on those who flout them. Once men's minds are darkened by idolatry, their wills are corrupted and their bodies degraded. The argument Paul uses here is similar to that in the Book of Wisdom, chapter 14, and the pseudepigraphical books as noted in chapter 4 above. In a vigorous phrase, Karl Barth has commented that the Gentiles are subject to God's wrath because their religion 'consists of one great confusion between the creator and his creatures'. But the confusion here is not that between species of creation; it is the fundamental mistake of idolatory to obscure the difference between the divine and human roles. For St Paul the consequence is seen to be that men imitate the beasts they worship. God abandons them, they lose their moral sense, degrade their bodies in sexual sin, and commit the usual long list of anti-social offences on each other, breaking all rules of conduct.

Although the examples of shameful passion given by St Paul in verses 26 and 27 are apparently almost universally regarded by modern commentators as referring to homosexual behaviour, first between women and then between men, the obligation of the biblical translators to render the Greek text as precisely as they can has slightly obscured this meaning. For verse 26 the New English Bible has: 'The women have exchanged natural intercourse for unnatural.' The King James Version has: 'changed the natural use to that which is against nature', and the Revised Version has the same. The Revised Standard Version, the Common Bible and the New International Version alter this to: 'exchanged natural relations for unnatural' and the Jerusalem Bible renders the phrase: 'their women have turned from natural intercourse to unnatural practices.' The Good News

Bible has 'The women pervert the natural use of their sex by unnatural acts', and the Living Bible paraphrases: 'the women turned against God's natural plan for them and indulged in sexual sin with each other.'

The Greek words *phusis* and *chresis* used by Paul mean 'nature' and 'use'. So clearly, the King James Version translation is precise and literal, but it does not indicate what practices 'against nature' might, in fact, be, and the later versions are hardly more definite, except by implication as in the Living Bible version. Paul would be aware of lesbian practices from his contact with Greek and Roman culture, but it is possible that all he means here is heterosexual intercourse per anum. Most variations of sexual behaviour other than vaginal intercourse were disapproved of in the Jewish tradition, but it seems more likely that lesbian practices are repudiated.

The description of male homosexual practices in verse 27 is quite direct and produces no difficulty in various translations. Paul links the shameless or indecent acts among men with their lust for each other, but does not expressly mention sodomy or pederasty. Some doubts have been expressed about the introductory phrase 'giving up natural relations with women', for this could mean that Paul is only condemning those men who have been first heterosexual and then deliberately pervert themselves with homosexual practices. If that interpretation is correct, then only this kind of pervert, and possibly men of bisexual nature, are being reproved, but it is probably unrealistic to suppose that Paul himself could have thought in this way. If the argument is pressed, then it could be that we have an example in these verses from Romans of the church's later interpretation being mistaken in including genuine homosexual men and women with Paul's condemnation, but this is really an attempt to read the old texts with modern presuppositions. It seems better to accept the view that Paul is adapting for his purpose a standard piece of Jewish propaganda, familiar to all his readers and unquestioned at the time. The *Satyricon* and other similar writings give lurid descriptions of the secular permissiveness of Roman life at this time, and Paul's condemnation could be taken as a typical piece of preacher's polemic against the sins of the day. The readers may be expected to fill in the details for themselves.

Among the Christians in Rome, therefore, those converted from Judaism would find little new or strange in Paul's argument at this stage of the Epistle. Gentile converts would probably have heard such condemnation from Stoic sources, and perhaps be aware that Roman law officially disapproved of homosexual behaviour, irrespective of rumours about disgraceful goings-on in the dissolute imperial court. It might seem, therefore, that Paul is expressing here little more than the conventional moral disapproval of secular vice, just as in chapter 3 he will string together a series of quotations from the Psalms to bring the Jews under condemnation. It all goes to demonstrate a topsy-turvy world in which the good is unachievable by Jew or barbarian, and therefore a world ready to be justified by God's free grace alone if only it will abandon its pride in either works or law.

Undoubtedly, Paul is determined to remove every excuse so that he may clear the way for the gospel, but the question remains how far his denunciation of the gentiles is a reiteration of his Rabbinic traditions, and how far he has subjected them to reassessment in the light of his Christian experience. In general terms, Paul has repudiated the Torah as a means of salvation, but he has no time for antinomianism: the loving liberty of the Christians will fulfil and exceed all that the law requires in terms of human care and responsibility. It is one of the paradoxes of the Christian ethic that law and love will point in the same direction in most aspects of practical living. So, does the condemnation of homosexual behaviour in Romans here reflect a continuation of the Jewish attitude which Paul, at this stage in his thought, has seen no need to revise after his conversion, or is it a freshly worked judgment, a Christian view, which happens to be the same as the Jewish one?

This question, which also arises for the Corinthian Epistle, has seemed crucial to many modern Christians, and for some can be almost decisive of the whole question of the morality of homosexual behaviour. These two verses in Romans 1 are often cited as the clearest possible demonstration that homosexual behaviour is forbidden in the New Testament. It is argued that their meaning is clear, and that although they are used as part of the criticism of the secular world, a consequence of idolatry, they also stand in their own right as fully Christian precepts.[9]

The recognition that Paul is quoting a standard list of sins needs some further explanation. Mention has been already made to the Noachian commands in the Jewish tradition. The Rabbis held that although Gentiles could not be expected to obey all the provisions of the Jewish Law, as descendants of Noah, so their reasoning ran, there were seven minimal requirements they must obey if they wished to be saved. Six of these requirements are listed in the Midrash on Genesis 2.16 as the prohibition of idolatry, blasphemy, injustice, murder, incest and theft. The prohibition against incest is explained by reference to Genesis 2.24: Adam is united to his wife, 'which implies not to his neighbour's wife, nor to a male, nor to an animal'. An editorial footnote to this comment adds that in Hebrew usage, 'incest' includes adultery, pederasty and bestiality.[10]

It is clear that this Noachian Code forms the basis for many of the household codes found in the New Testament, and the six precepts are included in the lists given by Paul here in Romans 1 and also in I Corinthians 6. Further, the so-called Apostolic Decree settled at the Council of Jerusalem in 49 CE (Acts 15.28–9) contains three of the Noachian precepts and some early texts of the decree add the 'Love your neighbour' commandment in negative form. This minimal law for Gentile Christians, as the Jerusalem church saw it, refers primarily to food laws, but with the prohibition of fornication added, and that presumably given the wide meaning including all forms of sexual misbehaviour, it became a set of moral precepts widely used in the early church.

Paul was at the Jerusalem Council. It would be likely therefore that he would use this 'official list' of sins not only as a rebuke for pagans, as the Rabbis also had done, but also as a simple reminder to Christians of what they were meant to avoid. What the Gentiles ought to discern as part of the Natural Law, what the Jews had been taught in their Pentateuchal Codes, what the Council of the Apostles had decided in Jerusalem all pointed in the same direction. A fair conclusion seems to be that Paul, if asked, could have provided a number of reasons for his condemnation of homosexual behaviour in this Epistle.

(b) I Corinthians

This Epistle is part of the correspondence Paul has with the church at Corinth. He writes from Ephesus around 55 CE to a city and congregation he knows well from his previous eighteen months stay. They are close to his heart, he has written before, their reply is to hand, and he has heard other disquieting news.

After a warm greeting, Paul deals with various points from their letter, justifying his own previous instructions against their queries which he regards as partly reflecting a worldly attitude, and partly the antinomian error. Paul argues that they are to be separate from the world's standards in morality, but they cannot live totally apart from other men.

The concept of the Kingdom of God is treated by St Paul, as generally in the New Testament, in two senses. Sometimes it is regarded as the present reality, realized eschatology as Dodd has named it, and sometimes it refers to the future hope and consummation of God's will. Here the future sense is implied. The unjust will have no part in the coming Kingdom. Some of the Corinthians had been sinners in the ways listed – Paul may have had personal knowledge of the previous life of some of the converts – but now they have been through the purifying waters, dedicated to God, and justified. They are free, but not free to do anything, as the Corinthians seem to be implying. The Epistle continues with a number of cases where Paul sets out in a casuistic style the moral obligations of the Christian life. In striking a right balance between Christian freedom and licence, Paul finds himself waging war on two fronts at the same time. He has to correct those who think the truly spiritual man can ignore petty moral conventions, and yet he has to reassure his Gentile converts that the Council in Jerusalem makes him free to protect them from any attempts by the Judaizing party to make them subject to the precepts of the Mosaic Law.

The list of offences which includes homosexual perversion as sins excluding from the future Kingdom is cast in the form of a rhetorical question. The precepts are broadly similar to those in Romans, but more specific and more focussed on individual acts of sin concerning sex and property. The style is again that of a household code, a domestic list of things a Christian does not do. Such lists abound in the New Testament and opinions differ among scholars as to their sources. Clearly the Noachian code can be detected as one, and given the already noted Rabbinic inclusion of homosexual behaviour as a form of fornication, Paul could simply be reiterating that. But such lists from Plato and from Stoic sources were widely circulated in the Hellenistic world, and in the Gospels and some Epistles there is another form which seems to depend more on the Decalogue with the addition of the love commandment.

It is difficult to be certain how far Paul chooses the particular offences in this list on the basis of what he knows of the previous life of the Christians at Corinth. It is a personal letter, and he continues 'Such were some of you' (v. 11). Commentators usually stress the immorality of Corinth and assume that such offenders had been converted and brought into the church, but it is also possible that the list is unstudied, a reflection of the offences from the Holiness Code: once he has begun on incest, the other prohibited sexual activities are added for good measure. In any case, it is quite clear that Paul warns the Corinthians against homosexual behaviour, and in much more specific terms than in the Epistle to the Romans. He writes specifically 'catamites' and 'sodomites'.

The Greek words *malakoi* and *arsenokoitai* have precise meanings. The first is literally 'soft to the touch' and metaphorically, among the Greeks, meant males (not necessarily boys) who played the passive role in homosexual intercourse. The second means literally 'male in bed' and the Greeks used this expression to describe the one who took the active role. Whereas in other biblical texts referring to homosexuality, the translators have wrestled to make precise sense of vague expressions, in this verse of I Corinthians, the older versions have euphemistically avoided conveying Paul's bluntness to their readers.

The King James Version had 'effeminate, and abusers of themselves with mankind', which to modern readers would probably convey 'rather feminine types who indulged in mutual masturbation'. The Revised Version is the same as the King James, but the Revised Standard Version uses 'homosexuals' to include both the Greek words with a footnote 'two Greek words are rendered by this expression'. The Common Bible changes this to 'sexual perverts'.

The New English Bible compromises between explicitness and euphemism by referring to 'homosexual perversion' but the Jerusalem translators into English have 'catamites and sodomites', following Moffatt's accuracy of 1913, rather than their own French antecedent which reads: 'ni depraves, ni gens de moeurs infames'. Etymologically, the word 'catamite' is a Latin form of the Greek 'Ganymede'. Ganymedes, the son of King Troas, and the most beautiful of all Greek youths, was appointed wine pourer of the gods, and cupbearer to Zeus. The myth is said to have gained immense popularity in Greece and Rome because it afforded a dubious but welcome religious justification for a grown man's passionate love for a boy. The Good News Bible has 'homosexual perverts', the Living Bible has 'homosexuals' following the unamended Revised Standard Version, and the New International Version has 'homosexual offenders'.

The general trend of these newer translations is to leave no doubt that Paul means to condemn homosexual behaviour, the Common Bible altering the Revised Standard Version to meet the objection that the emphasis is placed on behaviour or perversion, and not on the homosexual condition as such. Whether or not Paul would have understood the modern distinction between the condition and behaviour is unascertainable, but his choice of words here strongly suggests that he is warning the Corinthians against the institution of homosexual behaviour between mature men and youths, so commonly recorded in the secular literature of the time, and forbidden, as we have seen in some of the inter-testamental writings. The words 'sodomite' or 'paiderastia' might have been used instead of these secular Greek ones, but it is clear from the vocabulary of the Pauline corpus of letters that *paidion* is only used in a positive sense, to render the ideas of childlikeness or teachability as Christian virtues. He does refer to Sodom once, in Romans 9.29, as a reminder of the forbearance of God who has saved a remnant, and not judged all Israel like Sodom. He does not use the word '*malakos*' except in this verse of Corinthians, and it otherwise appears only twice in the New Testament: in the Synoptic Gospels of Matthew (11.8) and Luke (7.25) where it means soft living in contrast to asceticism, but there is no obvious sexual implication.

The word '*arsenokoitai*' re-occurs in the similar context of I Timothy 1.10. Perhaps it seems a pedantic point to labour the 'homosexual behaviour' meaning of this verse in Corinthians, but the range of translations shown above, and the very limited use of the words in the New Testament has led some modern commentators to query their meaning. It does, however, seem clear that Paul intended to be specific and that his Corinthian readers would have no difficulty in understanding what he meant.

A comparison between the reasons Paul gives for condemning homosexual behaviour in Romans and Corinthians shows that he uses different words, and concepts, and this difference may be somewhat obscured in those translations which concentrate on the notion of sexual perversion. Thus, in Romans, the offence is to change from natural to unnatural relations, but in Corinthians, it is the particular roles of the two people involved which are identified for repudiation. This difference is balanced of course in the NEB translation by the reference to 'such perversions' in Romans, and to 'mistake' in Corinthians, the Greek word in both cases being derived from the same verb '*planaw*'.

This verb has a variety of meanings in Greek literature, the Septuagint and the New Testament, all derived from its basic concept of wandering, or going astray. Wandering sheep or stars out of their courses can be thus described by '*planaw*'. In the St Matthew's Gospel parable of the sheep which has gone astray (Matt. 18.12 ff.) it is used by Christ to explain his mission. In the Lucan equivalent, the ordinary word for lost is used which perhaps suggests not so much that the sheep has wandered off as that the shepherd has to look for it. The sense of pastoral care implied was used to good effect by the Bishop of Chester in the 1987 Synod debate.[11]

The words in question are '*planias*' in Romans 1.27, and '*Planasthe*' in I Cor. 6.9. The sense of pastoral care does not seem to be meant in Romans. Paul has in mind the alternative and more theological meaning – wandering away from God's truth, or led into error, and in Romans 1.88ff., the context is those who have chosen to turn the truth of God into a lie, and have been therefore abandoned by God and dishonour their own bodies (v. 24). Although some translations of *planais* in Romans 1.27 have 'such *perversions*' (NEB, NIV,) the RSV and others have 'their *error*' and this makes clearer that the basic fault is to choose idolatry, from which immorality flows, and not merely wrong moral choice in terms of sexual preference. Paul is here using the language of judgment, not care.

The use of '*me planasthe*' in I Cor. 6.9 is typical of a similar judgmental use. It occurs in the Greek text as a warning clause which stands by itself, and serves as an introduction to the list of pagan vices which continue to the end of v. 10, in the Hellenistic style. Such were some of you, St Paul continues until you were washed and justified in the name of Christ. The English translation can be 'Do not be led astray', or 'do not be deceived'. The NEB version 'makes no mistake', seems weaker, and does not sufficiently suggest the dualistic sense of the usual Greek meaning, that the forces of evil are involved. What catamites and sodomites do is brought together with a list of other offenders who go astray as idolators, adulterers, etc. Strictly speaking, Paul uses *'planaw'* in Corinthians and Romans to condemn pagan ways, and thus to prepare them for the good news of the gospel.

So far we have established that Paul's condemnation of homosexual behaviour in the Corinthian Epistle appears in a list of offences against sexual morality and respect for property and the context is a dialogue between the Corinthians and himself on certain precepts of his original letter which they question. He has dealt with incest, separation, arbitration within the community, and in parenthesis reminded them of the pagan life-style they have abandoned since their conversion. It would be possible to argue at this point that no special Christian reasoning has been offered for the disapproval of homosexual behaviour, but merely the reiteration of a standing Rabbinic and Stoic tradition. However, the construction of this Epistle is less ordered than in Romans, and a fresh approach to questions of sexual morality appears in subsequent verses. These provide in effect a Christian theological basis for repudiating all forms of sexual behaviour except within monogamous marriage.

In the remaining verses of chapter 6, Paul comments on an argument from the Corinthians that 'they are free to do anything'. He agrees as far as food regulations are concerned, having in mind, no doubt, the Apostolic Decree, but he disagrees with regard to the use of the body. The body is for the Lord and the Lord for the body, therefore human lust is excluded, since God who raised Christ's body will also raise ours. He then takes the example of the prostitute to illustrate this.

Paul argues that human beings are a union of body and spirit, and that the whole personality is involved in sexual intercourse. It is not just an external act 'outside the body' as some Corinthians may have supposed. Therefore, in the act of fornication, a Christian might be said to be joining a part of Christ's body, that is himself, with a prostitute. It is a vigorous metaphor, and obviously must not be taken literally, but it goes far to explain why Paul finds sexual relationships outside marriage so abhorrent. This abhorrence would apply even more forcefully to homosexual unions.

In verse 18, Paul describes fornication as a sin against one's own body. Adultery and Sodomy are equally intimate physical acts.

Fornication here presumably extends beyond intercourse between unmarried people. The use of the Greek word *soma* translated 'body' is a complicated one in the New Testament, and especially so in I Corinthians, but it will suffice to say that Paul is using it in these verses to include intimate personal relationship. The Christian, indwelt by the Spirit, has an intimate relationship with Christ, and he takes the view, against the agnostics, that human flesh and spirit are so interdependent that they must be regarded as, in effect, a unity.

The reference to 'the twain shall become one flesh', from Genesis 2.24, by Paul in verse 16 is interesting because it posits a kind of ontological reason for the practice of chastity and monogamous marriage. The 'one flesh' relationship can be understood as a sacramental union of which intercourse is the effective sign, and those Christians who argue for the indissolubility of marriage understand this to be the case. In the Hebrew tradition, man is thought to have been created by God as originally the androgynous Adam, and Philo for example comments 'when the true companion Eve is created, love supervenes, and brings together and fits into one the divided halves as it were of one being'. The same myth is referred to by Plato in the *Symposium*. This exegesis of Genesis 2.24 placed the Rabbis in a difficult position, recognizing as they did both polygamy and divorce. They therefore adopted a different interpretation, seeing the commandment to become one flesh as a Noachian one addressed, not to the Jews, but to the Gentiles and requiring them not to practice incest, homosexuality, or bestiality, thus bringing the verse into conformity with the Leviticus 18 injunction for the Jews.

It is most likely that Paul would have been aware of the Rabbinic interpretation of Genesis 2.24, and also familiar with Jesus' own repudiation of that exegesis and it may well be that he accepts the androgynous myth as to the nature of human sexuality. With this background and his typical Jewish reaction to homosexual practices, there seems no doubt that even though this is another generalized polemic against the pagan way of life, Paul would be ready, if asked, to justify his condemnation of homosexual behaviour in I Corinthians 6 as properly based on his theology of marriage as a one-flesh union between men and women exclusively.

Paul very rarely refers directly to sayings of Jesus, but in chapter 7 when he moves on to the next query from the Corinthians, he distinguishes clearly between the dominical principle against divorce, and his own observations on related matters concerning marital problems. This section starts with a quotation from the Corinthians: 'It is good for a man to have nothing to do with woman'. He disagrees with this ascetic view on several grounds, of which the negative one against fornication is not the most important. As most commentators point out, Paul is not in principle against marriage: in this respect he follows the Rabbinic precept that it is a duty, perhaps lessened if the parousia is imminent, and he himself has a special vocation to celibacy for the sake of his missionary calling. Times of abstinence are recommended, but this was also a Rabbinic precept. Divorce is prohibited, and he is clearly aware of the teaching of Jesus which reversed the Rabbinic view that Genesis 2.24 applied only to sexual offences outside marriage among the Gentiles. Polygamy and divorce are now banned though Paul is realistic enough to recognize that some women, under Jewish law, and some men, under Roman law, may have already found themselves legally separated. If reconciliation is not possible, he advises against second marriages, and where one partner is not a Christian, he does not find that an obligatory ground for divorce.

Paul's firmness over these matters is, of course, a matter of thorough scrutiny in connection with the present dilemma about remarriage, a subject outside our scope. For our purpose it is sufficient to note that Paul reflects the reinterpretation of Genesis 2.24 positively to stress the permanence of the 'one-flesh relationship', and negatively to exclude all other forms of sexual behaviour. It seems fair to conclude that taking the course of the arguments put in I Corinthians 5–7, Paul's thoughts about human sexuality are expressed in terms of 'within marriage only' and that this is a new approach, following the teaching of Jesus, and marking a Christian viewpoint distinct from either the Rabbinic or secular traditions of his time. Given that approach, he evidently holds, but does not think it necessary to elaborate, the view that homosexual behaviour is to be rejected among Christians.

Before leaving our study of these two undoubtedly Pauline references to homosexual behaviour, there remains one difficult question to be faced. This concerns the supposed identification of pederasty with Paul's condemnation. The moral objection to the sexual abuse and corruption of minors inherent in the custom is obvious enough, and St Paul was reflecting a widely-felt disapproval of it, irrespective of his own reasoning. But was it only pederasty that is being condemned? Since it was such a common practice in the Hellenistic world, and quite familiar to the Romans, though less approved by them, it has been strongly argued by Professor R. Scroggs, Professor of New Testament at Chicago Theological Seminary, that we should ask ourselves the question: What exactly is Paul denouncing? He finds some evidence in first-century literature of same sex relationships between equals, but these are rare, and the implication is that St Paul, and nearly everyone else who condemns homosexual behaviour at this period has the institution of pederasty in mind. There was no first-century equivalent of a Gay Lib Movement for consenting adults.[12]

(c) I Timothy

St Paul's First Letter to Timothy appears from its introduction to have been written from Macedonia, with the intention of setting out formally the instructions Paul has already given to Timothy as the temporary leader or personal representative of the Apostle for the church at Ephesus. If this was indeed the situation, the three references to homosexual behaviour in the Pauline corpus are conveniently addressed to three of the most significant original Christian congregations, at Rome, at Corinth, and at Ephesus. A possible date would be around 55 CE, the letter being written some months after I Corinthians and preceding Galations and Romans.

Although traditionally regarded as a genuine Pauline letter, many scholars have recently doubted his authorship, identifying four main difficulties. These concern the theological content, the vocabulary used, the type of church organization described, and the apparent incompatibility between the biographical details given in the Pastoral Epistles and what is otherwise known of the Apostle's movements. No attempt to resolve the question of authorship would be appropriate here, but if Paul did not write it personally, the possibilities are that Paul dictated it to a secretary who was free to use his own words and expressions to some extent, or that it was composed much later, well into the second century CE, simulating apostolic authenticity with a few direct quotations from St Paul himself.

The reference to 'perverts' is again condemnatory, occurring within a list of offenders whose behaviour is said to 'flout the wholesome teaching of the gospel'. It is not suggested that the Ephesian Christians are doing such things, but that they are troubled by inadequate teachers of the moral law (v. 7). These are probably Jewish teachers, expounding the precepts of the Torah as binding on the Christians, though not perhaps Judaizers in the sense of insisting on the ceremonial precepts; they are inadequate, Paul suggests, in not understanding the full implications of the gospel of love and faith.

This kind of interpretation of these verses fits well an early date for the Epistle, reflecting the controversies of the times, but those commentators who accept a later date see a more bourgeois morality implied here, less dependent on the Torah than on second-century conventional Gentile attitudes, to which Christianity is said not to be in opposition. In either case, the list Paul gives is more markedly cast in the decalogue form than those in Romans and Corinthians, and rather fierce examples are chosen. Paul uses the word *arsenokoitais* as in Corinthians, and this has resulted again in a wide range of translations.

The King James Version has 'them that defile themselves with mankind'; the Revised Version has 'abusers of themselves with men'; the Revised Standard Version has 'sodomites' which suggests that its translators' reticence in I Corinthians was a matter of style rather than of distaste for the word. The New English Bible has 'perverts' which is consistent with their translation of Romans and Corinthians, provided it is remembered that they have homosexual perversion in mind in each case. The average reader, without a Greek text to compare, might, of course, assume that the dropping of 'homosexual' in this third reference means that Paul is here referring to other forms of perversion. The French Jerusalem has 'les gens de moeurs infames', and the English Jerusalem recasts the whole phrase 'those who are immoral with women or with boys or with men', which is not a literal translation, but does try to express in a modern idiom what Paul probably thought.

The Good News Bible has 'sexual perverts', the Living Bible 'homosexuals' and the New International version has 'perverts'. Since the other offences in this list tend to be gross examples of offences within the decalogue categories, such as matricide, kidnap, and perjury, it seems most likely that homosexual behaviour is again being vehemently condemned.

Those who regard I Timothy as a second-century work note that this emphasis on serious and unusual crimes is not typical of Paul and reflects a more general approach, indicating as perhaps the whole Epistle does, that there is no particular church or setting in mind. Similarities have been noted with the style of Philo's commentary on Genesis, and the polemical lists of sins in some of the inter-testamental writings, and equivalent Hellenistic lists. Phrases such as 'the wholesome teaching which conforms with the gospel' seems redolent of a more settled pastoral situation than existed in the church at Ephesus after Paul's stay there and its tense conclusion, but this does not, of course, necessarily argue that the unknown later author was unaware of Paul's attitude to homosexuality. Indeed, even if this Epistle is contemporaneous with the *Didache*, considered later, there is no innovation at this point.

(d) Summary

Taken together, St Paul's writings repudiate homosexual behaviour as a vice of the Gentiles in Romans, and as a bar to the Kingdom in Corinthians. In taking this attitude he conforms to the precepts of the Rabbis, to popular secular moralism, and also, by implication, to the dominical precept limiting sexual activity to monogamous and permanent marriage. If he wrote the relevant section of I Timothy, it would be consistent with his thought to call such behaviour forbidden by the moral law though that is not a characteristic expression for him.

All these references, however, arise in parenthesis and he assumes that homosexual behaviour will have been abandoned on conversion if it had occurred before. Since he suggests the man 'married' to his stepmother at Corinth should be excluded from the congregation – a similar punishment to being cut off from the worshipping community required by the Holiness Code for the Jews – it seems unlikely that he would have taken a different view of a homosexual offender, if he had been required to adjudicate on such a problem. At this very early stage of the development of the Christian church, forgiveness is largely focussed on sins before conversion, and the discipline of those who offend after baptism is still to be worked out in detail. That he would have had no hesitation in denouncing pederasty, and all that went with it in Greek and Roman culture can hardly be doubted. As a man of his time, deeply immersed as he had been in Jewish traditions, yet not without respect for some aspects of Greek philosophy and Roman law, his conversion to Christ gave him no cause to suppose that pederasty could ever be an acceptable feature of life in the Kingdom of Christ.

Yet, in estimating the importance of St Paul's teaching for today, the churches face the awkward fact, posed by Scroggs and others, that there is a considerable difference between the ancient institution of pederasty and the freedom gay men and women now seek to commit themselves, within the Christian family, to the only kind of permanent loving relationship, and a physical expression of that relationship, open to them. There is no definite evidence in the New Testament that such a relationship was recognized by the early church as posing a different question from pederasty, yet it is unlikely that nothing of its kind existed. Some Christians judge this argument from silence leaves them free to work out a new answer on general principles; others conclude that the biblical condemnation taken as a whole extends to all forms of homosexual behaviour, and not only to the particular form of it found in pederasty.

6

From St Paul to Sir John Wolfenden 1957

Introduction

The Christian attitude to homosexual behaviour is often said to be remarkably consistent throughout church history. From the middle of the second century to the end of the nineteenth, many records show that homosexual offences were declared sinful and those found guilty of them rigorously punished. The condemnations in the Old Testament and St Paul's Epistles are reiterated in similar terms by the early church fathers both in their biblical commentaries and in their pastoral works, often with vehemence. A number of conciliar decrees confirm their judgment. With the rise of monasticism, and the development of more detailed regulations for the Christian life, a range of specific offences and appropriate penances is formulated, notably in the Penitentials, and this ecclesiastical discipline is matched in many respects by the secular law under the Christian emperors Justinian's Edicts providing the pattern on which mediaeval Europe was to depend until the Reformation.

The scholars of the Reformation re-examined the biblical texts, and noticed some ambiguities in them, but they did not reject the traditional interpretation, which continued unchanged until the call for reassessment associated with the appointment of the Wolfenden Committee in 1954. This consistency is not perhaps surprising, for the Christian church has seldom modified the ethical traditions it inherited from Judaism; the major precepts of the Law and the Prophets concerning marriage and sexual problems have been maintained in the church. Only for divorce and the status of women has any significant change been made, and that mostly in the twentieth century by some Protestant churches sensitive to the twin pressures of secularism and modern understandings of sexuality. The Roman Catholic Church has tried to maintain its traditional insistence that procreation is central to the right use of sexual acts, and continues to repudiate both contraception and homosexual intercourse as incompatible with this doctrine. The Anglican churches have debated the possibilities of change in a much freer way, but it remains true at present that no major Christian Denomination has officially ceased to hold that homosexual behaviour is sinful, or falls short of the ideal of chastity in personal relationships.

The apparent consistancy of the tradition was demonstrated by Dr Sherwin Bailey in his pioneering book, *Homosexuality and the Western Christian Tradition*, published in 1955 and since reprinted.[1] His review of the whole Christian era was an important initial achievement, albeit highly compressed, and the pattern he set has influenced all subsequent studies. In recent years however, further research has raised some doubt that the Christian attitude has been uniformly hostile to homosexual relationships throughout this long period.

A major challenge to the consistent hostility thesis has been provided by John Boswell, assistant Professor of History at Yale University, in his *Christianity, Social Tolerance and Homosexuality*, published in 1980.[2] Boswell, a Roman Catholic who is sympathetic to Gay Lib, tells his tale twenty five years after Bailey and from a different perspective. Boswell covers fourteen centuries in great detail, and his strength lies in mastery of the literary documents of that period. Compared with Bailey, Boswell's book is relatively light on biblical scholarship, though he often follows Bailey's exegesis and sometimes elaborates it. His chief purpose seems to be to encourage the world-wide gay community to recognize that not all church history is against them. He argues that Christian people through the ages have understood and indeed shared in homosexual passion and friendship on a scale the official record of hostility almost totally conceals. Boswell has been criticized by other scholars, but it is clearly no longer safe to claim history shows that homosexual behaviour in its many aspects thrived in Greece and Rome, was banished by the Christians, and has only revived in our modern secular and pluralistic society. Thirty years of study have shown it is all much more complicated than that.

A thorough study of early Christian attitudes to human sexuality has just been written by Peter Brown, who is Professor of History at Princetown.[3] Covering the period from soon after St Paul's letters were written until the death of St Augustine in 430 CE, he sets out the distinctive flavour of these formative years. It is impossible to do justice to this major work here, but Brown provides some new material about how the Christian attitude against homosexual behaviour was strengthened which is likely to cause much re-thinking. He shows that the notion of renunciation of the body as then understood was related to discussions about such fundamentals as how the earthly human body could become the heavenly resurrected one. In short, a male soul allocated in perpetuity to a male body could not on earth even for a moment wisely force that body into female poses.

Serious work to establish the correct meaning of the biblical texts independent of the subsequent Christian interpretation of them has continued through the three decades since Bailey's book was first published. From the textual quotations and exegetical suggestions I have adopted in Part three of this book, I hope this subject has already been adequately covered, so I do not refer to it further here. Much good modern study of that question has to be ignored here, but in chapter 7, covering the period after Wolfenden, the arguments of the New Morality school are covered. These do not rest chiefly on the exegesis of particular biblical texts relating to homosexuality, but on an analysis of the fundamental of New Testament ethics. The 'New Morality' view that the whole development of a natural law tradition by the church, and the legalism and casuistry built on it, conflicts with that ethic, always was and still is a mistake does need attention, both in this historical survey, and also in Part five.

Some detail of the legal history is inevitable if we are to understand the interplay between morality and law in a country that has always claimed to be Christian. As Europe's off-shore island, England inherited and maintained the prohibition of sodomy as a capital offence, enforcing it first by church and later by state law from Henry VIII onwards. In Victorian times the harshness of the penalty was mitigated to penal servitude for life, with lesser punishments for attempts to commit sodomy and indecent assault. This reform meant that homosexual people who kept their activities private were left tolerably free from prosecution, but that measure of freedom was suddenly removed, by a carelessly worded amendment to an Act of 1885 intended to protect young people from sexual exploitation, suppress bothels, and raise the age of consent for girls to sixteen years.

The Act as such had the support of bishops in the House of Lords, and was a mark of the successful campaign by Josephine Butler and her colleagues in the Christian Welfare and Purity Movements to rescue girls and boys from prostitution. The amendment added a new offence, the misdemeanour of gross indecency, applying to males of any age, with a maximum punishment of two years imprisonment. The new offence was so widely drawn that it went far beyond any notion of protecting the young from assault. It meant that in future, any homosexual behaviour less than sodomy, among adults in private and with consent, could be punished by the Criminal Law. No doubt such behaviour was morally reprehensible to the Victorian mind, but, like the other sexual sins fornication and adultery, it was only previously a criminal offences when aggravated by special damage to a vulnerable person. The new clause opened the way to informers and blackmailers, and led to a series of 'monstrous martyrdoms' of which Oscar Wilde was among the first of the famous victims.

The problem of under age prostitution eased in the following years, and it became police policy not to seek out homosexuals unless complaints were made or public scandal arose. In the thirties, progress in medical and psychological understandings of the homosexual orientation, notably as the pioneering work of Sigmund Freud became better known, tended to shift attitudes towards a belief that homosexuality was an illness resulting from inadequate parental relationships in childhood rather than a deliberately chosen perversion. The situation changed in the aftermath of the Second World War, when a period of more aggressive police prosecution began, in connection with spy scandals. However, public disquiet at the spate of convictions in the 1950s obliged the Government to set up the Wolfenden Committee, which recommended the repeal of the 1885 amendment.

The Committee asked the churches to submit evidence and this was provided by specially appointed working groups of the Anglican, Methodist and Catholic Churches. They agreed in advising that the law should be changed, on the ground that homosexual behaviour between consenting adults was sinful, but not a proper matter for the Criminal Law. After the Wolfenden Committee recommendations were make known this evidence was published and debated in the Church Assembly and the Methodist Conference. Both bodies expressed approval of the change in the law, but that did not necessarily mean they agreed with all the evidence submitted on their behalf; the moral debate was still to come. After a long campaign to create a sympathetic public opinion, in which the discreet support of Bailey and several prominent Christians was significant, initial Government hesitation was overcome, and Parliament passed the new Act in 1967. This was in fact in line with similar changes already made in some European Countries, and some but not all American States.

The passing of the 1967 Sexual Offences Act seemed to many at the time a watershed where not only the secular and Christian moralities divided but also where a sharp division occurred between Catholic and Protestant moral teaching on homosexual acts. That popular impression is to some extent true, but conceals a more complex situation. Until the Twentieth Century, in British history, on questions of morality, state and church often spoke the same language. That had of course also been the experience of most European countries and for those parts of the world they once colonized. The great division of the Reformation left an indelible mark on the shape of Christian faith, but had less effect on Christian morality. Moral rules tend to be more tenacious in society than the institutions that promulgate them.

The separation between Christian and State morality was a slow process, responding to changes in political philosophy over some two hundred years. In its clearest forms, Napoleonic France had introduced a new Legal Code which reflected a definite anti-clericalism, and some precepts of Catholic morality were ignored. Bismarck had attempted similar changes in Germany, for the same reasons. The standard Lutheran teaching regarded the state as God's agent for the good ordering of society, but the emergence of Nazism forced the Confessing Church to repudiate this concordat, and Barth and Bonhoeffer took a leading part in formulating a distinctive Christian ethic.

At the same time, Archbishop William Temple in England, and his colleagues in the slowly developing Ecumenical Movement realized that the European States were drifting into another war, and that only a search for world peace and just society based on a Christian vision which transcended national loyalties would avert it. Their protests were unheeded in the thirties, but were trend-setting in post-war discussions. The third component in the climate of thought was the already mentioned new perceptions about human sexuality, in which the Christians shared. Thus, although Bailey and his collaborators could in no fair sense be called radical, their work in asking for a change in the law took place in a climate of opinion among informed Christians that their ethical system was in mutation, not before time. A new way of thinking ethically for personal decisions about sexual behaviour was in fact under way, though not much publically discussed until 1963, when the Quaker Report and *Honest to God* were published.[4]

Distinct from the Protestants, the Western Catholic Church has faced Fascism somewhat as it had found accommodation with Napoleon, taking a long view, and it was firm that there could be no departure from its traditional teaching. The Second Vatican Council took the new emphasis on the relational aspects of sexuality seriously, but it did not change the rules about marriage, contraception or homosexual behaviour. Only in America did Catholic Bishops attempt modification. The Orthodox Churches were either in strongly protected positions, politically, or in Marxist countries so embattled that they could spare little energy for speculation about these, to them, secondary matters.

The 1967 Act was therefore not so much a watershed as a sign of the times in British social awareness, and probably, one can say with hindsight, the highest point of liberal tolerance reached here in this century. Since then, the mood has changed, and become more uncertain and anxious. Attempts to revive the old morality have become much stronger, and by 1989, teaching in support of Gay Liberation has become more proscribed in England than it was in 1967, not least in the churches. Although a spate of reports by expert working parties since 1967 have advocated in some measure that the request of practising homosexual men and women to receive an uncritical acceptance in the Christian family should be approved, this has not happened, and seems frankly less likely that it did in 1954.

Chastity required

(a) The early church period

As Christianity spread round the Mediterranean, its local communities began to establish a separate identity. Just as the Jewish Diaspora had resisted uncompromisingly, at least in principle, the life-style of the Greeks and Romans, so the Christians found themselves in opposition to much of the contemporary conventional morality. In particular, the sexual ethics advocated by St Paul and the sub-apostolic writers were clearly incompatible with those of the declining Empire, and yet, like the gospel itself, they needed formulation in a more logical and coherent way if they were to be successfully commended to the new converts. An early example of how this was attempted is given in the *Didache*, a manual of instruction on Christian morals and church order ascribed to the Twelve Apostles, but best dated early in the second century and probably from a Jewish Christian source.[5]

The manual begins by describing the two love commandments as the way of life, and then follows a rather arbitrary selection of sayings of Jesus chiefly from the Sermon on the Mount. The second chapter of the manual starts with a household code in the decalogue form similar to those in the New Testament, introduced as 'The second commandment of the Teaching'.

It continues:

> Do not murder; do not commit adultery; do not corrupt boys; do not fornicate; do not steal; do not practise magic . . .

In chapter three, reasons are given for obeying these precepts; lust, foul language, and leering are said to lead to fornication and adultery, but pederasty is not mentioned again.

The converts from paganism to whom the *Didache* and similar early Christian manuals are addressed will have come from many different backgrounds. There were Jews to whom the new morality was a liberation from anxiety and wearisome attention to the detail of the Torah, without departing from the basic precepts they had learnt in the synogogue. There were simple peasants, artisans and fishermen whose life style had from their birth reflected the decencies of family life in stable small communities, just as much in Italy and Egypt as in Samaria and rural Galilee. For them not much in the Christian household codes would have come as a surprise.

For urban converts, the contrast between their old life and the new would often have been stark. In the great cities of the Roman empire, and not only in the capital itself, few could have grown up untarnished by the pagan life style. Among those presenting themselves for baptism in Corinth, Ephesus, Alexandria and Athens, as in Jerusalem and Caesarea, were men and women who had participated in the mystery religions and perhaps shared in cultic sexual acts or been forced into prostitution. The practice of exposing unwanted children, especially girls, meant that some had only survived because they were taken into slavery or brothels. People of respectability and privilege, of wealth and deprivation, of decency and decadence, married, divorced, polygamous, living together in friendship or lust, all jostled together in the early Christian congregations, and they were attracted to the new faith for a wide variety of reasons. Then, as now, in a missionary situation, the Apostolic Fathers had to work out how best to teach the obligations of belonging to the new community, and how high to set the fence to be jumped in terms of repentance and changed life for many who were the victims of a decaying civilization.

The laws and customs of this pagan world were not, until the time of Constantine, much influenced by the Christians, and so there is a sense in which the morality of the early church has the character of rules for an alternative society yet to be established. The Kingdom of God is to come, and this eschatological expectation that paganism will be destroyed encourages the local Christian leaders to exercise a distinctive jurisdiction in moral leadership. Thus, though marriage still has to be solemnized according to local civil law, Christians should choose their partners from their own community, and have the approval of their local bishop or pastor. The civil ceremonies are to be followed by a eucharist of thanksgiving and dedication.

One of the most attractive early Christian authors, Justin Martyr from Shechem in Samaria, wrote an *Apology* for the Christians addressed to the Emperor Antoninus Pius. Composed about 155 CE, after an appeal for respect for the truth against ancient customs, Justin argues that in following the truth of Christ, Christian moral standards are worthy of more respect than the contemporary mores, and takes as an example the custom of exposing children and giving them away for prostitution, even to the extent of mutilating them for 'the purpose of sodomy'. Such brutalities are done 'in the name of the mother of the gods' and so the defence of the superiority of Christian morals is used as an argument against the pagan deities.

Parallel with the Christian denunciation of pagan sexual vice, the early Christian writers frequently appeal for stable monogamous marriage among the Christians, and the avoidance of fornication, adultery, and all forms of unchastity. A typical example is given by Clement of Alexandria, a Greek contemporary of Justin, who advises all Christians, young and old, to 'hasten to accomplish marriage', the remedy for temptation to adultery.

In their attempt to explain Christian ethical training, the Apologists also found the Neo-Platonist teaching of Philo and his followers useful. This teaching laid strong emphasis on ascetic attitudes to the body, and Christian teaching tended to coalesce with it in stressing the moral superiority of the unmarried and the chaste. Philo's attitude to homosexual practices has already been noted (Part 3), and it was reiterated by the church Fathers with a vehemence which suggests that they preferred his view of the matter to the caution of the New Testament.

A notable early example of their rigorous view is provided by Tertullian, the Carthaginian lawyer converted in Rome in 195 CE. One of his later treatises concerns modesty, *De Pudicitia*, written about 217 CE, and this demonstrates the determination of church authorities to achieve strict control of the sexual behaviour of its members. Thus, in chapter four, he links together adultery and fornication, forbids secret marriage, insists widows should remain inviolate and concludes with a general denunciation which seems to include homosexual behaviour:

> All the other frenzies of passions – impious both towards the bodies and towards the sexes – beyond the laws of nature, we banish not only from the threshold, but from all shelter of the church, because they are not sins, but monstrosities.

Tertullian wrote this after he had become a Montanist. Montanism was an ascetic movement within the second-century church, seeking to distinguish the spirit-filled community from the worldly forms of Roman Christianity, and was eventually condemned for its unorthodoxy. This movement was only one form of Christian reaction against the difficulties of living in pagan society, and the search for holiness through separation led eventually to the courageous but sometimes excessive mortification practised by the Desert Fathers. World negation could not, however, be the whole answer and the bishops eventually found themselves responsible for dioceses of largely nominal Christians, after Constantine had tipped the scales towards making the Empire Christian by the Edict of Milan in 313 CE.[6]

(b) The Christian empire

There is some uncertainty how far pre-Christian Roman Law was officially used to inhibit sodomy. The Lex Scantia of *c*.226 BCE long pre-dated the so called 'marriage' between Nero and Pythagoras reported by Tacitus, and that may have been little more than a licentious joke, matching the ribaldry of Caesar's soldiers against his reputed youthful service as a catamite. Ridicule was the usual public reaction to those who were known to be active adult sodomites. The Lex Scantia was not much used except in aid of political vendettas, though rules to protect the young were later made more effective. By *c*.250 CE, homosexual prostitution which had previously been tolerated and heavily taxed as a source of state income was suppressed. The Christian Emperors Valentinian and Theodosius increased the penalties for these offences in their new Code of 390. Male prostitutes were dragged from the brothels and burnt.[7]

The Theodosian Edict shocked Rome, but failed to eradicate homosexual vice throughout the Empire, and the Christians continued to teach against it. Influenced by this teaching, but also perhaps to use it as a means of destroying his opponents, the Emperor Justinian, as part of his general policy of legal reform, issued two Edicts concerning homosexual practices in 538 and 544 CE. Neither of them changed the Theodosian code or its penalties, but added new exhortations that those guilty of these offences should repent and seek forgiveness as a better way than risking the consequences of conviction. Justinian claims to be moved by the fear that the divine vengeance wrought on Sodom would destroy his Empire if this vice continued. Thus, the Christian attitude was firmly set into the law of Christendom.

In the church of the East, early in the fourth century CE, the Cappadocian brothers, Basil and Gregory of Nyssa, both record disciplinary regulations for practising homosexuals, assessing the gravity of the offence as similar to adultery, rather than fornication, with penances between four and fifteen years, though full repentance would mitigate this. In the same period, the Councils of Elvira in Spain, and Ancyra (Ankara) in Turkey passed canons prohibiting homosexual behaviour. In the Spanish canon, bestiality and sodomy are treated together, a reflection of Leviticus, and in the Turkish equivalent, the specific point is the refusal of communion to unrepentant pederasts. These Conciliar decisions were of local application and possibly indicate that homosexual prostitution was a particular problem in these countries, but it was probably still endemic in the Mediterranean lands, east and west. In any case, later canons re-enact the same rules, or more comprehensive versions, and if repentance is not forthcoming, flogging, castration or death by burning are the suggested penalties. (Note: Using the flames of purification for unrepentant sinners was acceptable to the mediaeval mind. Joan of Arc and Thomas Cranmer were burnt.)

The theologians of the now officially recognized church had to continue the struggle against pagan cults. Thus, Arnobius and his pupil Lactantius, later tutor to Constantine's son Crispus, repeat the now familiar challenge that the sexual frenzies associated with the old deities are repugnant. Not only are incest, child exposure, and subsequent prostitution mentioned, but the phallic symbolism in statue and art associated with Bacchus is described as an example of the false religion of those who unjustly accuse the Christians.

A good description of church discipline at the end of the fourth century is provided by the *Apostolic Constitutions*, a collection of ecclesiastical laws compiled by the church in Syria. Book seven of the *Constitutions* is an expanded version of the *Didache*, conflating the clauses of the Decalogue with dominical sayings from the New Testament and references from the Old Testament. The commandment against adultery is amplified as follows;

> Thou shalt not commit adultery, for thou dividest one flesh into two. They two shall be one flesh, for the husband and wife are one in nature, in consent, in union, in disposition, and the conduct of life; but they are separated in sex and number. Thou shalt not corrupt boys; for this wickedness is contrary to nature, and arose from Sodom, which was therefore entirely consumed with fire sent from God. Let such a one be accursed, and all the people shall say 'So be it'.

The biblical references to support this instruction are given as Genesis 1.14; Leviticus 18.20; and Genesis 19; and it is interesting that St Paul's Epistles are not referred to here, though they are in other sections. The instructions are set in a form which permits liturgical use with a congregational response inserted at appropriate points.

Close attention to the problem of homosexual behaviour is given by St John Chrysostom in his biblical commentaries. Chrysostom, originally a lawyer and monk, became Patriarch of Constantinople in 398 CE, and was nicknamed 'Golden mouth' because of his accomplished preaching. His commentaries were probably written while he was still at Antioch and are in the form of a series of *Homilies*. He comments on Romans, I Corinthians and Titus to set out at length the full Christian arguments against homosexuality as a form of lust, and he is not content merely to re-iterate the standard criticism of pagan pederasty.

He begins by arguing that both the men and the women to whom Paul refers have chosen this deliberately, since heterosexual activity was available to them. They refused the pleasures of natural sex because they decided not to obey what they knew of God's will by natural reason, and therefore God withdrew from them and they became dominated by Satan. The women are the more disgraceful as they should have a stronger sense of shame. The men who make themselves mad in this way are of less use than animals or eunuchs, and deserve to be driven from the society of the church and stoned. The Epistle of Jude and the destruction of Sodom are cited for those who doubt that the punishment of hell awaits them, and the moral is drawn that all this depravity is the consequence of turning away from God and enjoying a life of luxury.

St Augustine of Hippo, who had been a Manichaean, and then a Neo-Platonist before his baptism in 387 CE, writes about homosexual practices in his *Confessions*, *c.* 400 CE. The reference occurs in parenthesis in Book three where Augustine is describing his Manichaean period, and is considering afresh the presupposition that it might be possible for the Christian duties to love God and his neighbour to clash with man-made regulations. If they do, he concludes that God must be obeyed, but often human customs agree with God's commands, and a Christian may not opt out at his own whim. He takes Sodom as an example:

> There are those foul offences which be against nature, to be everywhere and at all times detested and punished; such as were those of the men of Sodom: which should all nations commit, they should all stand guilty of the same crime, by the law of God, which hath not so made men, that they should so abuse one another. For even that intercourse which should be between God and us is violated, when that same nature, of which he is Author, is polluted by the perversity of lust.[8]

This passage shows greater restraint than that from Chrysostom, and while firmly identifying the sin of Sodom, echoes Paul's two reasons for condemning homosexual practices – they are contrary to nature, and a lustful perversion with interferes with men's relationship with God.

One of the standard criticisms of the traditional Christian attitude to sexual behaviour is that, under the influence of Augustine and monasticism, a largely negative view of sexual activity became firmly established, love-making in particular being a sign of mankind's dominance by the sinful lusts of the flesh, redeemed only by the concession of God in the act of conception. There is no doubt a sense in which this is irrefutable, the preference for virginity is a recurrent theme in the writings of the church Fathers, latin as well as Greek. But apart from those who became monks and took the vow of celibacy, there were some Christian leaders who experienced happy marriage and were prepared to defend it on more positive grounds. Clement of Alexandria, for example, was one of these; Tertullian also was married; and Augustine himself cohabited for some fifteen years with a woman who bore him a son and shared a contented domestic life within the then accepted bounds of concubinage. Only after his move to Rome did Augustine abandon her, and she probably became the good catholic 'widow' of whom he writes tenderly later in the *Confessions*.

Augustine was no stranger to sexual desire and often expressed embarrassment at the force of this fire in his loins. In a soliloquy he writes:

> I do not consider anything more capable of sending a man's mind plummeting from its lofty heights than a woman's charm and the touch of their bodies (Sol. 1.10)

There is one section in his *City of God* where Augustine notes with heavy sarcasm the Roman custom of invoking a group of lustful deities to assist the initial union of marriage. His derison takes the form of suggesting that a healthy male needs no such assistance to perform his sexual duty. In later life, Augustine was involved in controversy with a younger man, Julian, bishop of Eclanum, who takes a markedly liberal view of the rights of married people to make love day or night when it pleases them. Although Augustine disapproves, he argues with an explicitness which shows him to be, like Luther, no stranger to sexual vigour. Since his own co-habitation started when he was eighteen years old, and he was clearly markedly heterosexual, it is not surprising he only mentions homosexuality rarely. In one of his sermons he does lament that his pastoral work gives him too much evidence of adultery, far too little of chastity.

The retreat from the world into asceticism was chosen in its most determined form by the monks of the Egyptian desert, but that did not allow these hermits to escape from sexual temptation. Apart from the way memory and imagination could prey on these lonely saints, even if dismissed as the wiles of the Devil to disturb meditation on God, in their isolation they still needed some kind of support system for food and other necessities, and they hungered for companionship.

Their cells had to be reasonably near a village and its water supply. They could not altogether avoid human contact with the inhabitants, and pilgrims disturbed their tranquillity. Did the friendly spiritual encouragement of a veteran monk towards a novice ever cross the boundary into pederasty? Apparently sometimes it did, and the Abbots made rules against it, not always successfully. The vocation to celibacy was not the same as a denial of all human relationship; it was the concentration on some good things by restraint towards others. At one stage in this process of sorting out how to manage relationships in a close-knit religious community, Augustine wrote to some nuns over whom his sister had been Superior:

> The love which you bear to one another ought not to be carnal, but spiritual: for those things which are practised by immodest women, even with other females, in shameful jesting and playing, ought not to be done even by married women or by girls who are about to marry, much less by the widows or chaste virgins dedicated by a holy vow to be the handmaids of Christ.[9]

The quality of cosmopolitan life did not change in the later Empire as fast as the Christians hoped. In particular, the need for Christian schools was soon felt, the protection of the young from corruption and finding a place to send those who needed rehabilitation were of much concern. St Benedict and his community of monks at Subiaco, and later at Monte Cassino, founded in 525, well knew the problems from their own youthful experiences in Rome, and as the monastic communities developed, they became a useful resource not only for hospitality and refuge, but also gradually for Christian education and learning. Sending children to the Desert had seemed an earlier solution, but not all the monks could cope with such distraction. Drawing on earlier models, John Cassian, who was for a time at the monastery in Bethlehem before settling at Marsailles in 415 CE, wrote there a set of rules for the monastic life which were used later by St Benedict. His warnings about homosexual temptation included advice that monks should not share the same donkey, lift their habits too high when washing, sleep in the same cell or anoint another brother with healing ointment. They are never to hold hands, nor when working together speak to each other except through the monk in charge.

Becoming a monk or nun did not remove a man or a woman from sexual temptation or fantasy, it remained a present force in their lives and imaginations, hence the strict rules of Cassian and others to restrain its expression, and limit occasions of temptation. But the similarity of expression between the general Christian renunciation of the flesh and the discipline of the monks concealed a genuine difficulty because, despite this negative theology, most Christians continued to fall in love, marry and have children.

In his recent book, *The Body and Society*, Peter Brown throws much light on the different views of sexuality taken by Augustine and Cassian which the quotations above do not adequately show. The difference is considerable. In his later life, Augustine as a bishop in Africa was expected to affirm marriage, not damn it, and this he tried to do. But he never lost his conviction that as an *immediate* consequence of the Fall, Adam and Eve had felt their bodies touched with a disturbing new sense of the alien, in the form of sexual sensations that escaped their control. As a result of their act of disobedience in eating the forbidden fruit, they felt themselves naked, and thereafter all mankind found their sexuality developed a momentum of its own, at war with the soul. This was not just a matter of youthful lust of the flesh, it was a concupiscence that only death could remove.

For Cassian, such despair about sexuality was too severe:

> When a thing exists in all persons without exception, we can only think it belongs to the very substance of human nature, since the fall, as if it were 'natural' to man. When a thing is found to be congenital, how can we fail to believe it was implanted by the will of the Lord, not to injure us, but to help us. The struggle of the flesh and the spirit against each other is not merely harmless, but is in fact extremely useful to us.[10]

This meant for those whose vocation was withdrawal from the world an opportunity to learn through sexual temptation the depths of their own egotism, and imperfect dedication. Their fantasies were signs of forces beyond their consciousness which still needed to be changed. Unlike Augustine, Cassian thought that human nature could strive towards improvement and achieve it. But this was not a pre-Freudian concept of frustrated libido. Sexuality as such was not important, it was a sign of far heavier beasts within the soul, anger, greed, avarice and vainglory. That could be as true of both homosexual and heterosexual temptation, in the religious life. And also true in ordinary life, married or single. Augustine's severity allowed insufficiently for human will and free choice.

This emphasis on asceticism was however by no means the only alternative for Christians facing up to their sexuality at these times. For contrast, these lines from a poem by Ausonius for his former pupil Paulinus, who was thinking of becoming a monk show a romantic affection if nothing more:

> As long as I am held within this prison body, in whatever world I am found, I shall hold you fast, Grafted into my being, not divided

by distant shores or suns. Everywhere you shall be with me, I will see with my heart And embrace you with my loving spirit.[11]

Ausonius became tutor to the future Roman Emperor Gratian, and was made a Consul, dying in *c*.395 CE. His library was notorious for a large and most disreputable collection of homosexual pornography. Although his poetry shows some sign of Christian faith, his advice to Paulinus is clearly unsympathetic to the claims of vocation. Paulinus disregarded it, and became a monk, and later Bishop of Nola in Spain.

(c) The mediaeval church

The Christian church gradually took firmer hold of the culture and social life of Europe as the Christendom of Charlesmagne approached, and although this was a triumph of a kind, reality required some acceptance of the existing customs. Not everything secular could b baptized, and the church had to watch with suspicion, but without success in quelling it, the steady development of a new ethos centred on romantic and courtly love. There were two kinds of Christian obedience, religious and world denying, secular and world affirming. It was the world of Dante and Beatrice, and of Peter Abelard and Heloise, witnessing to the Christian humanity, and of St Bernard of Clairvaux, and Peter Damian, the Abbot of Fonte Avellana among those who tried to replace the increasing leniency of the monastic rules with greater strictness.

For many monks, the Benedictine rule or variations were accepted as the supreme guide to Christian holiness, though the somewhat freer systems of the Friars, Franciscan and Dominican, were a popular alternative. Regulations to control sleeping arrangements in both monasteries and nunneries clearly reduced opportunities for sexual licence, and the third Lateran Council of 1179 condemns 'incontinence against nature'. By this time the Corpus of Canon Law governs church life throughout Europe and is applied in England.

Further evidence of the need to suppress homosexual behaviour is found in the *Penitentials*, regulations originating in the Celtic church. In line with the attitudes of the mediaeval scholastics and the decision of the church councils, there are many examples in the *Penitentials* of how seriously the various manifestations are to be punished. These handbooks for confessors developed systematic regulations to govern all aspects of human sinfulness as a practical expression in specific cases of the general principles of the Western councils and Canon Law. A wide range of homosexual offences was recognized with appropriate penances according to the gravity of the act. Sodomy was the most serious offence, and the penalty for it could be death, but this penalty had to be carried out by secular authorities, and the church was seldom willing to ask for this extreme punishment. Among the lesser homosexual offences were various forms of physical contact, ranging from those intended to induce orgasm to mere kissing. Lesbianism among lay people was punished with a three-year penance, or seven years for nuns. Boys under twenty were treated more leniently according to age.

It is difficult to know how widespread homosexual offences were in the Middle Ages, but the existence of these regulations, and their application to secular as well as monastic communities, show their continued existence. There were periodic outbursts of scandal and indignation when a notable ecclesiastical or civil personality was convicted, and this would be followed by a reissue of the regulations and solemn exhortations to discourage future offenders.

As early as 744 CE, Boniface writes to the King of Mercia that 'the people of England have been living a shameful life, despising lawful marriages, committing adultery, and lusting after the fashion of the people of Sodom', but there is no certain evidence that the English were exceptional in their sexual licence. A fierce and detailed attack on homosexual behaviour is offered by Peter Damian, abbot of Fonte Avellana in his *Liber Gomorrhianus* of 1051 CE. He finds the regulations of the *Penitentials*, of which there were many continentals versions as well as the Celtic, far too liberal in the penances they required, and he lists three degrees of male homosexual offence, mutual masturbation, inter-femoral connection, and sodomy. For all three, he argues, monks and clergy must be removed from their orders, but this severity was received with protest, and eventually the Pope, Leo IX, decreed that only those who were persistent in sodomy should be thus degraded.

The vigour of some mediaeval poetry expresses the fascination with, and difficulty of controlling, the lusts of the flesh; Chaucer's tales gives examples, and the story of Sodom was sometimes used as a morality play. An anonymous fourteenth-century English poet, comparable with Chaucer, but known chiefly for the legend of *Sir Gawain and the Green Knight*, also wrote a long poem based on the three biblical epics of the deluge, the destruction of Sodom, and the death of Belshazzar. It illustrates the theme of God's attitude to sins of the flesh and commends purity. The title of the work is *Cleanness* and in modern translation the incident at Sodom is described thus:

The men uttered these words in a loud fierce shout; If you value your life in these parts, Lot, push out those young men who went in a little while ago, so we can teach them about love as our pleasure requires, as the custom of Sodom is to men who pass by.

After a narrative section, Lot replies:

I shall teach you a better device in accordance with nature. I have a treasure in my house, my two lovely daughters, unspoiled by any man. Though I say it myself, there are no ladies more beautiful in Sodom. It is better pleasure to join naturally with them.[12]

The poem takes the Genesis narrative literally, and reflects the standard view of the times – heterosexual behaviour should have been accepted as a more agreeable alternative. The early English legal treatises *Fleta* and *Britton*, which date from this period, make sodomy a capital crime, going beyond the French Councils of Paris and Rouen which maintained the traditional punishments of degradation and penance. Presumably this was intended as a deterrent in principle, and in practice the actual discipline of the church was expressed in refusal of the sacraments, or in an extreme case, as with King William Rufus, the witholding of funeral rites.

(d) Scholastic teaching

In the later mediaeval period detailed consideration of homosexuality is given by St Thomas Aquinas in the *Summa Theologiae* II.II.qq.153, 154 where he lists homosexual practices among the six species of lust. The others are fornication, adultery, incest, seduction, and rape, and all of them are condemned as contrary to the natural order of the venereal act which right reason shows to be for the preservation of the human race. Among the species of lust, homosexual practices are the most grievous form of sin because they corrupt this principle most directly. In response to the query that homosexual acts are less sinful than adultery, seduction, and rape, which injure another person, Thomas argues that this breach of the divine law injures God, himself the creator of it. This argument is not, of course, conclusive, for heterosexual breaches of the divine law have the same effect as well as harming other humans, but in Thomas' appreciation, the offence against God is the more serious matter.

The *Summa* is a comprehensive conflation of ideas taken from the Bible, Aristotle, and Augustine. Aquinas deals carefully with Aristotle's teaching that homosexual practices are a form of behaviour which belongs to the animal order rather than the human. Based on his observation of homosexual behaviour among animals when deprived of their natural mates. Aristotle had argued it was a species of bestiality rather than of lust because of its irrationality. Aquinas called Aristotle 'The Philosopher whom it was impertinent for most people to criticize', and built much of his own natural theology on his teaching.

St Thomas's sense of importance of the natural order makes it impossible for him to deny God intends people to marry, but he shares with other scholastics the conviction that reason not passion must inform behaviour, and therefore sexuality is always potentially dangerous. He introduces his discussion of sexual intercourse with the quotation from Augustine's soliloquy already noted, and some of his references to Aristotelian physics may seem bizarre to us, but he is clear that procreation is the right use of sex. Any other use is against reason, and so he condemns contraception, anal intercourse, and other homosexual activities. The central idea of nature held by St Thomas originated with the Aristotelian view, in this context 'the specific difference which gives form to each thing', but the prolonged debate among Christian theologians about the dual natures of Christ overlies this simplicity, and Thomas will have been familiar with it.

(Note: The teaching of Aquinas has remained in many respects the dominant influence in the theology of the Western Catholic Church, and his argument that homosexual behaviour is not only contrary to reason but also contrary to the natural order for human sexuality has proved to be the definitive ground for all subsequent rejection of homosexual behaviour by the Catholic Church. An authoritative reiteration appeared in the Vatican '*Declaration on Certain Questions concerning Sexual Ethics*', approved by Pope Paul on 6 November 1975, where it is stated that scripture attests 'to the fact that homosexual acts are intrinsically disordered and can in no case be approved of'. The texts from Romans, Corinthians and Timothy are referred to in a footnote, but the language of the Declaration is Thomist.)

(e) The Reformation

The political and religious upheaval of the Reformation broke for ever the Catholic unity of Europe and the penitential theology of the Reformed churches revived the ancient Christian understanding of the full freedom of God's grace for the individual, in many ways a radical release from the legalistic casuistry of the later mediaeval church. Luther could cry '*simul peccator, simul justus*' without intending thereby to proclaim antinomianism, but in sexual ethics the re-enhanced primacy of the scriptures ensured that there was no great change. The crucial issue of the time was the freedom to marry for those who as monks and nuns had vowed celibacy. Some possibility of divorce by local church authority replaced the old procedure of papal annulment of marriage. The condemnation of homosexuality continued.

Before turning to Luther, whose writings on the conflict between flesh and spirit are voluminous but who seems to have been quite uninterested in the problem of homosexuality, it is important to recall the developments in biblical studies that preceded the Reformation proper in the later stages of the mediaeval period. The French Jewish biblical commentator, Rashi, already quoted on p. 65, had revived a style of commentary on the biblical texts which avoided elaborate allegorizing and concentrated on the clarification of basic meanings in the original Old Testament. His work was widely circulated, and despite the persecution of the Jews and the burning of their sacred books in the fourteenth century, particularly in France, Judaism continued to be regarded officially by the church as the one heresy God allowed. The Jews were not to be forcibly converted nor subjected to inquisition, and their centres of learning and libraries, particularly in Eastern Europe, were available to Christian scholars. The best equipped biblical scholar of the later middle ages was Nicholas of Lyra, himself a converted Jew who became a Franciscan and a doctor of the Sorbonne in Paris. His commentary on the Bible, written soon after 1300 CE, was very popular and refers frequently to Rashi, whose Hebrew he, of course, understood. The 'Lyra' biblical commentary was one of the first to be printed, its precision widely admired among the Reformers, and many English Cathedrals still have copies of it among their collections of incunabula. The Vulgate Bible, printed in Basle in 1498, had the Jerome text on each page surrounded by the *Glosses* of Anselm and the *Commentary* of Nicholas. Luther used the Basle Bible extensively, and in his lectures on Romans, quotes and comments on Nicholas' work.

Since Nicholas of Lyra's commentary was approved by the Reformers for its stress on the '*sensus literalis historicus*' and was reckoned the best commentary since Jerome, the interpretation given to the Sodom, Gibeah, and Leviticus passages deserves mention at this point. Nicholas comments on Genesis 19.6:

> Lot went out to them lest they should enter his house for nefarious intercourse and assault his guests.

Then, in an extended note on verse 7 he considers the problem whether or not Lot was justified to offer his daughters to prevent the greater evil, the vice against nature. His argument proceeds in a scholastic style, first suggesting that although natural law requires protection of guests, and a lesser evil may be used to prevent a greater, nevertheless, as Augustine has argued, chastity is ordered, and therefore Lot was not in his right mind in making this offer. Nicholas concludes that even though human law permits prostitution and hence fornication, leaving the punishment to God's judgment, fornication must not be encouraged, and Lot should not have attempted to safeguard his guests by unlawful means. The distinction between natural law and human law is standard scholastic teaching.

This comment shows that Nicholas interprets '*ut cognoscamus eos*' as clearly sexual in meaning, the vice against nature, and illustrates the systematic tidiness looked for in the biblical text as to the moral motivation of its characters – Lot is declared 'confused' to avoid the text becoming an argument for the end justifying the means.

For the rape at Gibeah in Judges 19, Nicholas notes that most commentators maintain that sodomitical intercourse is intended, but he then quotes Josephus with approval, to suggest that they were really looking for the woman and made the homosexual demand only to force her to be surrendered. He repeats the conclusion that it would have been mortal sin to surrender the daughter, referring back to the Sodom comment, and concludes that the Levite's woman was actually his wife.

For Leviticus 18.22 Nicholas comments briefly:

> Such intercourse is contrary to nature and is called the sodomitical vice after the city of Sodom, which is recorded to have been utterly destroyed on account of such wickedness.

It is clear from these comments that Nicholas has no doubt of the literal meaning of the Sodom story, but has detected the ambiguity in the event at Gibeah.

Luther delivered his *Lectures on Romans* in 1515 and 1516 at the University of Wittenberg while he was still an Augustinian monk of the Catholic Church, but also Professor of Biblical Theology at the University. His lecture notes, preserved by his son, found their way to the Royal Library in Berlin where they were overlooked until the present century. In considering the closing verses of Romans 1, Luther is reticent about the particular categories of sins, at least as far as his notes show, and he observed that the glory of the body lies in chastity and continence and its disgrace consists in unnatural abuse. Bodies are ordained to an honourable marriage, and to chastity which is still more honourable (this is some years before he married Katherine von Bora and he inverts the order in his comment on the fruits of the Spirit in Galations 5). Among the humiliations of the body more disgraceful than adultery and unchastity, is the 'pollution of an even worse turpitude'.

He then details various forms of uncleanness or effeminacy, such as lascivious thoughts, petting, especially of a woman's body, rubbing of the hands, and obscene movements. He also refers to nocturnal emissions and distinguishes these from sexual intercourse with a person of the same or other sex. At this point he asserts that God can forgive all such sin, or harden the sinner in it and condemn him, as he chooses. In his lecture notes on Galatians, he describes lust as various *'species libidinis'* and notes that he has defined these in detail before and does not need to interpret them further, his purpose now being to concentrate on explaining justification. It is, of course, characteristic of Luther's theology to take a somewhat negative view of human nature outside grace, and therefore not to mention the argument of unnaturalness stressed by previous mediaeval authors and, in fact, Nicholas of Lyra. Luther's comment on Genesis 19 also shows his characteristic widening of interpretation to include heterosexual vice and general corruption of society. God had to destroy Sodom because it became ungovernable through these consequences of idolatry, and the church takes the same risk – hence the need for reform.

Reference has been made earlier to Calvin's interpretation of the story of Sodom's destruction in his commentary on Genesis (see p. 45). Although Calvin suggested the townspeople used subtlety in the ambiguous wording of the demand 'to know' the visitors, he concludes that they were, in fact, determined on a crime 'the atrocity of which would not suffer the destruction of the place to be any longer deferred'. In similar vein, his commentary on Romans 1.27 makes clear that he has no doubt about the sinfulness of 'that which even the brute beasts abhor', but he is not drawn into further particular comment, preferring to emphasize in a typical way the general sinfulness of man. His comment on I Corinthians 6.9 makes the same point. However, Calvin moves away from the old negative attitudes to sexuality and marriage more confidently than Luther does, and regards the rule of celibacy for the clergy which had been established in the fifth century as a mistake. By fresh studies of the creation stories at the beginning of Genesis, he re-claims for Christianity that sense of the good vocation to family life and child-bearing which belonged to Judaism, and he refurbishes the status of women in a way that eventually enabled the Protestant Churches to accept some of the demands of feminism more readily than the Catholics could.

Reformation interests were concentrated on the new life of faith, and the kind of attention the early church, with its Jewish background, gave to Leviticus well-nigh vanishes. The Sodom story as an example of the plight of sinners is much more studied. The mental picture of God's wrath expressed in fire and brimstone had a strong hold on the mediaeval mind and was vividly illustrated at the time by a painting by Dürer entitled '*Lot and his daughters*', which is now in the National Gallery of Art, Washington. The whole town is depicted engulfed in flame as the three of them look on appalled.

Few people would have seen Dürer's painting at the time, but the influence of illustrations in early printed books was, of course, widespread and important. One of the best engravers of the sixteenth century was Theodore de Bry who worked in Frankfurt and specialized in providing the pictures for the very popular histories of the exploration of America. One of these engravings, perhaps to be dated 1593, shows Balboa throwing 'some Indians who have committed the terrible sin of sodomy, to the dogs to be torn to pieces.' De Bry never crossed the Atlantic himself, and the brutalities he depicts are offensive to modern eyes, but would not have surprised European readers of the time who were accustomed to cruel death for much less serious crimes.

The Law in England

(a) Church and state attitudes

The post-Reformation situation in England was one in which the old Catholic moral theology was, in many respects, retained in the Anglican tradition, though the new canons of 1604 CE were a greatly simplified summary for the administration of the new established church. State law took over jurisdiction in homosexual offences.

Back in Saxon times, the Laws of King Alfred, dated about 980 CE, begin with the decalogue and extracts from the Pentateuch, but are, of course, largely a modification and codification of Saxon customary law. The laws were administered by the Sheriff and bishop sitting together in court, but when the Normans arrived William I separated the secular and ecclesiastical jurisdictions.

This change was not motivated by anti-clericalism, for William was a sincere churchman and a great collaborator with Lanfranc, Archbishop of Canterbury, in bringing canonical order to the church in England, but he retained the common law tradition in England, under the control of his own judges. The discipline of the clergy, matrimonial causes, and offences against sexual morality, however, continued to be within the jurisdiction of the ecclesiastical courts.

The Western Canon Law developed rapidly at this time and was finally codified by Gratian as the *Concordantia Discordantium Canonum* of around 1140 CE. This became also the Canon Law of England, though subject in principle to the king's approval and in practice to local variation in minor respects among the dioceses. The traditional prohibitions of homosexual behaviour from the early councils and papal decretals were maintained in the canons.

There seems little doubt that the next English king, William Rufus, was justly accused of homosexual behaviour, and his successor Henry I held a Council in London to pass extra canons for the reform of clerical and moral abuses, including one (twenty-eight) in which 'those who commit the shameful sin of sodomy, and especially those who take pleasure in doing so' were condemned by a weighty anathema, until by penitence and confession they should show themselves worthy of absolution. Clerics guilty of this crime were not to be promoted, but deposed, and laymen deprived of legal status. Only a bishop could absolve, except for monks. The next royal scandal concerned Edward II, brutally murdered at Berkeley Castle in 1327.

Reformation theology in its continental form advocated a separation between church and state law – the left and right hand of God's rule as Luther saw it. Support for this view was readily found among the European princes in the wake of the Holy Roman Empire, the growing sense of nationalism, and the independence needed for commercial expansion. The English solution was a compromise.

(b) The Act of 1553

As part of Henry VIII's policy of asserting the royal supremacy over ecclesiastical matters, he caused an Act to be passed in 1553 which transferred jurisdiction 'for the detestable and abominable vice of buggery committed with mankind or beast' to the royal courts. The preamble to the Act complained that 'there was not yet sufficient punishment' for the crime, and this suggests that the church courts were very reluctant to pass a death penalty. Sodomy was thus made a felony, for which hanging, mutilation, or deportation were the usual punishments. The Act related only to sodomy, and jurisdiction in other homosexual offences remained with the church. Henry's original Act was limited in operation 'until the last day of the next Parliament', but was reintroduced three times in his reign, temporarily repealed by Edward VI in 1547, restored by him the next year, repealed again by Mary in 1553 with the probable intention of reviving the ecclesiastical court's jurisdiction, and finally became a permanent part of English law when it was re-enacted by Elizabeth I in 1563, the preamble stating that since the repeal 'divers ill disposed persons have been the more bold to commit the said most horrible and detestable vice of buggery aforesaid, to the high displeasure of Almighty God'.

This new law was enforced only occasionally in the next 275 years as far as public records indicate, but these would, of course, only report the more notorious cases.

(c) Capital offences

The death penalty was still being occasionally exacted in the nineteenth century, examples of which were an army trooper, caught with the Irish Bishop of Clogher in 1822, and two labourers in Bristol whose execution the local newspaper reported in 1800 without any further comment. But as Blackstone observed this was still the usual punishment for all felonies. The bishop escaped to Scotland and died there in 1843.

The problem of proof, also referred to by Blackstone, caused anxiety, especially when public opinion began to protest that too many kinds of crime incurred capital punishment. Sodomy has sometimes been interpreted to cover a wider range of offences than anal intercourse, and by a court decision of 1781, both penetration and emission of seed were required to be proved. By the 1820s, with the establishment of a regular police force, more than a hundred crimes ceased to be capital, but Sir Robert Peel reinstated the old rule that only penetration was needed for sodomy, and this offence remained capital despite an attempt by Lord Russell to gain Parliamentary support for a change. The armed forced had their own disciplinary rules, and all forms of homosexual offence were harshly punished, four members of HMS Africaine being hanged for buggery in 1816. The army had similar punishments. The Cambridge criminologist, Sir L. Radzinovitz has noted that in London in 1826 there were more death sentences for sodomy than for murder.

The death penalty was finally removed in 1861, when the punishment of penal servitude for life was substituted. To establish the crime it was necessary to prove only anal penetration and not seminal emission. At this time the jurisdiction of the ecclesiastical courts was substantially curtailed. All matrimonial causes were transferred to a division of the High Court, and church courts ceased to be concerned with sexual offences except where clergymen were involved, and not always then. The civil courts had, meanwhile, come to deal with indecent assault as one of the types of 'offences against the person' and, under this heading, homosexual practices other than sodomy could be included when a complaint was made. The 1861 Act laid down a maximum of ten years for attempts to commit sodomy, or for indecent assault, and thus the viciousness of the old law was mitigated.

(d) The Criminal Law Amendment Act of 1885

The result of the 1861 Act was that homosexuals who kept their physical activities private among themselves were left tolerably free from legal prosecution, but in 1885 a Bill was introduced into Parliament 'to make further provision for the protection of women and girls, the suppression of brothels and other purposes'. At a late stage of the Bill's passage through Parliament an extra clause was added which provided that:

> Any male person who in public, or private, commits or is a party to the commission of, or procures or attempts to procure the

commission by any male person, of any act of gross indecency with another male person, shall be guilty of a misdemeanour. . . .

The stated purpose of the extra clause was to provide for the protection of men and boys, as well as women and girls, from assault, the main object of the Act. Since everyone knew there were many male prostitutes and boy catamites to be found in the parks and railway stations of London at this time, it may have seemed sensible to make this extension. But, as a late addition, the clause escaped any serious examination, and perhaps unintentionally made a much wider change in the law. Gross indecency in private could include a range of activities far short of sodomy, and the clause was quickly dubbed 'the blackmailer's charter'.

The extra clause is commonly known as the 'Labouchere Amendment' because Henry Labouchere, a Liberal-Radical MP and editor of the journal *Truth*, was the author of it. The original bill had passed all stages in the Lords and was being considered by the Commons in a committee of the whole House when Labouchere moved his amendment. It was a late night session, between 11.30 p.m. and 2.55 a.m. with a handful of members present, and one of them immediately intervened to ask the Speaker if the new clause was within the scope of the Bill as it dealt with a totally different class of offence. The Speaker ruled that at this stage of the Bill anything could be introduced by leave of the House, and the Attorney-General, Sir Henry James, said that the Government accepted the amendment, asking successfully at the same time that the punishment should be a maximum of two years' imprisonment.

The very short report of the debate in Hansard does not make clear what Labouchere intended his clause to achieve, and maybe he didn't know himself. Whoever it was who affixed a title to the new clause seems to have supposed it was dealing with a public offence, at least primarily. Earlier in the debate a clause had been passed raising the age of consent for girls from thirteen to sixteen, and it seems that Labouchere was trying to extend this ordinary legal protection to boys as well, without wanting to fix an age limit of sixteen. His clause, in fact, had no age limit at all.

The summer recess beckoned, and no one was inclined to pick the Bill to pieces again, and so the last words for it were spoken by the Bishop of Winchester:

> The Bishops were interested in this question as the natural guardians of the morals of the people. . . . They were most anxious that the Bill should pass their Lordships' House, and he believed, whatever faults might be in the Bill, it was calculated to do a great deal of good, and it would be a great strength to the country. It was said,

truly, that you could not make people moral or chaste by Act of
Parliament, but a great deal might be done to prevent things which
were immoral and unchaste. . . . Living in a Diocese in which there
were more naval and military stations than in any other part of the
country, he happened to know how terrible were the conditions of
the streets of those places, especially in connection with this prostitution of infants.

(e) Child prostitution

The bishop's sentiments no doubt reflected the general wish of both
Houses of Parliament that the Bill would help to clean up the streets
and protect the young. Public indignation had been stirred up by an
investigation carried out by W. H. Stead, the editor of the *Pall Mall
Gazette*, into the traffic in procuring young girls for prostitution. His
horrifying discoveries were published in his newspaper, and a government Commission, chaired by the Archbishop of Canterbury (Benson),
with Cardinal Manning and the Bishop of London (Temple) as two of
the other four members, was set up to enquire into the report and
confirmed its truth in July 1885.

Labouchere's motives in adding the extra clause have been scrutinized in recent years and the relevant factors can be briefly summarized. One may have been the Government's wish to take a firm
line following the trial for homosexual behaviour of certain officials in
Dublin the previous year. The session was nearly at its end, with an
election pending, and the pressure of the Purity Society and Josephine
Butler and her associates to achieve the main object of the Bill in
protecting young women was probably irresistible even when the
complication of Clause 11 was added. Although Labouchere himself
may have thought the Bill likely to interfere overmuch with personal
liberty, and indeed, during the trial of Oscar Wilde some years later,
suggested that his intention was only to introduce a wrecking amendment, his opportunist intervention failed in its main purpose, and led
instead to the immediate flight of many known homosexual men from
London. Wilde called the consequences of the new Clause a monstrous
martyrdom, and was himself the most famous victim of it. The loosely
drafted clause should have been properly scrutinized by Parliament or
later restrictively interpreted by a Court of Appeal, but this never
happened.

(f) The rescue work of the church

The passing of the 1885 Act has to be set in the context of the long
campaign by Joseph Butler, Ellice Hopkins, General Booth of the
Salvation Army, together with several Bishops and lay readers, to
improve the conditions of women throughout the late Victorian

period. The hostels for rescued prostitutes was their most substantial achievement, and they succeeded in changing the age of consent and tackling the problem of venereal disease by legislation. The need for this work continued into the twentieth century, and in 1918, Mrs Randall Davidson, the wife of the Archbishop of Canterbury brought together the already existing Diocesan committees for rescue work among women under a new centralized body called 'the Archbishop's Advisory Board for Spiritual and Moral Welfare Work.' The eventual direct successor of this body is the present General Synod Board of Social Responsibility.

The Reformers knew that the double standard was the source of the anger to women, and that needed an educational programme to commend purity among men. By implication, homosexual prostitution would also be discouraged, and after several attempts, an organization to concentrate on rescue work among boys was set up called the White Cross League. Over the years, the League held many public meetings and published pamphlets commending various aspects of purity. It's best seller was called *The Blanco Book*, provided free to all in the Armed Forces, and suggesting they kept themselves away from the French brothels and pure for the women they were fighting to protect at home. In partnership with the London Diocesan Welfare Committee, they organized workers to befriend and rescue boy prostitutes, and in 1911 established a residential house for them at Clapham Common, known as the Shelter Home. An ex-police constable from Hastings, Mr Pritchard, was the Warden and he divided his time between patrolling places in central London where the boys were to be found, notably the main railway stations, administering the Home, and finding local work for the boys he took there. His handwritten diary recording the work day by day survives, and sometimes his efforts at rehabilitation seemed to be successful, though he could seldom do anything more than provide a steady job for those boys willing to co-operate. The underlying causes of deprivation were noted but little could be done. The home was eventually sold, and the proceeds were given to the Anglican Franciscan Order who agreed to take some boys at one of their houses in Dorset.

Reforming the Law

(a) An enquiry needed?

Child prostitution gradually ceased in the stringencies of war and did not reappear after it in the same way at public places. There were occasional scandals, and the sad story of Sir Roger Casement may be mentioned as an example of how evidence of homosexual behaviour could be used at that time. Landing from a German submarine on Tralee on the south west of Ireland, on Good Friday in April 1916, and intending to involve himself in the rebellion, he was caught, charged with treason and convicted. It lay within the power of the Home Secretary to recommend a reprieve, and there were cogent political reasons for doing that rather than provide another martyr for the Irish cause. He was not reprieved, but in papers published since it has been revealed that in Casement's private diaries, discovered at the time of his trial, he declared himself an active pederast. The Cabinet knew this, and pondered if there was in this fact an excuse for leniency on the ground of 'insanity'. The medical advice offered them was that Casement was abnormal but not insane, and the Archbishop of Canterbury, Randall Davidson, in a private letter to the Lord Chancellor, took the same view. Casement, he wrote, was not out of his mind, but mentally and morally unhinged, and should be reprieved. Davidson continued that he had much experience of these morbidities every month of his life, and we know from other sources that he was greatly troubled at the time about some clergy in London known to be homosexual.[13]

During, and immediately after the Second World War, there was a rapid increase in the number of homosexual offences known to the police. The Wolfenden Committee Report of 1957 showed that between 1931 and 1955 the increase had been from 622 to 6,644. Of these, 390 and 2,504, respectively, had been proceeded against in the courts. Such a rise in detection and prosecution must have been the result of a change of police policy at the highest level, acted upon perhaps by keen junior officers seeking promotion. Offences of this kind, particularly in the public lavatories of London, were relatively easy to detect.

The defection of Guy Burgess and Donald Maclean to the Soviet Union in March 1951 was probably the real cause for this rise. They were both reputedly homosexuals, and in America particularly there was anxiety about security, homosexuals being assumed to be prone to blackmail. It seems that the Home Secretaries, Herbert Morrison, followed by Sir David Maxwell Fyfe, together with the Metropolitan Police Commissioner, Sir John Nott-Bower, and the Director of Public Prosecutions, Sir Theobald Mathew, pursued a common policy of encouraging the police to step up the number of arrests for homosexuals offences. Corroboration of this 'new drive against male vice' announced at the time by the Home Office is suggested by Peter Wildeblood, a journalist on the staff of the *Daily Mail* who was convicted of homosexual offences in the same trial as Lord Montagu in 1954.

However, the immediate situation was marked by a polarization between those who were critical of the rise in prosecutions and those who felt that these were a symbol of a new malaise in society that had to be firmly resisted. The popular papers tended towards ridicule and caricature. Early critical reaction to the rise in prosecutions was expressed in the correspondence columns of the *New Statesman*. Kingsley Martin, the then editor, was in strong sympathy with a move to change the law, and subsequently gave support to the Homosexual Law Reform Society. A young Anglican ordinand, Mr Graham Dowell, wrote a letter to the periodical *Theology* in January 1952, suggesting this was a matter for Christian concern and the then Editor of Theology, Dr Alec Vidler asked Sherwin Bailey to respond. This he did, and it was followed by a vigorous educational programme by the Church of England Moral Welfare Council. Their main achievement was the production of an Interim Report, *The Problem of Homosexuality*, in January 1954.

The Interim Report was not for sale to the public, but was distributed widely to Members of Parliament, students at Theological Colleges and anyone who had good reason for wanting one (but not clergy generally nor members of the Church Assembly). It quickly achieved a circulation of 3,000 copies, astonishing in the circumstances, but it should be remembered that public trials for homosexual offences were much in the news. More significantly probably than this, however, was the decision of the Moral Welfare Council, at its meeting on 3 December 1953 to send a letter to the Home Secretary requesting an official enquiry into the whole subject of homosexuality. The letter said a report would follow (i.e. the Interim Report) and asked *inter alia* that the enquiry should consider the legal penalties, the adequacy of prison treatment, blackmail, new psychological knowledge, and the right of the state to take cognizance of male but not female private immorality among adults . The duty of the state to protect young people was said to be self-evident. This letter set the agenda for the future debate precisely, though it cannot have pleased the then Home Secretary overmuch who had just stated in the Commons that homosexuals were exhibitionists, proselytizers and a danger to others. (Note: The Interim Report was written by Bailey though this was not acknowledged at the time. Its significance justifies a proper summary, printed as an appendix to this chapter on p. 122.)

The issue was raised in Parliament at the end of the year. At question time in the Commons on 3 December Mr Shepherd asked the Home Secretary what were the numbers of cases involving male perversion in 1938 and 1952 respectively, and what complaints he had received from the police as to their lack of power to deal with these cases. It was obviously an expected question, and Sir Maxwell Fyfe replied with figures showing a similar increase to those already quoted above from the later Wolfenden Report. The figures given were for a combined total for cases of sodomy, bestiality and 'unnatural offences' in general, so they are not strictly comparable with those in the Wolfenden Report, but they undoubtedly registered a dramatic increase for the period.

On 28 April Mr Desmond Donnelly raised the matter again in an adjournment debate in the Commons as follows:

> I wish to raise the question of a Royal Commission to investigate the law relating to and the medical treatment of homosexuality

and he explained that he only wished to criticize the laws in so far as they applied to people over the age of consent. He then reminded the House of the unsatisfactory way the Labouchere amendment had originally been passed. Donnelly's speech included four main points:

1. The present law contained several anomalies, not least in that it did not apply to women.
2. Prison was the worst possible place to treat adult homosexuals.
3. Police methods of dealing with homosexual offenders were unsatisfactory. This was particularly so when accomplices were employed as agents provocateurs, or when people were vaguely charged with conspiracy to commit the crime, which might mean anything, rather than the crime itself – for which more precise evidence was needed.
4. The law should not interfere in a moral issue of this kind.

He thought this point was well made in the Church of England Moral Welfare Council (Interim) Report, which he quoted:

> In no other department of life does the State hold itself competent to interfere with the private actions of consenting adults. A man and a woman may commit the grave sin of fornication with legal impunity, but a corresponding act between man and man is liable to life imprisonment, and not infrequently is punished by very long prison sentences.

Sir Robert Boothby spoke second, and referred to the prejudice against homosexuals, their persecution by the police, the happy field for blackmail provided by the present law, and the distress felt in the country about recent cases. Delving into history he continued:

> The basic laws dealing with the problems are enshrined in the ecclesiastical doctrines of the Middle Ages, and are really derived directly from the Jewish Law, with the inevitable emphasis on

reproduction of a race struggling for survival many centuries ago. Solomon could have a thousand wives, but homosexuality was punished by death. It is significant that no laws, however savage, have in fact succeeded in stamping out homosexuality. In France where they have the Napoleonic Code, which is far less severe than the laws in this country, there can be no doubt at all that the problem of homosexuality is far less intense than in this country. All the laws relating to this subject were enacted before any of the discoveries of modern psychology. I do not rate modern psychology too high, but I think it has significance. I am not sure that with all his bias and with all his defects, Professor Freud will not go down in history as a considerable figure . . . The duty of the State, as I see it, is to protect youth from corruption, and the public from indecency and nuisance. What consenting adults do in privacy may be a moral issue between them and their Maker, but in my submission it is not a legal issue between them and the State. . . . To send confirmed adult homosexuals to prison for long sentences is in my opinion not only dangerous, but madness.

Boothby then quoted from a British Medical Journal paper by Dr S. Jones who wrote of prison sentences: 'It is as futile from the point of view of treatment as to hope to rehabilitate a chronic alcoholic by giving him occupational therapy in a brewery.'

Replying for the Government, Sir Hugh Lucas Tooth, the joint Parliamentary Under-Secretary at the Home Office, announced that the Home Secretary, along with the Secretary of State for Scotland, agreed to the appointment of a departmental committee to examine and report on the law of homosexual offences and the parallel problem of the law relating to prostitution. In answering other points in the debate, the Under-Secretary took a much more optimistic view of the amount of psychiatric help available in prisons to those convicted than anyone with specialist knowledge at the time was inclined to think the facts warranted. He assured the House that one of the difficulties was the refusal by many prisoners of the help that could be offered. The official announcement of the composition of the 'Wolfenden Committee' as it has since been usually called, was made on 26 August 1954.[14]

(b) Church support

Following the Commons debate, a rather fuller discussion of the problem of the current law and the incidence of homosexual offences took place in the House of Lords on 19 May. This was introduced by the Earl of Winterton, who had been born in 1883, two years before the passing of the Act now under attack. Lord Winterton began by saying that the whispering campaign against the police was unjustified. He hoped that the law would not be changed, and he strongly disagreed with the views expressed in the Moral Welfare Council (Interim) Report, that the social consequences of homosexual practices were less serious than those from pre-marital and extra-marital sexual activity. He said:

> I contest the view that they are more evil and more harmful to the country than the filthy unnatural disgusting vice of homosexuality. I think that the particular sentence from the report which I have quoted is an astonishing doctrine to emanate from an organization of the Church of England.

Later in the debate Lord Brabazon of Tara was to agree with the views expressed by Donnelly and Boothby 'in another place', and to admit he was agreeably surprised by and supported the attitude taken in the Moral Welfare Council Report. Lord Jowitt, the Lord Chancellor, also expressed some agreement with the Report, and told the House of his surprise when appointed Attorney General some years before, after a legal practice mostly concerned with commercial cases, that ninety-five per cent of the many blackmail cases he had to deal with concerned allegations of homosexual offences. The Bishop of Southwell spoke for the bench of Bishops.

> English Law, as it stands at present, regards these offences with quite exceptional severity. . . . I am sure that it is a highly debatable question whether sin could, or should, rightly be equated with crime. There are many sins of which clearly the law cannot possibly take cognisance: it is impossible to send a man to prison for unclean thoughts, for envy, for hatred, for malice or for uncharitableness. On the other hand, there may be things for which a man may be sent to prison which are not in any real sense sins at all. I venture to think, without any suggestion of condoning these offences, that we may have to ask ourselves seriously whether making this particular kind of moral wrong-doing a crime may be only aggravating the total problem. And, in the present state of public opinion we are on very dangerous ground there, because one of the results of the immense volume of social legislation in recent years is that the popular mind tends to equate right and wrong with legal and illegal. People tend to say: 'The law does not forbid it, so it is all right'. It would be most disastrous if it could ever be said: 'You see, after all, there never was any harm in it, for the Government have now said that it is not illegal any longer and even the Church seems to think it all right.'

> On the other hand, I think it is a big question whether the moral

welfare of society is rightly served by making this particular kind of sexual offence a matter of criminal procedure for the law. .... If the law is going to take cognisance of these offences between consenting parties, what is the ground for differentiating between male and female perverts? ... If the law protects a boy from assault by a man, why does it do nothing to protect a girl from assault by a woman? Obviously in all these cases the offender must be restrained and punished, and, if possible, reformed. Almost nowhere, I think in the whole field, is the relation between retribution and rehabilitation so difficult and so delicate as at this point.

... we must not allow our judgement to be clouded by passion on this subject, and heaven forbid that I should in any way seem to minimise the gravity of the problem before us! But further medical and psychological knowledge may lead us to a more enlightened or, at any rate, to a different approach to the whole question, and to yield to a clamour for vindictive action or for even harsher punitive measures may easily defeat our ends.

We have to disinfect our minds of the idea that the state of being a homosexual or an invert is necessarily, in itself, something morally reprehensible. It is something which happens to a man, like colour-blindness or paralysis or anything else.... Rather does it make a demand from us for sympathy and understanding; and society through all its agencies, ought to be co-operative in trying to help people so frustrated and so conditioned, whether men or women.

Certainly the Church, like nearly everyone else, would vehemently repudiate what I might call the 'behaviourist' plea – the suggestion that a man in this condition is not a free and responsible moral agent, so that he simply says: 'I am made that way: I cannot help it'. And here the specifically religious contribution, surely, is the reminder that, by the Grace of God, a man can triumph over his disabilities and turn even the most crippling limitations into achievement. These forms of unnatural association are, of course, morally evil and sinful in the highest degree, because they are a violation of natural law, or, as the Christian would say, of the purpose of the Creator also, who, when he created man in his own image, created them male and female.

The Bishop of Southwell had reminded the House in an earlier part of his speech that:

As St Paul said about this point a long time ago, once the creature is confused with the Creator, once people cease to believe in God and, therefore, in ultimate moral obligations, everything begins to go bad on us, and natural instincts and affections become unnatural and perverted.

This speech *in toto* was an early indication of the attitude the Church of England would consistently take in the ten-year-long battle to implement the main recommendations of the Wolfenden Committee. Homosexual behaviour was still thought to be sinful by the church: Romans 1 still stood, but should not be the concern of the criminal law. Although the Bishop of Southwell could claim to be one of the more learned of the bishops in the House of Lords at this time, it was and is the practice for bishops who are acting as chief church spokesmen in such debates to be briefed by either the appropriate department in Church House or from the secretariat at Lambeth Palace. It is clear that in this speech, the points made by Southwell were much in line with the recommendations of the Moral Welfare Council Interim Report.[15]

Appendix: Moral Welfare Council Interim Report

The first chapter of the Report, entitled 'Variations in the Homosexual Pattern', reiterates with more precision the points made about this in Bailey's *Theology* article. The second chapter deals with 'causes of inversion', and sets out briefly what were thought at that time to be the chief causes of the homosexual orientation, namely an ineffective or absent father, a clinging or dominating mother, a broken family. Other contributory causes mentioned are a congenital factor, the influence of school friends, and the accidental lack of female company.

The third chapter, 'The Moral and Religious Aspects', is the main section of the Report, and in effect offers a refutation of the argument that for an invert, homosexual love-making is as natural as heterosexual intercourse is between men and women. This refutation is cast in orthodox terms. Heterosexual love, it is argued, is *sui generis*, connected with God's purpose in creating man as a male–female duality, and his establishment of an ordinance towards which sexual activity is directed, namely, union in 'one flesh', in the specific context of marriage. A homosexual 'union' cannot be in terms of 'one flesh', and an invert is not a female with a male appearance; he is a man with many male characteristics, but lacking heterosexual desire. This last point is substantiated by reference to Dr Kinsey's report that a male invert responds to the same sexual stimuli as a normal male, his reactions being characteristic of the man, not of the woman. Further, the chapter continues, homosexual physical expression has and can have no relation to procreation and the family whereas, between man and woman, it always has at least implicitly this relation. Even some types of caress are immoral for homosexuals, which are morally legitimate for heterosexuals 'within marriage'.

Having made this rather sharp distinction between the significance of homosexual and heterosexual physical activity, the chapter then deals with the situation faced by a homosexual, and a pastoral rather than judgmental attitude is taken. Homosexuals are said to be like normal unmarried women who can learn to live with only transitory friendships and a prospect of eventual loneliness. They can accept their situation and sublimate their sexual lives and achieve personal fulfilment in various socially useful ways. 'Homosexual marriage' would not solve the problem any more than extra-marital concubinage does for a woman. Repentance of past sin, forgiveness and grace, especially through Holy Communion, are the means of liberation for the invert; he will still have his old instincts, but will have power to avoid 'occasions of sin', in brackets defined as 'association with perverts'. Priests are asked to offer the ministry of reconciliation, and to work with psychiatrists sympathetic to Christian understandings, and the public are asked to help by strengthening the moral foundation of society, supporting the law in defence of the young and of public decency, and by insisting on justice for the homosexual.

The fourth and final chapter of the Interim Report is entitled 'The Law and the Male Homosexual'. The law as it then was is reviewed, with a preliminary point that it is the state's duty to protect the young from seduction and assault, and therefore any change in the law should not endanger the welfare of young people. The influence of the Code Napoleon in removing private homosexual acts between consenting adults from the cognisance of the Criminal Law is noted and then attention is drawn to the difference of treatment accorded to males and females in relation to homosexual practices in English law. The Report then argues that fornication and adultery present much clearer evidence than private homosexual practices of consequent damage to society; the risk of illegitimate children from the former and the risk of the break-up of the family unit from the latter are clearly apparent, but the law does not punish fornicators or adulterers as criminals. The individual aggrieved (father or spouse) may bring a civil action for damages. It is also noted at this point that the penalties for soliciting are far more severe for male prostitutes than for females.

The chapter then deals with subsidiary considerations which point towards a change in the law. As it stands, the law encourages blackmail, encourages adult homosexuals to seek young companions who will not report them, discourages normal friends who run the risk of being assumed to be homosexuals themselves, provides an undesirable opportunity for the police to use *agents provocateurs*, and prevents homosexuals from seeking psychiatric help because they risk prosecution if they reveal their activities. A final note in the chapter recommends that the age of consent in a new law be retained at twenty-one. Although for heterosexual intercourse this is only sixteen, homosexual intercourse as an unnatural activity involves a different principle, and no risk should be taken of precipitating an unnecessary life-long inversion by participation too young. Retaining the age at twenty-one would also continue to give protection to young National Service men.

7

The Limits of Tolerance Shift 1957–79

Introduction

The previous chapter surveyed the long period of history from the beginning of the Christian church until the appointment of the Wolfenden Committee. For some fourteen centuries, with minor variations, the laws of Christian countries had conformed with the biblical precepts and punished those found guilty of homosexual behaviour. The Wolfenden Committee recommended that it was no longer appropriate for the Criminal Law to be concerned with what consenting adult homosexual people did in private. This was in effect a reversion to the kind of policy intended by the 1881 Act, so quickly and unreflectively put into reverse by the Labouchere amendment in 1885. It may be that the wide scope of the new offence of gross indecency among males of any age Mr Labouchere introduced was never seriously intended. Perhaps its scope would have been curtailed much earlier if the police had not on the whole used its provisions sparingly until they had to react to political pressure in the Cold War period.

By keeping the age of consent at twenty-one, and other exceptions, the Wolfenden Committee proposals did not imply abandoning the principle of protecting the young or those at risk of assault. This change had already been made in other countries, but the English Parliament was slow to approve, and between 1957 and 1967 energetic lobbying was undertaken. Many Christian leaders were known to be in support, and though that was not surprising to members of Parliament who had all been given the Moral Welfare Council Interim Report, the popular impression that the church was going soft on sin in this regard became the focus point of a much wider debate about the character of Christian morality.

In 1959, Lord Devlin, a Roman Catholic and one of the most eminent of the Law Lords, observed in his Maccabean Lecture that 'in matters of morals, the limits of tolerance shift'. His concern with the relationship between law and morality of which this lecture was a profound examination, arose directly from discussion among jurists about the proposed change in the criminal law, and although in many ways he was himself an innovator, he advised that law should not follow shifts in public opinion too quickly. The delay in Parliament allowed sufficient time for public acceptance. The Christian support for the 1967 Act was based on a strong conviction that the criminal law should not buttress morality in this respect, but on the question of the morality of homosexual acts, more than thirty years of debate have proved indecisive.

This chapter surveys first how the Act was passed, and how the Christian influences which helped to make that possible were themselves affected by the contemporaneous assessment of what came to be called the New Morality. Attention then moves to the spate of reports by working parties of the churches between 1967 and 1979 which tended to argue for a change in the Christian moral attitude to homosexual behaviour. The survey ends with a record of the main debates among official and representative church bodies which have uniformly found themselves voting against such departure from traditional Christian teaching. The limits of tolerance have not shifted that far.

At the start of the 1987 debate on the 'Higton' motion, the General Synod of the Church of England appeared to be in some danger of being driven into a tight corner by a pressure group and media expectation. Escape was provided by passing with near unanimity a cautious and carefully worded amendment by the Bishop of Chester. The Lambeth Conference of 1988, in one of its closing sessions, when a mass of resolutions prepared in Sections were being finally approved, had a short and somewhat unpremeditated discussion about the possibility of adding an extra clause about homosexual rights. The outcome showed no great change from what had been agreed in the previous Conference of 1978, a clear sign that opinions are sharply divided between different parts of the Anglican Communion.

Parliament Accepts the Change – 1957–1967

The Wolfenden Committee deliberated for three years, holding sixty-two meetings and taking evidence from over two hundred witnesses, of which many were expert in the field, and many were, in fact, representing public and professional bodies with carefully prepared memoranda. Christian opinion in a direct sense was expressed by the Church Commissioners, the Church of England Moral Welfare Council, and by the Roman Catholic Advisory Committee set up for the purpose, but neither the British Council of Churches, nor any of the Free Churches, nor any other religious body was apparently officially consulted. Among the judges called was Mr Justice Devlin, who was later to write that his appearance before the Committee started the train of thought which led him eventually to take his stand for the principle that the law should sometimes be used to enforce morality. The Wolfenden Report's chief recommendation on homosexuality was the abolition of the law relating to private homosexual acts between consenting adults on the ground that it was not

> proper for the law to concern itself with what a man does in private unless it can be shown to be so contrary to the public good that the law ought to intervene in its function as the guardian of that public good.[1]

The Report was received with wide approval, but it was clear that the Conservative Government was by no means eager to implement its proposals with legislation as the then Home Secretary, Mr R. A. Butler, explained. However, Lord Pakenham, a Roman Catholic, and later to become the Earl of Longford, moved a debate in the Lords on the Report in December 1957 supporting the principal recommendation of the Committee. The Archbishop of Canterbury (Fisher) agreed with him.

The Archbishop had been informed of the work undertaken in the previous five years by the Moral Welfare Council, and had seen and commented privately on the evidence that body provided to the Wolfenden Committee. In fact, the Roman Catholic evidence (from an advisory group led by Monsigneur G. A. Tomlinson, and probably written by Norman St John-Stevas, now Lord St John of Fawsley) had taken the same view as the Moral Welfare Council in supporting a change of the law for consenting adults. The evidence from both groups had been published separately in 1956, so the Archbishop's agreement with Lord Pakenham was no surprise and reflected a common policy.

In the next few years, several motions to get things moving were put down on the Order Papers of both Houses of Parliament by private members. Support grew, but the Conservative Government showed little enthusiasm. They expected controversy, and their hesitation was strongly re-inforced by the trial for espionage in 1962 of the Admiralty clerk William Vassal, who had been blackmailed by the Russians because of his homosexual activities. The Profumo affair soon followed and led to the resignation of Mr Harold Macmillan as Prime Minister, in favour of Sir Alec Douglas-Home. In October 1964, a Labour Government was formed under the leadership of Mr Harold Wilson, and Lord Arran and Mr Leo Abse put down fresh motions. After jumping various procedural hurdles, and another election which strengthened the Labour majority, the Sexual Offences Act was passed in July 1967, by eighty-five votes in the Commons, and sixty-three in the Lords, both Archbishops supporting it. In the Lords, the debate was enlivened by the opposition of the Chief Scout, Lord Rowallan, and of an ex-Lord Chief Justice, Lord Goddard who described the Bill in the memorable phrase 'the buggers' charter'.

Writing twenty-two years after these events, it is not easy to distil from their course over a decade which factors were most important in changing parliamentary and public opinion. It was, I have already suggested, the high point in the post-war mood of liberal tolerance in England, the political mood was innovative, and the change in the law may have been simply a reform whose time had come. Some other European countries had already made the change, including some with large Catholic populations influenced by the French Code Napoleon, to the distress of the Vatican. In American States, the situation varied, but the trend was towards amilioration of old puritanical statutes. Scotland and Northern Ireland had to make the change later via their own Legislatures. The Republic of Ireland did not, and has not; their law was held to be in contravention of the European Convention of Human Rights by the Court in Strasbourg in 1988. By what the *Economist* called Irish co-incidence, the barrister who put that case to the European Court was Mrs Mary Robinson, who happened to have spent her childhood at the house in Dublin where Oscar Wilde was born.

Christian Influence 1957–67

There are some grounds for thinking that the Christian influence in favour of a change in English and Welsh law was significant especially at the early stages. There is no doubt that behind the scenes Canon Hugh Warner as secretary of the Church of England Moral Welfare Council, and even more its lecturer, Dr Sherwin Bailey, were active lobbyists for the reform. They were supported throughout by their chairman, the Bishop of St Albans (Michael Gresford Jones) and upon him fell the task of reassuring Archbishop Fisher in an exchange of confidential letters arising from the Archbishop's reading of his advanced copy of the Council's evidence to the Wolfenden Committee. Sherwin Bailey, incidentally, also helped the British Medical Association prepare their evidence, which argued that on balance the social consequences of a change in the law would be beneficial.

The Council's evidence was published separately, as was a similar report from the Methodist Citizenship Department; the Catholic evidence was printed in full in the Dublin Review. Soon afterwards, the Church Assembly and the Methodist Conference debated the Wolfenden Committee recommendations, with the reports from their working parties to hand, and cautiously agreed the law should be changed. As the Government hesitated, further steps were taken to argue the case in public, notably by the homosexual Law Reform Society with some Christian backing, and then the already simmering internal debate among the churches about the character of Christian morality in the contemporary world exploded into new life with the publication of the Quaker Report in 1963. Honest John Robinson, as he was known, joined the fray,[2] and Christian leaders found themselves fighting a war on two fronts. They were committed to supporting the Wolfenden proposals as public policy, but at the same time they had to defend their own moral tradition generally for anxious Christians who had learnt about the new morality movement from the newspapers and didn't much like what they read. The new Archbishop, Michael Ramsey, who followed Fisher in 1961 found himself in the thick of it. Fortunately, he was a scholar not easily frightened.

(a) The Moral Welfare Council evidence

This evidence was published in an extended form by the Church Information Office in 1956 under the title *Sexual Offenders and Social Punishment*. It was a substantial work of 120 pages, including most of the unpublished material of the Interim Report of 1953. (See appendix to previous chapter.) Four appendices were added to the text submitted to the Wolfenden Committee to fill out the picture for a general readership, and the second of these deals with the pastoral care of homosexuals and includes a case study of an imaginary undergraduate 'Peter', who is distressed to find that he

> feels for his room-mate Alan the sort of regard he ought to feel for a girl. (orig. publ. *The Student World* 1955)

This case study was written by the Franciscan Brother Michael Fisher, who was working in Cambridge at the time. 'Peter' is advised that the church will accept him, and he must accept himself as he is. He will need someone with whom he can confide, and will have to share the loneliness and friendship of Christ. In Appendix One, however, a reprint of a previous essay of 1955, Bailey includes a re-statement of the standard morality:

(*a*) all homosexual acts are intrinsically sinful;
(*b*) almost all homosexual acts are free, and therefore morally imputable – i.e. they are capable of being treated as blameworthy; . . .[3]

Bailey had submitted his own book *Homosexuality and the Western Christian Tradition* to the Wolfenden Committee as personal evidence, and it is this, rather than the Council's Report which is still studied today. The Report itself may still be available in specialist libraries, and gives a good flavour of the way a church body at the time thought the case could be presented to a Departmental Committee of the Government. It dealt of course with prostitution as well. Of its six recommendations, the fourth most directly concerns this study:

> There should be no departure in specific instances from the generally accepted principle that the British law does not concern itself with the private irregular or immoral sexual relationships of consenting men and women.

This recommendation reflects the crucial criticism of the law made by the Moral Welfare Council in its original letter to the Home Secretary in 1953, and set out more fully in the Interim Report of 1954. Fornication and adultery, which are not criminal offences, cause far more social damage and distress, family break-up and illegitimate children than does homosexual behaviour between consenting adults.

(b) The Church Assembly Debate, 1957

By the summer of 1957, the Wolfenden Committee Report was ready for printing, and its main recommendations were known. The Church Assembly debated them on 14 November, in a composite motion covering both homosexuality and prostitution:

> That this Assembly generally approves the principles on which the criminal law concerned with sex behaviour should be based, as stated by the Wolfenden Committee, and also its recommendations relating to homosexuality; but it is unable to accept all its recommendations relating to prostitution.

It soon became clear that the recommendations concerning prostitution needed more study and the motion was split up into three for voting. The first part, referring to the principles, was accepted on a show of hands, and so was the third part, slightly reworded. The second part, relating to homosexuality, was narrowly approved, the count showing 155 votes in favour, 138 against, a majority of only seventeen out of a total vote cast of 293, less than half of the Assembly's total membership.

In opening the debate, the Bishop of Exeter was chiefly concerned with principles. The criminal law existed to protect both the rights of the individual and the community, but where neither was infringed, this law had no place. In mediaeval Christendom, it had been assumed that the purpose of the criminal law was also to enforce the observance of a particular moral code, but he thought this was inconsistent with Christian ethics. He supported the view of the Wolfenden Committee that morality was a matter of free choice and responsibility; the work of the church in training souls was to dispense with coercion and establish a position in which acts were freely chosen because, and only because, of their rightness.

The Bishop then considered other examples of human behaviour, where the distinction between sins and crimes was already commonly accepted, citing fornication, adultery, drunkenness, gluttony, heavy gambling, and homosexual behaviour among consenting women in private. But the law was not wholly consistent, and there were traces still of the older mediaeval conception in the treatment of homosexual practices between adult males. He also believed that the proposed change in the law, while not removing the risk of blackmail, would lessen it. Few things had horrified him so much as the evidence given in the Report of the attitude of certain chief constables, who had issued an instruction that the police were not to prosecute the black-mailer, but both of them for their homosexual activities. He thought that there was a certain robust objectivity about the Committee's Report. The Committee had denied that it considered homosexual practices to be necessarily symptoms of disease, or that it thought homosexuals necessarily suffered from diminished responsibility. And they were rightly careful to protect the young and mentally defective from exploitation. In conclusion, he rested his case on the manifest injustice of the present law in selecting one particular form of sexual behaviour for treatment as a criminal offence while others were left outside the law. The law could not make people chaste, but only try to create conditions in which it was difficult and not easy to be immoral. The task of teaching chastity and strengthening character belonged to the church, and he did not think any researchers into the etiology (*sic*) of homosexuality would add anything to what the church knew already about the desperately sick heart of man, and the restorative powers of the grace of God.

The Bishop of St Albans seconded the motion, dealing with the prostitution aspect, and Mr O. H. W. Clark, a Church Commissioner and member of the Assembly Standing Committee, hoped for a middle position, between the re-creation of a Calvinist position in which all sexual offences were regarded as crimes, and a total separation between sin and crime. Whatever the moral theologians said, he believed that the public at large did ascribe to the law a moral force so that if an action was not forbidden by law it was not wrong in their judgment. He hoped that no decision would be made until public opinion had time to be convinced. The Rev. Kenneth Ross, Vicar of All Saints, Margaret Street, quoted figures from the Kinsey Report which seemed to him to justify the conclusion that over 500,000 men in the British Isles over sixteen years old were habitually committing homosexual acts which under the present law could lead to imprisonment. The magnitude of the problem was such that perhaps 2,000,000 people were occasionally committing homosexual acts, but in 1955 only 2,000 of them were proceeded against. It was inequitable to maintain the present law. Chancellor Garth Moore, a senior canon lawyer, took the view that morality and the law could not be completely dissociated, but that in this particular matter, over which the law had no effective control, it would be better to remove it to the realms of morality; the motion would not be licensing vice, but upholding a true morality which was not to be enforced by coercive measures. Mr Goyder from Oxford, read the relevant passage from Romans chapter 1, and drew the conclusion that in this respect the old law was not wholly abrogated. 'This was a crime worthy of death because it was contrary to God's whole order, and undermined the whole order of humanity.'

In his concluding remarks, the Archbishop of Canterbury told the House that the bishops would soon have to speak on behalf of the church in the House of Lords, and it would be helpful to them to know what the Assembly thought. Taken as a whole, the mood of the debate was a little sombre, as if the Assembly sensed that any forceful expression of opinion would be out of place. They had, in fact, of course, been presented with a *'fait accompli'*. The Moral Welfare Council had not sought their opinion before presenting their evidence to the Wolfenden Committee, yet nothing could not be gained by publicly repudiating it.[4]

(c) The Methodist Conference, 1958

The Methodist Church Citizenship Department co-operated with the Public Morality Council in submitting evidence to the Wolfenden Committee and then set up a working party to examine its recommendations, reporting to the Methodist Conference in 1958. The most important part of the statement read:

> The Department registers the judgment that the Wolfenden Report is a sane and responsible approach to the difficult questions with which it deals. We are generally agreed that the functions of the law, at any rate in relation to sexual behaviour is, as the Report states, the preservation of public order and decency and the protection of the citizen, particularly the young and vulnerable citizen. It is not the function of the law to interfere with private behaviour unless it can be shown that such behaviour is detrimental to the public good in an extraordinary degree. Thus, adultery,

fornication and prostitution, though they are grievous sins, are not offences for which a person can be punished by the criminal law. Sin and crime are not synonymous terms.

The Department agrees with the recommendation that homosexual behaviour between consenting adults be no longer a criminal offence. We considered with the utmost care the arguments of those who oppose this Recommendation and who fear that the removal of the ban of illegality would lead to an increase in homosexual behaviour. We believe that this possibility has been exaggerated and that there are weighty reasons why this suggested alteration in the law should be accepted. Such alteration would remove the anomaly which discriminates between male and female homosexuals; it would mitigate the evil practice of blackmail; and we believe it would help towards the creation of a healthier attitude on sex questions generally. The elimination in this field of ignorance and false emotionalism is of paramount importance. The Department is in general agreement with the remaining Recommendations relating to homosexuality and particularly with the suggestion that research be instituted into the aetiology of homosexuality and the effect of various forms of treatment.[5]

The Methodist Conference considered this statement and endorsed a resolution approving the Wolfenden Committee recommendations. This in effect matched the outcome of the Church Assembly debate held in the previous year.

(d) The Homosexual Law Reform Society

Apart from the churches, whose initial pressure was largely confined to Government and Parliamentary circles until the Church Assembly and Methodist Conference openly supported the proposed change in the law, the most important of the other lobbying groups who received a measure of support from Christians was the Homosexual Law Reform Society, started by Mr A. E. Dyson, then a lecturer in English in the University of Wales, and a young Anglican curate from Birmingham, the Rev. Andrew Hallidie Smith. Dyson and Smith had seen one of their fellow students at Pembroke College, Cambridge, commit suicide, probably in connection with anxieties about homosexuality.

The Society began with Hallidie Smith as secretary, and A. J. Ayer as president. In March 1958 a letter to enlist support for the reform, sponsored by the Society, was printed in *The Times* and this was signed by an impressive list of thirty-three public figures, among whom were Lord Attlee, the Bishops of Birmingham and Exeter, A.

J. Ayer, Isaiah Berlin, Sir Robert Boothby, J. B. Priestley, Bertrand Russell and Barbara Wootton. The letter began:

> The present law is clearly no longer representative of either Christian or liberal opinion in this country and now that there are widespread doubts about both its justice and its efficacy, we believe that its continued enforcement will do more harm than good to the health of the community as a whole.

> The case for reform has already been accepted by most of the responsible newspapers and journals, by the two Archbishops, the Church Assembly, a Roman Catholic committee, a number of Non-Conformist spokesmen, and many other organs of informed public opinion. In view of this, and of the conclusions which the Wolfenden Committee itself agreed upon after a prolonged study of the evidence, we should like to see the Government introduce legislation to give effect to the proposed reform at an early date and are confident that if it does it will deserve the widest support from humane men of all parties.

After a large public meeting organized by the Homosexual Law Reform Society on 12 May 1960, at which the Bishop of Exeter (Mortimer) described the present law as a 'monstrous injustice', and Mr Kingsley Martin moved a resolution asking the government to implement the Wolfenden recommendation without delay (carried unanimously by over a thousand people present), Mr Kenneth Robinson, a member of the society's executive committee, a labour MP and future Minister of Health, introduced the matter again in the Commons. No effective progress was made, and despite the opportunity of a free vote, it became clear that the issue was polarizing, at least temporarily on party lines.

(e) The Quaker Report, 1963

A small group from the Society of Friends was among the first to express a firmly liberal Christian point of view. The pamphlet *Towards a Quaker View of Sex*, published for them by the Literature Committee of the Friends Home Service Committee in 1963, was in fact largely concerned with homosexuality, the response to a request for guidance from Quaker students faced with difficulties of this kind. Although in no sense an official statement of the Society of Friends, it caused some anxiety in drawing attention to the normality of adolescent masturbation, the steady increase in physical familiarity casually allowed, and the suggestion that

> light-hearted and loving casual contacts can be known without profound damage or 'moral degeneracy' being the result to either partner.

Turning to homosexuality, but 'without alacrity' the report observed that although a homosexual orientation is usual among boys in the eleven to seventeen age group, and a boy's first love will be for another boy, this could be far from casual, and if it be denounced, the shock might make it harder for him to reach a satisfactory sexual adjustment later. Female homosexuality is then discussed in the context of its greater social acceptance, but the emotional dangers for young women in such relationships, and the stresses of older women who seek in female partners what could only be provided by a male, are described more critically.

After a quotation from a sermon by Bishop John Robinson about our 'utterly mediaeval treatment of homosexuals' the report challenges the traditional condemnation of homosexuality in direct terms:

> It is the nature and quality of a relationship that matters: one must not judge it by its outward appearance but by its inner worth. Homosexual affection can be as selfless as heterosexual affection, and therefore we cannot see that it is in some way morally worse. Homosexual affection may, of course, be an emotion which some find aesthetically disgusting, but one cannot base Christian morality on a capacity for such disgust. Neither are we happy with the thought that all homosexual behaviour is sinful: motive and circumstances degrade or ennoble any act, and we feel that to list sexual 'sins' is to follow the letter rather than the spirit, to kill rather than to give life. Further we see no reason why the physical nature of a sexual act should be the criterion by which the question whether or not it is moral should be decided. An act which (for example) expresses true affection between two individuals and gives pleasure to them both does not seem to us to be sinful by reason alone of the fact that it is homosexual. The same criteria seem to apply to us whether a relationship is heterosexual or homosexual.[6]

In the next section of the report, headed 'A New Morality Needed', it argues for a conviction that love cannot be confined to a pattern. The group observe that it is unfortunate that sexual intercourse takes place between Adam and Eve only after expulsion from the Garden (a point surprisingly made since biblical literalism is not an obvious feature of the report elsewhere), for this provides an excuse for thinking that sexual intimacy is associated with a sinful or disobedient state. Bailey's suggestion that 'I love you' should properly be said in the context of a possible marriage, is countered by the suggestion that it is the waywardness of love in tending to leap every barrier which provides its tremendous creative power. Finally, the group, mostly teachers, doctors, and psychologists, reassure their readers that several of them have, in fact, found it possible 'to give substance to the traditional code, conscious of their debt to Christ in showing what love implies'.

(f) Time for Consent, 1967

Norman Pettinger is a retired American theologian whose main work has been in Dogmatics and Process Theology, especially concerned with the New Testament, but in 1967 his article in the magazine *New Christian* entitled 'Time for Consent' set out the basic argument for accepting homosexual behaviour among Christians. The article became a book of the same title, in several editions up to 1976. His main points are expressed in Chapter 5 as follows:

> What a homosexual person is seeking is love; in this respect he is like all human beings. I do not mean simply love which is given to him. I also mean love which he can give.

> We shall do well to recognize that very few human beings are called to the celibate life.... For most of us the expression of our created nature as lovers 'in the making' will be by loving another person, and with this there will go the desire for sexual expression of love in physical contacts of various kinds.

> It remains true that if the homosexual person is to be accepted, he is expected by religious leaders to refrain from any physical acts which give external expression to his impulses.... The attitude which demands of the homosexual no physical expression of his love seems to be inhuman, unjust and above all, unchristian. I do not understand it, nor can I find any reason to support it.

Pittenger then describes the kinds of physical contact in which homosexual men and women are likely to engage, and notes that none of them are in themselves peculiarly homosexual, for they are also practised by many heterosexuals, though some may find particular acts distasteful.

Pittenger faces squarely the realistic expectations of stability and fidelity for a homosexual partnership. Since there can be no natural children of the couple, some adopt successfully, but it is recognized that the relationship must be based on the love of the partners for each other. Pittenger recognizes that such partnerships break up, often through jealousy, when one partner has a brief affair with someone else, and both partners have to decide whether or not such freedom is likely to be acceptable. Open or closed situations are possible, as they are in heterosexual marriage.

Pittenger hopes that counsellors will prepare homosexuals for disappointments of this kind, and assist them to establish relations 'which will be by intention as permanent and faithful as can be possibly managed'.

In his final chapter, entitled 'An Ethic for Homosexuals', six suggestions are made of a practical kind; these may be summarized as:

1. Do not accept one's homosexuality without questioning it, testing one's capacity for relationship with the other sex and taking advice.
2. Accept the fact once established as 'given', without shame;
3. Remember that God loves the homosexual just as he is – that is the whole point of the Christian gospel;
4. A homosexual should be a responsible person; it is bad manners and irresponsible to attempt the seduction of others;
5. A homosexual should try to develop close friendships with people he esteems and likes;
6. If a homosexual does find a person whom he loves and who loves him in return, he must decide whether or not physical contacts are permissible.

Pittenger himself concludes they could be, provided that they are

expressive of his total self, that they are genuinely desired by his friend, and that they promote increasing love between them.

For behaviour in the past that has not reached these standards, Pittenger affirms that God forgives, and God still loves: this is the assurance of Christian faith.[7]

(g) The New Morality

It would be an over-simplification to claim that the Quaker report of 1963 launched the New Morality. Indeed the phrase had been used as long ago as a Vatican Statement in the twenties which condemned it. But in 1963, the kind of Spirit-cum-Humanity intuitions of the Quakers coalesced with those of an even more famous publication – *Honest to God* by John Robinson, the distinguished Cambridge New Testament scholar who was working at this time as the Bishop of Woolwich. Robinson's book was rushed into the best seller list on a wave of media interest. The poignancy of a scholarly bishop in court at an obscenity trial, defending the publication by Penguin of an unexpurgated edition of D. H. Lawrence's notorious *Lady Chatterley's Lover* because of its literary merit, adding to the fun, and to the sales! Many who bought *Honest to God* were surprised to find that it was a sophisticated if readable account of recent movements in theological and ethical thought. To understand what the good bishop was writing about, it was really necessary to have, already, more than a smattering of church history, and some feel for extentialism. Chapter six of this perhaps undeservedly best remembered of Robinson's many books was headed 'The New Morality', and introduced the non-specialist world to situation ethics. That approach had been tentatively suggested by the Swiss, Emil Brunner, and developed by the Americans, Paul Tillich and Joseph Fletcher among others. At the centre of the new morality principle was the proposition that the usual official method of making Christian ethical decisions was over-dependent on a mediaeval notion of Natural Law, and this was almost as habitual for the Protestants as it was for the Catholics. This supra-natural ethic, like all supra-natural definitions of God himself, was now redundant, ought not to have happened, and needed to be replaced by the New Testament ethic summed up in the slogan: 'Nothing is prescribed in advance but love.'[8]

A proper consideration of this thesis must wait until Part 5 of this book, but Robinson and several other authors in similar vein rescued the study of Christian ethics from the doldrums it had slept in since the Christian Socialist Movement a century earlier. Church of England ordinands of the sixties were still being trained in their colleges by a syllabus heavily weighted on the Bible, Doctrine, and Church History, from which Christian ethics had been demoted from the status of an examination subject, because, it was said, few people were available to teach it properly. The real reason was that even fewer knew what to teach; the Logical Positivist Philosophy had so dominated pre-war Oxbridge, where most of the teachers had been trained, that Christian ethics had become the Cinderella subject among academic theologians.

Faced with the searching demand from the logistic philosophy that unless the Christians could prove that their rules were based on something more objective than emotion, they should shut up, most Christian moralists in the thirties had lost their confidence, and the war added to their impotence. (The next generation, people like Hugh Montefiore and David Jenkins found their vocation through it.) Apart from those like Temple who knew his way through this labyrinth, and remained undaunted in his pursuit of a post-war society based more on Christian principles, the outlook seemed bleak. Even Mortimer, who had held the Oxford Chair in Moral Theology before moving to Exeter, and had become the chief episcopal voice in the Anglican support of the Wolfenden Committee, worked most on explaining and defending the old Catholic morality and helping Fisher with the revision of Canon Law.

The fresh work of the Continentals, Karl Barth, Brunner, Thielicke and the earlier social ethicist Ernest Troeltsch were available in translation, as was Bonhoeffer, but the world of Fascism which had confronted them and made them press for a new tougher and less world affirming ethic, accepting the cost of discipleship as they called it, was somehow more alien to the liberal English student of the sixties than the German language they used. (Barth was as fierce as any Catholic on the evils of homosexuality because he was strong both on creation, and on the absolute imperative of God's word.) But it was Fletcher and Robinson who brought the British moral theologians suddenly back to work, as the ethics examination was hurriedly restored for ordinands.

Perhaps this is too slick a judgment. Certainly the churches were unprepared for sophisticated discussion about personal morality. It was true that in a succession of Lambeth Conferences marriage and particularly contraception had increasingly been a preoccupation, but for many people the Ten Commandments, rather than any thorough-going reflection about the primacy of love, and what that might mean as a radically different kind of obedience, had been the received basis for Christian behaviour. C. S. Lewis had tested the water a bit in his much admired radio talks and very popular little books, and his comment on the Decalogue, written by his wife-to-be Joy Davidman, *Smoke on the Mountain*, but very much a combined effort, made plain that at least Christians worked out their obedience to these precepts in non-legal ways. But despite the mastery Lewis had in his academic life of Mediaeval Romantic literature, and the allegory he found in it of the Love of God, all this was far from the trenchant challenge of the Confessing Church theologians of Germany, from whom Robinson drew much of his ethical thought.

Stronger links with Continental thought were forged by the British biblical scholars than the moralists before the war, and there had been since 1920 a strong shared awareness of the Christian responsibility towards Social Order among those church leaders who were pioneers of the Ecumenical Movement. Chief in this dialogue were Archbishop Temple, Reinhold Niebuhr, and Nathan Sodorblom, but their attention had been centred on global and international ethical issues, fascism, persecution of Jews, the right uses of capital and economic power. These Christian leaders perceived that the causes of the 1914–18 war were not in fact resolved, and the drift into another conflict was inevitable unless the churches, with their international perspective and network of contacts, could do better than the moribund League of Nations in alerting public opinion.

Faced as they rightly were with this great danger, church leaders had little time for pastoral ethics, and the advice given to individual Christians about private behaviour tended to remain as it had been since the late Victorian Revival Movement for personal purity. The useful little books provided to guide clergy in the twenties and thirties were continually re-printed. Peter Green's *Problems of Right Conduct* was a standard work on many clergy bookshelves. Based on his experience as London vicar, even that was thought too political for some tastes. Thus it was that when the New Morality thinking hit the Christian public in the sixties, they were ill-prepared, just as in a similar way, Dietrich Bonhoeffer's *Letters and Papers from Prison*, written while he awaited martydom by the Gestapo in 1945 emerged twenty years later as the great new spiritual discovery. These were turbulent times for Christian ethicists and a spate of books and reports disturbed and reassured by turns.

The Gay Christian Movement

It has been noted earlier that several Christian leaders were active in the lobbying that led to the passing of the 1967 Act, especially through the Homosexual Law Reform Society and the Albany Trust. Their concern had grown through their pastoral and counselling work, and the realization that the old law was unsatisfactory. As the climate of public opinion changed, there was a need for some organization to advise and support homosexual people in an open way, and this was met by the Gay Liberation Movement and similar bodies which provided counselling and various publications describing the gay sub-culture. It was not a free for all situation, and in 1962 an attempt to print a list of homosexual prostitutes was declared illegal by the House of Lords as an attempt to corrupt public morals. By 1978, the Movement and others associated with it were confident enough to publish a Charter of Homosexual Rights, and a Carnival for International Gay Pride Week was held in Hyde Park, London in June 1979. Gay Lib was open to all, and it was thought by some church people to be overmuch identified with a radical political stance, and understandably enough, fiercely critical of the Christian tradition which could be said with some truth to have been the main cause of persecution in the past.

Christian gay people therefore created their own fellowship and support group, initially through 'Reach' and other societies linked with particular denominational churches, but some of these tended to be transitory, and eventually in 1975 The Gay Christian Movement was formed. It was ecumenical in membership, and in 1985 decided to include lesbians, hence its present name The Lesbian and Gay Christian Movement (LGCM). The basic conviction of LGCM is that:

> human sexuality in all its richness is a gift of God gladly to be accepted, enjoyed and honoured as a way of both expressing and growing in love, in accordance with the life and teaching of Jesus Christ; therefore it is their conviction that it is entirely compatible with the Christian faith not only to love another person of the same sex but also to express that love fully in a personal sexual relationship.

Given that conviction, LGCM describes its four principal aims as:

> To encourage fellowship, friendship and support among lesbian and gay Christians through prayer, study and action; to help the whole Church examine its understanding of human sexuality and to work for positive acceptance of gay relationships; to encourage members to witness to their Christian faith within the gay community and to their convictions about human sexuality within the Church; to maintain and strengthen links with other gay Christian groups both in Britain and elsewhere.

An opening Holy Communion Service for GCM was held at St Botolph's Church in the city of London, and the Movement was allowed to use space in the church tower for an office, and for counselling. St Botolph's is in fact an example of how an ancient city church can be used to develop a wide range of caring resources for homeless and unemployed people, and the work among homosexuals was only one aspect among many of the ministry led there by the vicar, the Rev. Malcolm Johnson, who is also Area Dean of the City.

Unfortunately, as one result of the publicity surrounding the Synod Debate in 1987 (see pp. 164ff.), much criticism was directed at St Botolphs for its willingness to allow the LGCM office facilities. Some of the literature said to be on sale was supposedly pornographic, though that was denied by LGCM. The tower was technically part of the consecrated building of the church itself, and a case was brought in the London Diocesan Consitory Court to have this use prohibited. Eventually, after some preliminary hearings, LGCM were advised by legal counsel not to defend the case and withdrew from the proceedings and from their premises. They found temporary accommodation in Camberwell, and are expected to be based in future at the Oxford Mission in Bethnal Green.

During the Meeting of the General Synod in February 1989, Mrs Muriel Curtis from Sheffield Diocese proposed a private member's motion primarily concerned to deplore any suggestion in school teaching curricula that homosexual and lesbian relationships were as acceptable as heterosexual ones. The third part of this motion asked that the entry concerning LGCM should be removed from the Church of England Year Book. In one of its earlier sessions that week, the Archbishop of Canterbury had responded to a question about a confidential report on homosexuality at the time awaiting proper consideration in the House of Bishops and refused to be drawn into premature discussion of it. Thus warned, and probably mindful of the danger of repeating ground already covered in the 1987 Debate the Synod decided to move to other business, and not vote on the motion. Perhaps the Rev. Malcolm Johnson summed up the mood when he said that the Synod 'had already insulted the lesbian and gay community enough'.

Roman Catholic Teaching

The observers of all this turbulence who belonged to the Roman obedience, as the Anglicans used once quaintly to call them, were not unfamiliar with the central proposition of the new morality, and as the possessors of the most coherent system of Christian morality, they were professionally accustomed to dealing with it in their own way for their own faithful, and for any fellow travellers within other churches who were alarmed at what all this portended. But the Vatican was itself in the midst of the disturbance to ancient wisdom brought on by the Agornimento, and in the Second Vatican Council of 1962–65, there was behind the scenes something of a tug of war between the Curia and those Bishops who found some of the traditional teaching difficult to connect up with the world they actually ministered in. This was particularly true for those whose Dioceses were farthest away from the still stoutly Catholic culture of Italy, Spain and Eire. The detail of this conflict is not well documented, for the Roman Church prefers not to wash its linen too publically. However, during the whole period under review in this chapter, official Roman Catholic Church teaching has maintained that sexual activity must be confined within heterosexual marriage, and this necessarily inhibits any form of homosexual behaviour. Some American Roman Catholics have suggested alternative views, not always without criticism from their own authorities, but the standard teaching has been restated in the Vatican Declaration of 1976, and repeated in a rather sterner fashion in the Vatican Letter to Bishops of 1986. It is convenient to set down a record of all the statements together at this point.

(a) Vatican II

In the Pastoral Constitution on the Church in the Modern World, one of the official documents produced by the Second Vatican Council in 1965 and known as *Gaudium et Spes* from its opening words in Latin, one of the specially urgent problems considered was 'fostering the nobility of marriage and the family'. The text apparently owes something to the arguments of Cardinal Suenens and others who pressed that the Church's teaching about marriage should be cast in positive form. This theme is firmly struck in paragraph forty-nine which speaks of conjugal love 'which is uniquely expressed and perfected through the marital act'. The whole paragraph seems careful not to represent the ends of marriage in terms of procreation first, followed by affection in the traditional way, though, of course, adultery, divorce, and contraception are forbidden elsewhere in the Constitution.

(b) Humanum Vitae

If the Constitution *Gaudium et Spes* was taken to indicate a developing approach to human sexuality within the authoritative teaching of the Catholic Church, the Encyclical letter of Pope Paul VI, *Humanae Vitae*, published two years later, showed that it had not entirely replaced the old teaching. The Encyclical reaffirmed the prohibition of artificial birth control, and in the preceding paragraphs referred to sexual activity between husband and wife as 'honourable and good as the recent Council recalled', but also observed that

> the Church, nevertheless, in urging men to the observance of the precepts of the natural law, which it interprets by its constant doctrine, teaches as absolutely required that any use whatever of marriage must retain its natural potential to procreate human life.

The footnotes to Paragraph 11 of the Encyclical give references to *Gaudium et Spes* in the first example and to the Encyclical of Pius XI, *Casti Connubii* of 1930, for the second. The stress Pope Paul puts on the Natural Law argument that procreation is the primary end of marital sex is, in effect, a reversion to the doctrine as it stood before Vatican II. It is also noteworthy that the church's position as interpreter of the Natural Law implies that without such guidance, natural man may be mistaken, which perhaps deliberately weakens the status of Natural Law as that was scholastically understood as God's way of enlightening the conscience of every man.

Neither in *Gaudium et Spes*, nor in *Humanae Vitae* is any direct reference made to homosexuality, though their emphasis on conjugal love and procreation were clearly directed only to heterosexual expression. The American edition of the *New Catholic Encyclopedia* of 1967 left no doubt:

> The homosexual act by its very essence excludes all possibility of transmission of life: such an act cannot fulfil the procreative purpose of the sexual faculty, and is therefore an inordinate goal of human nature, it is a grave transgression of the divine will.

In the European Catholic encyclopedia of theology, *Sacramentum Mundi*, of 1970 edited by Karl Rahner, SJ, a more ecumenical attitude is expressed in the whole article on 'Sex'. Although clearly influenced by *Gaudium et Spes*, it quotes also from Thielicke and other German Protestants. Homosexuality is described as a defective form of sexual behaviour, calling for some form of satisfactory 'pastoral solution'. St Paul's condemnation is said to have referred to the time of pederasty, and homosexual people are capable of entering permanent and total relationships 'seeking the totality of the other person, missing however, the Christian form of encounter with the neighbour. Although this Encyclopedia was given an *Imprimatur* for its English translation, it has, of course, no authority beyond that of its distinguished authors.

(c) The Vatican Declaration on Sexual Ethics, 1975

This is an authoritative rejoinder to any Catholic who might think the old teaching can be disregarded, but appears to be chiefly prompted by a continued anxiety in the Vatican that

> the corruption of morals has increased and one of the most serious indications of this corruption is the unbridled exaltation of sex.

In paragraph four of the *Declaration*, the norms of Natural Law and sacred scripture are defended as immutable against the assertion that they reflect a particular culture at a certain moment of history, and in paragraph seven the doctrine is affirmed that every genital act must be within the framework of marriage. In paragraph eight, the transitory and incurable categories of homosexuality are distinguished, and of the second the *Declaration* states:

> In regard to this second category of subjects, some people conclude that their tendency is so natural that it justifies in their case homosexual relations with a sincere communion of life and love analogous to marriage, in so far as such homosexuals feel incapable of enduring a solitary life.

> In the pastoral field, these homosexuals must certainly be treated with understanding and sustained in the hope of overcoming their personal difficulties and their inability to fit into society. Their culpability will be judged with prudence. But no pastoral method can be employed which would give moral justification to these acts on the grounds that they would be consonant with the condition of such people. For according to the objective moral order, homosexual relations are acts which lack an essential and indispensable finality. In Sacred Scripture they are condemned as a serious depravity and even presented as the sad consequence of rejecting God. This judgement of Scripture does not, of course, permit us to conclude that all those who suffer from this anomaly are personally responsible for it, but it does attest to the fact that homosexual acts are intrinsically disordered and can in no case be approved of.[10]

(d) New directions in Catholic thought, 1976

This study was prepared by a small group for the Catholic Theological Society of America. Commissioned in 1972 the Report was finally 'received' by the Commission in October 1976, and published the next year. A foreword explains that the reception of the study implies neither approval nor disapproval by the Society, who wish to make the research it contains available to members and a wider public. The study was already in draft when the Vatican Declaration on Sexual Ethics was issued, and appears to have been revised in several places to take account of it. Although concerned with sexual morality in general, a special section of the report considers homosexuality.

The Committee sets out a modern understanding of homosexuality. Homosexuals are said to have the same rights as heterosexuals to love, intimacy, and relationships, and Christian sexual morality does not require a dual standard. The rights and obligations are the same. Since homosexual friendships are not sustained and supported by society, they are tempted to promiscuity and therefore a pastor may recommend close stable friendships between homosexuals, not simply as a lesser of two evils but as a positive good. Although anything approaching a sacramental celebration of a homosexual 'marriage' would be inappropriate and misleading, prayer, even communal prayer for two people striving to live Christian lives, incarnating the values of fidelity, truth, and love, is not beyond the pastoral possibilities of a church whose ritual tradition includes a rich variety of blessings. The advisability of such an action must be determined by pastoral prudence and consideration of all possible consequences, including social repercussions.

In Guideline 7, the Committee turn to the principle of moral theology '*ubi dubium, ibi libertas*' – where there is doubt, there is freedom. Since the complexities, ambiguities, and uncertainties of homosexuality have only recently come to light, this principle should be applied in administering absolution and giving communion to homosexuals. The same principle allows counsellors and confessors to leave homosexuals a freedom of conscience, and this leads to the conclusion that

A homosexual engaging in homosexual acts in good conscience has the same rights of conscience and the same rights to the sacraments as a married couple practising birth control in good conscience.

The effect of the guidelines, therefore, is that this study recommends that the laity, having educated consciences, should make their own decision about the morality of both contraception and homosexual behaviour. The case of priests is also considered, and distinguished since those who have this vocation must accept celibacy. Candidates for the priesthood or religious life should therefore be confident that they can live up to the ideals and expectations of a celibate life and not enter it if they intend consistent homosexual behaviour, or are simply seeking an escape from confronting their sexuality and making it a creative force in their lives.[11]

(e) Vatican Pastoral Letter, 1986

This letter was produced by the Congregation for the Doctrine of the Faith in the Vatican and approved by Pope John Paul II. Addressed to the Bishops of the Catholic Church, it was published in October 1986.

The letter begins by referring to the public debate about the moral evaluation of homosexual acts, which often advances arguments inconsistent with the teaching of the Catholic Church, a cause of concern to all engaged in the pastoral ministry (Sec. 1). The Catholic moral perspective finds support in the more secure findings of the natural sciences, but its viewpoint is founded on human reason illumined by faith and the desire to do the will of God. The church is thus in a position:

> to learn from scientific discovery but also to transcend the horizons of science and to be confident that her more global vision does greater justice to the rich reality of the human person in his spiritual and physical dimensions, created by God, and heir, by grace, to eternal life. (Sec. 2.)

The Letter then recalls the explicit treatment given to the problem in the Congregation's previous Declaration of 1975, where a distinction was made between the homosexual condition and individual homosexual actions; the latter were described as being 'intrinsically disordered' and able in no case to be approved of. But in the discussion that followed the 1975 Declaration, the Letter says, an 'overly benign' interpretation was given to the condition itself as 'neutral or even good'. The letter seeks to correct this impression:

> Although the particular inclination of the homosexual person is not a sin, it is a more or less strong tendency towards an intrinsic moral evil; and thus the inclination itself must be seen as an objective disorder. (Sec. 3.)

In the following sections, four to six, the exegesis of sacred scripture is considered. Any view that scripture has nothing to say, approves, or is so culture bound that it is no longer applicable is said to be erroneous. Although the world of today differs from that of the New Testament, which itself differed from that of the Hebrew people, there is a clear consistency within the scriptures on the moral issue of homosexual behaviour. The church's doctrine is based on the solid foundation of a constant biblical testimony, for as the Vatican Council II (*Dei Verbum* 10) put it:

In the supremely wise arrangement of God, sacred Tradition, sacred Scripture, and the Magisterium of the Church are so connected and associated that one of them cannot stand without the others. (Sec. 5.)

The Letter then briefly reviews Genesis 3 on the Fall, Genesis 19 on Sodom, where there can be no doubt of the moral judgment against homosexual relations, and Leviticus 18 and 20 where those who behave in a homosexual fashion are excluded from the people of God. Against this background of theocratic law, St Paul, in I Cor. 9, is said to develop an eschatological perspective in proposing that such people will not enter the Kingdom of God, and in Romans 1, Paul, in the context of the confrontation between Christianity and the pagan world of his day, uses homosexual behaviour as an example of the blindness which has overcome mankind (Sec. 6).

In the next section, the immorality of homosexual behaviour is re-iterated on the further grounds that same sex activity annuls the rich symbolism of the marital relationship, and God's design. It is not a complementary union capable of transmitting life. Therefore (Sec. 9), the church must resist pressure groups within its own membership who argue for the removal of discrimination, or for changes in the law. Homosexual persons must not be treated with violence of speech or action; their dignity as persons is to be protected. That said, pastors must avoid the demeaning assumption that homosexual behaviour is compulsive and therefore inculpable.

Section 12 advises homosexual persons who seek to follow the Lord to enact the will of God in their life by joining whatever sufferings and difficulties they experience in virtue of their condition to the sacrifice of the Lord's cross:

> Homosexuals are called, as all of us are, to a chaste life. . . . As they dedicate their lives to understanding the nature of God's personal call to them, they will be able to celebrate the Sacrament of Penance more faithfully, and receive the Lord's grace so freely offered there in order to convert their lives more faithfully to his Way. (Sec. 12.)

The rest of the Letter suggests pastoral care in full accord with the teaching of the church, which will exclude any programme where the immorality of homosexual persons is not made clear. Ambiguous organizations must not be supported. In effect, these regulations suggest that gay clubs and organizations, which might give the impression of being Catholic, or want to use Catholic buildings for services or meetings, must be prohibited.

Although there is little new in this Letter, and it certainly reflects many reported statements of the present Pope, two aspects of it deserve special note. First, while setting out the standard teaching of the Catholic Church about the character of its moral authority, it does spell out the biblical tradition in more detail than usual, reflecting a sensitivity to the importance of that ecumenically. Second, as a guide to what the Vatican expects of its bishops, it gives specific warning against any kind of tolerant or sympathetic local official attitude to Gay Lib. Of course, it does not threaten punishment, but it does assume that with confession and grace homosexual Catholics will be able to live chaste (celibate?) lives.[12]

The official Roman Catholic teaching therefore remains clear, and the strong emphasis in *Gaudium et Spes* on conjugal love has provided no opportunity for any parallel recognition of the value of love between homosexuals.

Three Significant Reports – 1970–79

The apparent support shown in the 1957 and 1958 debates of the Church Assembly and the Methodist Conference for the proposed change in the law was by small majorities, an early sign that representative church bodies were not likely to find much unanimity on this controversial subject. It has been an oft-repeated pattern since, that an officially appointed church working party, with a balanced membership chosen to reflect a spectrum of theological views, pastoral experience and relevant specialist knowledge, after many hours of study and working together, find themselves able to agree recommendations, only to see their report coolly received. The present patterns of church democracy can mean that such reports are debated in a forum where the old attitudes are well-protected and quickly surface whatever criticism of them the new report makes. Such debates become sterile, and disillusioning to members of working parties who suspect their labours are not being taken seriously. Perhaps it is unreasonably optimistic to expect a controversial report to gain immediate acceptance in an instinctively cautious Synod or Conference, mindful as it has to be of local congregational opinion. The three Reports now to be considered (two Anglican and one Methodist) were not the only ones produced for the non-Roman churches in the period, but they are examples of a considerable shift in opinion from the initial cautious and divided view of the 1970 Report to the more adventurous approaches taken by the Methodists and Anglicans in 1979, the high point as it now seems to be ten years later, of the move towards liberalizing the old tradition. The first report was not published, the second accepted with qualification, and the third circumscribed with a cautious comment by the Board of Social Responsibility.

(a) Homosexuality reviewed, 1970

In September 1967, the new Church of England Board of Social Responsibility set up a working party who in the light of the 1967 Act were to review 'the situation concerning both male and female homosexuality', and report to the Board and to the Archbishop of Canterbury. He would decide whether or not their work should be published. This group was small, but included the Bishop of Lichfield as chairman, the Board's secretary, Mr Edwin Barker, and the Roman Catholic psychiatrist and author Dr Jack Dominian, with two members of the police. The report expressed the hope that pastoral care would be developed, and set out *inter alia* two alternative views of homosexual relationships, 'that they are always wrong', or 'that they may be a right relationship for the partners if it is the best they can achieve'. Perhaps because of this divergence of view within the group, the Report was not published but printed for restricted circulation (presumably to Bishops) in 1970.

The group were split on the question how far treatment could be successful in changing the homosexual orientation, and this was of some importance in shaping their report. The Wolfenden Committee had considered this question carefully, and had taken a good deal of evidence from medical officers and prison authorities of the availability and success rate of attempts to change the orientation of those in prison in the past decade for homosexual offences. They concluded the prospect of change was negligible for those whose orientation was firmly settled. It was possible, however, for treatment to lead to a better adaptation to life in general.[13]

In the group, some members thought that pastoral and medical care would enable most homosexuals to lead celibate lives as the Christian tradition had always required; others were less optimistic of change and preferred to argue that homosexual behaviour would have to be accepted as a second best.[14]

(b) A Methodist Report, 1979

This report was prepared by the Division of Social Responsiblity and the Faith and Order committee for presentation to the Methodist Church Conference of 1979, where it was received, but further study of some aspects of the Report was requested. It is a brief report, and only Section C, some twelve paragraphs, deals with homosexuality, but earlier, the Christian sources of guidance in seeking an understanding of human sexuality are listed: these are said to be the Bible, reason, the traditional teaching of the church, the personal and corporate experience of modern Christians, the understanding provided by the human sciences, and what may be called the spirit of the age. Applied to homosexuality these sources of guidance lead the authors of the Report to the conclusions that bear some similarity to those of the 1963 Quaker Report, but of course much study had taken place in between, and some of the new views on sexuality and morality had become widely assimilated into the churches. It would be fair to say that the distinguished group who prepared this report for the Methodist Conference were courageous in making plain their convictions. The paragraphs concerned (nos. C.9 and C.10) may be best quoted in full:

C.9 Christians affirm marriage because they believe that within it the creative, procreative and relational aspects of human sexuality can be expressed. Nevertheless, Christians have never asserted that marriage, procreative or not, is the only valid way of life – celibacy, for example, has at times been valued even more highly. It is recognised that marriages which have fulfilled their procreative character, have often failed in the quality of relationships which they ought to have created. It is because they set a high value on relationships within marriage that Christians ought also to argue that stable permanent relationships can be an appropriate way of expressing a homosexual orientation. *This involves an acceptance of homosexual activities as not being intrinsically wrong. The quality of any homosexual relationship is thus to be assessed by the same basic criteria which have been applied to heterosexual relationships. For homosexual men and women, permanent relationships characterized by love can be an appropriate and Christian way of expressing their sexuality.* This open acceptance of homosexuality will no doubt present problems at different levels in the life of the Church – it obviously removes the grounds for denying any person membership of the Church or an office in it solely because they have a particular sexual orientation.

C.10 It is the essence of the Christian Gospel to stand by and care for those in need. The Christian recognizes a common humanity and a personal constraint to show concern for others. In the context of homosexuality and bisexuality this means helping those in need to discover their basic sexual orientation and enabling them to come to terms with it. It also means encouraging and supporting those whose orientation is homosexual to form stable and lasting relationships, for men and women are made for relationships and their sexuality is involved in and fulfilled by these commitments. It is the quality of these relationships which matters, not the physical expression which they may take. Christians may need to counsel and support families in which one member realises that his or her orientation is homosexual. Christians who discover themselves to be homosexual may need special support if they are to come to terms with their sexuality and to retain their faith within the Church which a long anti-homosexual tradition.[15]

(Note. The request of the 1979 Methodist Conference for further study led to two subsequent reports to the Conference in 1980, and 1982. Neither of these proved acceptable to a majority of conference members, and a further group started work in 1988, expected to report to the Conference in 1990 or 1991. In 1989 the Ministerial Committee of the Conference voted by a small majority not to recommend a known lesbian candidate for the ministry.)

(c) The Gloucester Report, 1979

This report was the result of a request in 1974 to the BSR from the Principals of Theological Colleges for a study to be made of the theological, social, pastoral and legal aspects of homosexuality. This request appeared to set the agenda for the group in narrow terms, focussed on ordinands and the ministry, but it soon proved impossible not to extend the enquiry to the whole question of the morality of homosexual behaviour.[16]

Among those believing themselves called by God to the church's ministry, some will be of homosexual orientation, so there has to be a policy to determine whether or not they may be accepted. Sometimes an ordinand will disclose his situation in confidence, sometimes it will become obvious to those training him, sometimes it will be carefully concealed, or even unperceived by the candidate at the time. Either at the selection stage, if the question is raised, or during training, decisions had to be taken, and in the past policies had varied. Some College Principals took the view that the appropriate church authorities must be warned before ministry began, others retained confidences, and counselled how a ministry might avoid scandal.

The growth of the Gay Lib movement especially in Universities meant that some Theological Colleges faced an open challenge to their traditional discipline, difficult to manage without a clear uniform policy in the parent church. It was obviously very irresponsible to train a practising homosexual ordinand if his subsequent ministry would be unacceptable in most congregations once his life-style became known. Conversely, it could be argued that it was inconsistent for a church which proclaimed the acceptance of gay people to exclude them from its ministry. So the Gloucester working party had to face two questions: does the acceptance of gay people within the church mean accepting their style of love-making?, and if so, are the clergy to be included in that acceptance, or are they to be regarded as bound by a separate professional code of morality reflecting their special position, as for example is the case among doctors?

The membership of the working party was much larger than had seemed necessary for the 1967 Group, and its brief was far broader. It included four University Professors, one Theological College Principal, and six others, experts in various ways, two of them being women. The Group met twenty-seven times over three years, and received evidence from a great many people. In 1978, their Report to the Board of Social Responsibility, which was carefully described as 'a contribution to discussion' crossed the Rubicon and suggested that, for lay homosexuals:

> there are circumstances in which individuals may justifiably choose to enter into a homosexual relationship with the hope of enjoying a companionship and physical expression of sexual love similar to that which is found in marriage. (Sec. 168)

But for clergy, whose domestic affairs, insofar as they are common knowledge, inevitably affect their standing as leaders of the congregation and examples to the flock of Christ, such freedom of choice is not open:

> A homosexual priest who has 'come out' and openly acknowledges that he is living in a sexual union with another man should not expect the Church to accept him on the same condition as if he were married (Sec. 255)

and:

> a priest in this position ought to offer his resignation to the bishop of the diocese, so that he as the minister bearing responsibility for the Church in the locality could with the pastoral care appropriate to his office decide whether it should be accepted or not. (Sec. 256)

Obviously, if that view is taken of priests, then the situation for ordinands also needs clarifying:

> We do not think that a bishop is justified in refusing to ordain an otherwise acceptable ordinand merely on the ground that he is (or is believed to be) homosexually orientated. But an ordinand would be wrong to conceal deliberately from his ordaining bishop an intention existing in his own mind to live openly in a homosexual union after ordination or to campaign on behalf of a homophile organization. (Sec. 260)

The Gloucester Group in Sec. 168 did not go as far as the positive Methodist statement (C 9) that '*homosexual activities were not intrinsically wrong*' by their observation that '*there were circumstances in which individuals may justifiably choose to enter a homosexual relationship which might include physical expression.*' The Methodist opinion was expressly contrary to that in the Vatican Declaration of 1975, and the Anglican one could be understood as more ambiguously worded than either of the others. (The Anglican and Methodist groups were working at much the same time, and covering the same ground, but as I recall, there was no direct sharing of views.)

The Gloucester Working Party make clear in Sec. 167 and the earlier part of Sec. 168 of their Report that their suggestion for laity is an attempt to resolve the difficulty of those who have no choice in their homosexual orientation. They were seeking to shape a new formula which avoids the rigorism of the old tradition, but refuses to adopt a total affirmation of homosexual activity as an appropriate mirror of divine love. In terms of pastoral care, it is argued that the way forward for the church is not to condemn but to show concern for those who cannot conform to the norm of marriage. A homosexual relationship could not be regarded as the moral or social equivalent of marriage; it would be bound to have a private and experimental character. That said, if a homosexual couple decide in private conscience to enter into a sexual relationship, after careful consideration, their private conscience should be respected.

It is not surprising that the situation of parochial clergy, and therefore of ordinands was regarded differently by the Working Party. In a church divided on the moral issue it was unrealistic to suppose that a known homosexual relationship in the vicarage would avoid scandal, and therefore limit the scope of ministry. Perhaps a homosexual priest might be absolutely clear in his own conscience about his relationship, and regret that the church had no way of validating it. But as a member of a corporate community, he was under a moral (not legal) obligation to put his situation in confidence to his Bishop. Neither he nor an ordinand should be questioned directly, unless the Bishop or Archdeacon had grounds for supposing that a legal offence was being committed. The respect for privacy was otherwise very important.

The implication of these suggestions was, of course, though it was not drawn out sharply in the report, that a gay clergyman's future would much depend on what attitude his particular bishop would take. That had in fact been the situation in the past for those clergy who had been convicted in civil courts, and it continued where the offence occurred with an under-age person. The difference proposed in the Gloucester Report was that active gay clergy were expected to take their bishops into their confidence, even when neither scandal nor legal action threatened, and the hope of the Working Party was that the bishops would work out a common policy.

Section 168 of the Report comes towards the end of the chapter on theological and ethical considerations. The reference to clergy and ordinands comes from the chapter on social and pastoral care. In a tightly written report, reflecting the academic precision of several of its members, a précis of the arguments is likely to be misleading. But it can be said that the medical chapter of the Report included a thorough presentation of what was known about the development of sexual orientation and gender, the psychological understanding of homosexuality, and its treatment. The conclusion was that change was unlikely except for ambisexual people, and homosexuals were not responsible for their condition; it was not a sickness though, and they could be held responsible for the acts they chose.

The biblical chapter reviewed the usual texts and concluded that the evidence seems clearly to show condemnation of homosexual behaviour, but it is important to bear in mind how many moral and ethical precepts which in the Bible are presented as the direct commands of God have been re-interpreted in the course of Christian history and even in some cases abandoned as guides or moral standards for the conduct of individual or social life. The doctrine of the 'Holy War' is cited as an example. Similarly, the Old Testament commends marriage for all, but in the new divine society the option of celibacy is also approved. Given the fundamental importance of the doctrine of creation, this need not mean that procreation is the only pattern for sexual relationships; complementarity and companionship are equally part of the Genesis accounts, and so it could be argued that those who cannot achieve the ideal of marriage with the opposite sex should not be regarded as sharing in a special way the fallenness of creation, but find a place for themselves in the divine order wherein they may fulfil the sexuality that is theirs.

As the next chapter shows, the Gloucester Report was probably too radical for the church by the time it was published, and it has not been given very much sustained study. (It was notable in the 1987 Debate on the Higton motion, that it was seldom referred to, and the distinction it made between lay and ordained people largely forgotten.) When it came to the Synod in 1981, heavily qualified by critical observations from the Board of Social Responsibility, it was clear that its reception would be of a limited kind. The 1981 Synod debate is discussed in Chapter 8 below.

Uncertainty remained in the Church of England during the rest of the decade. After the 1981 debate, confidential guidelines were prepared for diocesan bishops by ACCM, the body concerned with advising them about the suitability of potential ordinands, but this was not of binding authority. Eventually, in 1986 the House of Bishops asked the BSR to set up another Working Party to report in strict confidence to them on questions concerning homosexuality and lesbianism. The report was to be ready in time for the Lambeth Conference if possible but was in fact only completed and circulated to bishops in strict confidence in the Autumn of 1988. They gave it a preliminary discussion at a meeting at Lambeth Palace that September, and considered it further at a residential meeting in Manchester in June 1989. Since the Report was written for the Bishops, it seems likely that they will continue to weigh its contents for some time, and no immediate publication is expected.

Neither the membership of this working party nor its terms of reference have been disclosed, though Mr Clifford Longley of *The Times* suggested in January 1989 that its Chairman may have been the Rev. June Osborne and it has therefore subsequently become known as the Osborne Report. Despite media hints that the unpublished report is quite radical in tone, it seems probable that, if its contents become known, they will be seen primarily as a review of the present situation and of the factors the bishops should consider if they seek to bring healing to what seems at the moment a painful and divisive issue to the church.

(Author's note. Alert readers will realize that since all Church of England bishops were at the Lambeth Meeting in September 1988, I have seen the Osborne Report, though in respect for its confidentiality I have not quoted from it in this book. As it happens, I was also a member of the BSR working group in 1970, and of the Gloucester Working party of 1979. My own thinking has obviously been influenced by all three studies, and by the debates I attended of the General Synod, the 1988 Lambeth Conference and several study groups organized by other churches in Britain and America.)

8

A Decade of Indecision – 1979-1989

Introduction

The Lambeth Conference of Anglican Bishops in 1978 considered homosexuality, and its report and resolution were known both to the General Synod and to the Board of Social Responsibility when it received the Gloucester Report. In 1979, the Board decided to publish it as Part One, adding their own critical comments in Part Two. The Synod debated the whole document in February 1981. The Synod debate proved once again how divisive an issue it was, and a lull set in, until the Private Member motion by the Rev. Tony Higton in 1987 attempted to reassert the traditional teaching. This did not succeed. The Lambeth Conference of 1988 after some hesitation in effect repeated its resolution of 1978.

It has been therefore a decade in which those who have worked for a change in the official Christian attitude among Protestant churches, and those who have sought firmly to re-assert the traditional teaching have both been frustrated by a refusal of middle ground people to commit themselves either way. Although what follows is mostly a record of four debates among Anglicans in England, two in the General Synod, and two in the international Lambeth Conferences, a similar experience of indecision has characterized discussions in other churches in Britain and in the world-wide confessional groupings. A brief illustration of this is given by including some of the resolutions passed by the American Episcopal Church's General Convention. In practice, the Anglicans function as a Communion held together less by a common theology than by a characteristic style, and by common roots, of which Canterbury and Lambeth are precious symbols rather than the central authority. One ear of many Anglicans is often tuned to Rome and Catholicity, the other to Geneva and the reforming Spirit. For this moral issue of homosexual behaviour, Rome has sent no new message and Geneva has never abandoned scripture, however hard it has tried to interpret the wisdom of our age concerning human sexuality.

Within the General Synod there is always a dialectic between the Catholic and Reformed traditions though it often seems that the voting pattern is dictated more by a refusal to take decisions which would decisively alienate either group than by a clear third middle way conviction. This style of dialectic and compromise, and the rather Christian club atmosphere of many debates creates problems for media reporters who may be expecting the Synod proceedings to mirror those of Parliament next door. The situations are actually very different. In Synod, there is no political party in power, and no cabinet. The civil service back-up is miniscule, and in so far as there is an initiator of policy, that is in principle the Holy Spirit, leading the church and moving individual members to find together a way forward towards a *consensus fidelium*. There was clearly no consensus to be found about the recommendations of the Gloucester Report. The Synod was equally clearly not prepared to endorse the Higton motion, and adopted instead a more moderate form of words which nevertheless linked homosexual acts with fornication and adultery as a falling short of the ideal of sexual intercourse within a permanent married relationship. But the process of amending a motion, and then further amending it left a set of statements which though passed by a large majority at the time, look on reflection frankly somewhat messy, and at the time obviously confused reporters. The day after the 1987 Debate, one newspaper carried the headline 'Pulpit poofs can stay'. As an example of expert caption writing it could be thought brilliant, as a description of the debate it was ludicrous.

Three other preliminary points deserve mention. While there are obvious long term benefits in holding open debates on controversial questions of Christian morality, it would be misleading to suggest that gay people have felt entirely free to express their own convictions in such gatherings. Although much was said about accepting the homosexual person, a residual aura of disapproval was clearly to be discerned in these debates, and the plain fact is that any homosexual person, male or female, clergy or lay, who bravely disclosed their true feelings took some obvious risks about their own standing in the church.

Secondly, although there is no Cabinet Government as such in the Synod, there has to be some element of business management in such debates. Synod members are skilled enough in procedure not to be deceived by covert manipulation, but senior Bishops and Administrators quite properly try to anticipate probable patterns of voting and what the mood of the Synod is likely to be. It seemed obvious both in 1981 and in 1987, that on neither occasion did the middle majority wish to be forced to a decision for or against liberalization.

To 'take note of' is the most non-committal form of motion available, and that safeguard was built into the 1981 Debate in advance. The Higton motion in 1987 attempted an explicit condemnation, but its rigour was blunted by the Bishop of Chester's amendment, printed on the Order paper sent out in advance and suggesting a suitable compromise. At Lambeth in 1988, a real tussle between some American and Australian Bishops on homosexual rights was saved by the bell.

Thirdly, there is the question of the pace of change in church attitudes. As guardians of the faith once delivered to the saints, church leaders try not to think like politicians with an eye on the next election. When does due deliberation become resistance to the leading of the Spirit? There can be no proper answer to that in theory, but in practice in church history, it seems that important changes occur when the time is ripe, and cannot be forced. Slavery for example is now thought to have been implicitly inconsistent with the gospel from the beginning, but William Wilberforce was born in 1759. The Church of England gradually changed its attitude to contraception between the wars; the Roman Catholic Church has not, but it is often alleged that many of its members think it should. The problems of urban decay and rural deprivation in Britain are 200 years old at least. In the past three years, the Christian denunciation of the proliferation of nuclear weapons has been heeded; CND was founded in the fifties. It might be said that the Bishop of Truro used this notion of due deliberation to good effect in suggesting in the 1981 Debate that the fourth-century church had got its christology wrong for some years by an over hasty decision, a point that few Synod members felt competent to dispute.

The Lambeth Conference, 1978

Most of the work of the Conference was done in three sections, the first one having as its general theme the question 'What is the church for?' It was chaired by Bishop Desmond Tutu (as he then was) and among the English bishops in this Section was John Yates, Bishop of Gloucester. The Section had a wide brief, and in Part four of its Report it dealt with particular issues concerning the church and society, including the family, sexuality and homosexuality. The Lambeth Conferences work under great pressure and tend to have a unifying and reaffirming role in the life of the Anglican Church, rather than being innovative in the style of Vatican II. Thus, a very interesting record of the developing and changing understanding of the Anglican attitude towards marriage and sexuality is to be found in the successive post-war Lambeth Report. What was said in 1978 about homosexuality follows on directly from its observations about sexuality in general:

Sexuality – masculinity and feminity (Lambeth Report 1.D)

The Lambeth Conference of 1958 recorded, in resolution 112, its profound conviction that the idea of the human family is rooted in the Godhead and that 'all problems of sex relations ... must be related, consciously and directly, to the creative, redemptive, and sanctifying power of God.'

God is not masculine. Neither is God feminine. God is the source of masculinity and femininity, and of all those human characteristics which are variously called masculine and feminine in different cultures. God's nature is reflected in the balance and interaction between them.

We, in time and space, are sexual creatures. God created us male and female. The wholeness of God can be most directly expressed in the give and take of love between a man and a woman. But this wholeness of God is also present in each individual person, whose total sexuality is expressed through the interplay of masculine and feminine qualities.

The Christian life holds in balance the masculine and the feminine qualities. God's wholeness sets us free. He calls us into mature relationships of inter-dependence with each other – to forgive as we are forgiven, to love as we are loved – our fragmented sexuality transformed by his wholeness.

We commend the study of this theme to the Church, as offering a true basis for all sexual relationships (see resolution 10 (1)).

Homosexuality (Lambeth Report 1.E)

Today we do not expect everyone to conform to a norm – a sort of average humanness – but rather to rejoice in variety; so the status and rights of homosexuals are being reconsidered.

Homosexuality has rarely received understanding either in Church or in society. Despite much research there is still considerable disagreement about its nature and causes. It is commonly referred to as a deviation, yet many homosexuals do not believe they are abnormal. They do not ask for sympathy, but for recognition of the fact that their homosexual relationship can express mutual love as appropriately for the persons concerned as a heterosexual relationship might for others. The majority of Christians would not willingly agree with this attitude. We assert however that an adequate understanding of, and response to, homosexuality will not be found until society as a whole, and Christians in particular, can approach the subject compassionately and without prejudice.

Questions relating to homosexuality are admittedly complex, and we note that these questions are currently the subject of serious study in some parts of the Anglican Communion. There are other places (e.g. in the Church of Africa) where homosexual behaviour has not emerged as a problem. This fact indicates the need for further study as to the possible relationship between homosexuality and environment. There is also particular need for further study of the Scriptural evidence such as Romans 1.18–32 which depicts homosexual behaviour as one of the manifestations of the fragmentation of life in a fallen world.

It is the responsibility of every local Church to become such a warm-hearted, Christ-centred, eucharistic fellowship, that people of every temperament and tendency might find their true unity and fellowship within the total family of Christ, where all are sinners, but all can find the grace and forgiveness of Christ in 'his accepting community' (see resolution 10 (3)).

Resolution 10 begins by affirming the Christian ideals of faithfulness and chastity both within and outside marriage, and its first and second paragraphs call for theology study of sexuality and diocesan programmes to promote the ideals of Christian marriage and family life. Paragraph 3 reads:

While we re-affirm heterosexuality as the Scriptural norm, we recognize the need for deep and dispassionate study of the question of homosexuality, which would take seriously both the teaching of Scripture and the results of scientific and medical research. The Church, recognizing the need for pastoral concern for those who are homosexual, encourages dialogue with them.

(We note with satisfaction that such studies are now proceeding in some member Churches of the Anglican Communion.)[1]

The Synod Debate, 1981

The Bishop of Truro, Graham Leonard, introduced the Gloucester Report as Chairman of the Board of Social Responsibility. He made plain that the Synod was asked only to take note of the Report, and that was reassuring to many, not only to those who had not had time to digest it, but also to those who were somewhat bewildered by the mass of paper in their hands. The tortuous path of the original

Gloucester text to the Synod had caused it to be bound up with three other documents, a foreword by Leonard, comments by the Board, and an official Report to the Synod by the Board. This was demonstration enough that the Working Party's work was not expected to gain an easy assent and therefore the debate was seen as a preliminary testing of reactions rather than an opportunity for decision. Conviction that delay was necessary was central to Leonard's introduction.[2]

The Bishop of Gloucester, spoke next, pointing out that the Working party had finished its work some three years previously, in an atmosphere less fraught and hypertensive than that of 1981 'but we knew even in those prehistoric days that whatever we produced was likely to produce more brickbats than bouquets.' Grasping the nettle, Yates set out the difference between the approach taken by his Group and that of the Board's criticisms:

> The working party – and I cannot emphasize this too strongly – tried to come to its estimate on the morality of homosexual relations firmly against the background of Christian marriage, heterosexual marriage, if you like, as the Christian norm. But even if you accept the norm and believe yourself or know yourself to be inescapably homosexual in orientation, what are you then to do to express, so far as you can, what you accept as God's will and purpose for sexuality? That is the issue, and it seems to me to be an issue to do with relationships and not to do with acts, and therein, I think, lies a great deal of the difference between at least two of the opposing schools of thought. So long as we are dealing primarily with the morality of certain acts and attempting to isolate them from relationships, we may be embarking upon a perfectly acceptable course but that course will not, on the whole, bring us within hailing distance of what the Working Party was trying to do, for it committed itself to relationships and the morality of them.

> The very cautious verdict of the Working Party about the morality within the realm of personal free choice, liberty and conscience, unbacked by any official sanction, that very guarded liberty accorded to an individual to enter upon a homosexual relationship, is not nearly enough for those who see homosexuality as some alternative sexuality as natural to some people as heterosexuality is to others. Of course not. But those who would adhere to the old tradition most strictly must, I think, be challenged in love to tell us what other course they recommend. Can you close the door, or keep it closed indefinitely and without any liberty? I have read and reread many times paragraph A17 on page 92 of this document, which is the response of the Board at that central point of the argument. The section to which I refer reads: 'There is a second view of sexual

behaviour which is held by many members of the Board. They believe that people with a homosexual condition do have, as the report accepts, a moral choice, but consider that the right choice is abstinence . . .' I cannot see that is a choice. I cannot see that that is now in the realm of a responsible choice.[3]

Bishop Yates suggested the church's magisterium should not direct in this matter, but circumscribe certain areas of behaviour within which the individual is free to make his own choice.

The next speaker was the Archbishop of Canterbury (Runcie) who apologised for intervening directly after two other Bishops. (He had news of Mr Terry Waite to announce). For the debate, he noted that the Gloucester Report had not received a warm welcome from those who would like the church to sound a clear blast on either side of this argument. Between four views, homosexuality seen simply as a sin, as a sickness, as a handicap which people have to cope with, or as a valid alternative, he inclined towards the third. He also stressed the decline in our day of the eclipse of friendship as a profound spiritual relationship, now too often surrounded with ungenerous suspicion.

> Kisses, tears, and embraces are not in themselves evidence of homosexuality. Hrothgar embracing Beowulf, Johnson embracing Boswell – a pretty flagrantly heterosexual couple! – and all those hairy old toughs of centurions in Tacitus clinging to one another and begging for last kisses when the legion was breaking up – all pansies? If you can believe that, you can believe anything. It is not, of course, the demonstrative gestures of friendship among our ancestors but the absence of such gestures in our own society which calls for special explanation.[4]

Particular points of criticism raised by members included the suggestion that the medical chapter included some as yet untested hypotheses, and that there was more possibility than the Report suggested that religious conversion could actually change sexual orientation, especially among the young. Sister Carol of the Community of the Holy Name spoke with moving clarity about the vocation to celibacy, a call which is not the same as abstinence or chastity, and does not repress or bypass sexuality: 'I cannot be fully alive nor wholly possessed by God until this aspect of my nature is liberated, orientated and surrendered to him.'

The biblical chapter was criticized by some members, mostly on the grounds of interpretation. The Working Party had taken a fresh scholarly look at the texts, and were by no means following the familiar Bailey type exegesis of twenty years ago, but the chapter was relatively brief, assuming perhaps more background knowledge of earlier discussions than Synod members actually had. In particular, the way biblical authority should be handled in the church in view of the Working Party was not entirely acceptable to the evangelical members, but in any case they had a fresh study of the texts from their own resources to set beside the report. This was *Homosexuals and the Christian Fellowship*, by D. J. Atkinson.[5] a book that was both scholarly and pastorally sensitive, based to some extent on experience with Christian Union students and others in Oxford.

Another view of the biblical texts was put by Canon Douglas Rhymes: 'We all know that in Leviticus, homosexuality is condemned. So, for that matter is the eating of pork, jugged hare and thermidor lobster . . .' His more substantial point was put in a quotation from Jack Dominian: 'The real evil of our age is not the permissiveness of sexual pleasure, but the impermanence of human relationships.' The Working Party had been told by representatives of gay organizations that the notion of homosexual 'marriage' did not commend itself to them, partly because it would imply a false identity with the heterosexual institution and partly because the social climate made long enduring or permanent relationships difficult for most gay people. Rhymes thought more help towards stability was needed.

The Rev. Robert Lewis, an incumbent of Thirsk, and previously Domestic Chaplain to the Archbishop of York, said the Synod needed to hear from people who knew this subject from the inside, of whom he was one. Homosexuals did not want tea and sympathy, but recognition as a fact of life which will not go away and which has to be accepted for itself. But that acceptance should include two kinds of restraint. There should be restraint in formally debating homosexuality in the church, and there should be restraint in any claim that it was a wholly valid alternative to the heterosexual condition. He ended with a *cri de coeur*:

> Remove the prejudice, yes, but do not, in order to put yourself in the right, maintain that black is white. I am telling the Synod that homosexuality, however inevitably some men and women and boys and girls belong in that condition, is a disability. It is part of the fault of things. Homosexuality is a cheat. So it is no business of the Church or any other group to make equal what is not equal. We are considering a mystery, and a mystery which I from my dunghill can only simply hold before my Maker, as I do every day, my Maker who knows best whose I am and whom I serve.[6]

After this speech, the debate continued for some time, but Mr Lewis had settled the outcome. Synod was reassured that to 'take note' uncommittally was the right course, and agreed that on a show of hands. Attempts to commend the Report for study in Dioceses, a small sign of approval, or conversely to add a note disassociating the

Synod from the conclusions of the Working Party were both quickly rejected. Enough was enough.

The Synod Debate, 1987

The diversity of views expressed in the 1981 Synod debate ensured that nothing further could be done to implement The Gloucester Working Party Recommendations. The mood of the church was in any case becoming more polarized. The Open Synod group probably hoped the bishops would be discreetly sensitive to the needs of homosexual clergy. The Anglo-Catholics were themselves split between those who wished to follow Vatican teaching, similar in this respect to the evangelicals though for not quite the same reasons, and those whose pastoral experience inclined them towards the 'Gloucester' view. The international fellowship of evangelicals were on the whole united in their disapproval of the Gloucester view on scriptural grounds, and some Anglican Provinces where the Low Church tradition was strong adopted resolutions which made it clear that the ordination of a person who intended to continue homosexual acts was impossible.

This polarizing movement found a synodical champion in the Rev. Tony Higton who was vicar of Hawkwell in the Diocese of Chelmsford, and co-director of an organization called 'Action for Biblical Witness to our Nation' (ABWON). His private member's motion put down in July 1987 quickly gathered 168 supporting signatures, and this strong support brought it to the top of the agenda for the next group of sessions. It was debated on Armistice Day (11 November 1987).

The media people were well alerted and in the days preceding the debate had printed various and sometimes inaccurate stories about gay clergy. Suggestions that it was the policy of ACCM, the advisory body for the selection of ordinands, not necessarily to reject candidates who were practising homosexuals had appeared in a Sunday newspaper, and the Chief Secretary of ACCM was reported to have said that the policy would continue until the Synod decided that it should change. This led to a preliminary skirmish the night before the main debate, when the Bishop of Bristol (Rogerson) explained that ACCM made recommendations to Diocesan Bishops who decided such questions, but that there could be a difference between 'homosexual' and 'practising homosexual', the adjective being added in the press reports.

Higton's motion read as follows:

This synod reaffirms the biblical standard, given for the well-being of society:

(i) that sexual intercourse should take place only between a man and a woman who are married to each other;

(ii) that fornication, adultery and homosexual acts are sinful in all circumstances;

(iii) that Christian leaders are called to be exemplary in all spheres of morality, including sexual morality, as a condition of being appointed to or remaining in office;

and calls upon the Church to show Christ-like compassion to those who have fallen into sexual sin, encouraging them to repent and receive absolution, and offering the ministry of healing to all who suffer physically or emotionally as a result of such sin.

It was clear from Mr Higton's opening remarks that his motion implied more than a rejection of the Gloucester Report, about which, of course, the Synod had never declared a decision:

Today the nation and the world are going to make a decision, not about sexual morality but about the credibility of the General Synod and of the Church of England. Whatever decision we take will send out a powerful message, either that the Church is courageously true to its biblical and traditional foundations or that it is not.[7]

Much of the arguments of the speech that followed depended on points made in a booklet, *Sexuality and the Church*, published by ABWON in preparation for the debate, and edited by Tony Higton.[8] The booklet was a collection of brief specialist essays by well-known Evangelical scholars covering the usual topics, the early church, the causes of homosexuality, the Gloucester Report, the 1981 Synod debate, and the biblical attitudes to hetero- and homo-sexuality, all from a conservative viewpoint. This booklet had been circulated to Synod members in advance, and Higton supplemented it largely with anecdotes and reported conversations with a range of people who had told him how disturbed they were about alleged homosexual activities among clergy, in Theological Colleges and schools. Higton argued that these immoral practices had to be dealt with in the life of the church before it could speak to the nation.

The debate that followed had three elements. First, although Higton's motion referred to fornication and adultery as well as homosexual acts, his own speech was focussed almost entirely on the third subject, and it was clear that no one wished to spend much time on the earlier two. With the television cameras very obviously present, it was not the moment for a general winge about sexual permissiveness. Second, with the Bishop of Chester's amendment already on the order paper, and known to have the support of the

House of Bishops, it was virtually certain that his motion or some variant form of it would be accepted (Synodical procedure allows for voting by Houses if requested), and then a motion has to pass in all three Houses. The Bishops could thus stop Higton's motion by preferring their own, and the chances were that the Clergy and Lay Houses would agree. So, procedurally, the central element of the debate was whether Chester's wording would find more favour than Higton's.

The basic difference between them was that Higton's second clause included fornication, adultery and homosexual acts as 'sinful in all circumstances', whereas the Chester amendment separated adultery and fornication, (clause two) from homosexual *genital* acts, (clause three) and seemed to distinguish them significantly. The heterosexual offences were described as being sins against the ideal that sexual intercourse belongs properly within a permanent married relationship (clause two), while homosexual genital acts were said to also fall short of this ideal (clause three).

The Bishop of London (Graham Leonard) was quick to point out the significance of the different wording in the clauses:

> If I am asked whether fornication, adultery or homosexual genital acts are sinful, I say as a Christian, in faithfulness to Our Lord and to scripture, that they are. I have done so in the past, in spite of the fact that some of us are constantly accused of being silent, and I will continue to do so in the future. They are instances of that disordering of human activity which springs from disobedience to God and to the divine ordering of creation. I believe that Our Lord makes this quite clear, in his own teaching and in the way in which he fulfils the teaching of the Old Testament.
>
> I would like to be able to support the Bishop of Chester's amendment, but I cannot, I am afraid, go with him in making clear judgments about fornication and adultery and a weaker judgment about homosexual genital acts. It will, I believe, be seen by the world as evading the issue, and what I say is borne out in this morning's papers. It may be that if Dr Forster's amendment is carried, that would make a great deal of difference to the Bishop's amendment. But further, the Bishop's amendment does not make clear whether these homosexual genital acts fall short of the ideal because of lack of fidelity, as in the case of adultery, or because they are sinful in themselves.[9]

The third element in the debate was a forlorn attempt to replace the condemnation of Higton, and the milder form of it in Chester's amendment by a general motion stressed permanency and commitment in sexual relationships, warning Christians of the dangers of sexual promiscuity, hetero- or homo-sexual, and asking for well-informed Christian education. This amendment was put down by the Rev. Malcolm Johnson, reflecting the views of LGCM:

> This motion seems to me to be a sort of moral M1, an open road, a motorway, down which we are being invited to drive at speed, recklessly knocking down everyone in the way and particularly those who are most vulnerable in our society. So we hit the single parent with condemnation and calumny; we injure the divorced; we maim the remarried, for in biblical terms they are adulterers. Many in this Synod and beyond have fought hard to recognise second marriages – how can we now say that adultery is sinful in all circumstances? Then finally we knock homosexuals into the gutter, for that is, I believe, the hidden agenda of this motion, once again to heap abuse on a minority group who in my view have suffered enough at the Church's hands. This motion is a negative piece of work, lacking in faith, lacking in hope and lacking in love.
>
> It is negative because it does not speak to the real world; it addresses only the first-time married and the promiscuous, and in the middle are many people seeking guidance. I believe that my amendment gives it. It is negative because it is aimed solely at those who fully accept the Christian ideal, so it can hardly be said to be for 'the well-being of society' since the majority are not committed Christian believers. It is negative because it refuses to face facts and denies the splendid variety of God's creation. Leaving aside all those who are branded as so-called adulterers and fornicators, it is a fact that approximately four per cent of our population, a larger number than the ethnic minorities, are exclusively or predominantly homosexual, about two and a half million people in the United Kingdom – far too large a number to be the result of a deficient upbringing or learned behaviour – and the vast majority of these people are not called to celibacy nor are they capable of it.
>
> Why can we not accept the fact that homosexuals will, by their nature, want to form same-sex relationships and will need positive guidance from us as they do so? I believe that my amendment offers that guidance, with its encouragement of stability, commitment and permanence in all relationships. Today we are faced, as we well know, with the scourge of AIDS, which demands a positive, helpful response from Christians. This motion obviously wants to combat promiscuity but, as it denies good, stable relationships, it will have the opposite effect. It is no good saying that homosexuals are promiscuous; we must ask why they are promiscuous. And if they have been given negative advice for two thousand years they have no guidelines except 'Stop it'.

Why are we frightened of opening our eyes to see the splendid variety of God's creation? He has made us black, brown, white, male, female, heterosexual, homosexual, tall, short, fat, thin, Thatchers, Kinnocks, Holloways, Brindleys. Blessed be God! When I was in America recently I sent to see the film *Maurice*, which is by the same team as did *A Room with a View* – and I hope that members will go and see it. It describes the tentative progress of a gay man towards self-realisation in Edwardian England, and so you can imagine the pain. The one line that had the American audience rocking with laughter and applauding – I gather the same is true in London – was E. M. Forster's immortal phrase, 'The English have always been disinclined to accept human nature'.

I do not understand why we cannot agree to disagree on this issue as we do on many others. Some priests marry divorced people in church, some do not. Some Christians agree with the ordination of women, some do not. Some support the Gloucester report in saying that there are circumstances in which a homosexual relationship can be accepted, some do not. Can we not in this time of transition agree to disagree?[10]

Malcolm Johnson's speech (of which only part is quoted above) was probably the most adequate declaration of the case for the recognition of the homosexual life-style made in either the 1981 or the 1987 debate, and it was listened to with respect but not much support. Tony Higton resisted it successfully,but with little patience for the argument, preferring to remind Synod that Johnson was Vicar of the church were LGCM had its headquarters, and quoting from some of the literature to be found there. Johnson's amendment was lost, 46 members in favour, 325 against.

The next speaker was the Archbishop Runcie, cooling tension by reminding the Synod that we all depend on the mercy of God:

There is a feeling that the Church has gone soft on the moral education of the nation. The message that we have to convey, and sometimes have failed to convey, is that the commandments of God are given to us for our true happiness. Jesus taught that the only right use of sex was in marriage. To many modern-minded people, this seems a harsh doctrine, but it is founded on a deep understanding of the true nature of the sexual act.

Homosexuality is more difficult. I cannot accept the extreme claim that homosexual unions are simply alternative lifestyles to Christian marriage. I do not deny, and cannot, that homosexual acts are condemned in the biblical and Christian tradition. It is our duty to teach the Christian ideal to our children and not to confuse them with options. But while there are both homosexual and heterosexual people whose conduct is undisciplined, self-centred and out of control, questions arise over our response to homosexuals who are seeking to behave responsibly towards other people, who are not sleeping around, not molesting children, not breaking up other people's marriages and friendships. In the face of much cruel prejudice, I want to insist that to be homosexual by nature is to be a full human being, that homosexuals have human rights like the rest of us. We need to listen to what such homosexuals say about their situation.

It seems to me that so serious a matter ought not to be dealt with by a single word within a composite motion, particularly when a report is under very careful preparation. There is a danger that we shall treat this whole matter as a choice between two lobbies. Lobbies do not like having to face up to complexities. Lobbies have their place, but the Church of England cannot be taken over by them. There is no escape from the need for reasoned, persistent, patient work on the issues.

The discipline of the clergy is very much at the heart of the life of the House of Bishops, and we have given, and are giving, particular thought to those with homosexual orientation. I do not believe that we need more legislation; rather, I believe that clergy behaviour is best left to their fathers in God within the present terms of the law.[11]

The Archbishop had given clear indication of his support to the amendment proposed by the Bishop of Chester (Michael Baughen). Baughen had been previously Rector of All Souls Church, Langham Place, the chief Evangelical Church in London. He was therefore able to speak with some confidence of success, and his main task was to explain that his wording was not soft, but based on a proper biblical exegesis:

My amendment moves the homosexual reference separately and specifies homosexual genital acts rather than Mr Higton's vaguer 'homosexual acts'. It does so because that is the biblical word; that is what it is referring to, particularly in I Corinthians 6 and Romans 1. In I Corinthians 5, immorality, greed and theft receive condemnation. They are described as wickedness and have judgment by the Church, as Mr Higton mentioned. But homosexual genital acts are not mentioned in I Corinthians 5. In I Corinthians 6, where they are included, the terms change. Those who do these things are called 'unrighteous'. The Greek word *planasthe* is used, meaning to 'wander away from'. The terms indicate a denial or a falling short of God's righteousness, and the doers of these things do not inherit the kingdom of God. Similarly in Romans 1.27 homosexual genital acts are called 'error' in our English translations and, again it is the same Greek word – *planais*, 'wandering away'. The force of it there is not that they are simply doing what is natural to them but that they have exchanged God's intention in nature for what is unnatural: they fall short of God's ideal. It is, in St Paul's words, 'living a lie', and, biologically, homosexual genital acts, like anal intercourse in marriage, are always a lie and a deception.

My amendment uses 'fall short' to be true to these scriptures but also to express love, sadness, sensitivity and understanding. The rich young man in Matthew 19 verse 20 fell short of God's ideal. Jesus told him what to do and was not deflected by the man's sorrow. Wrong was identified but was expressed with deep understanding. That is the precise balance that I have sought to achieve in this amendment.

While having no sympathy whatever with the flagrant promotion of homosexual lifestyles which draws many into its activities who are not orientated that way, we must recognise the enormous pressures of sexual urges in those who are genuinely and strongly homosexually orientated, not by their own action. They cannot choose marriage or to sin in adultery. If they 'burn', as St Paul puts it, they cannot marry. Those who pounce on the words 'fall short' here as weaker than 'sin' should see the 'also' in the sentence which links it to 'sin' in the previous sentence, and thus to the same need for repentance and compassion. It is not, I underline, a weaker expression but a more gentle one, fully in the spirit of Romans 3 verse 23, 'All having sinned and come short of the glory of God'.[12] (Synod Report pp. 930–2)

Despite the assurance by Baughen that the word 'also' in clause 3 linked with 'sin' in the previous clause, there was clearly some anxiety among synod members that the expression to 'fall short of this ideal' without qualification could be interpreted as giving of some measure of tolerant acceptance to homosexual behaviour. The additional words in clause two, that fornication and adultery required repentance and compassion were a clearer expression of the gospel. So a further amendment was put by Dr Forster of Durham to include these extra words also in clause 3. This was accepted, and the motion was put, the chairman ordering a count of the whole Synod, with the following result: Ayes 403, Noes 8, Abstentions 13. The motion was therefore carried, in the following amended form:

This Synod affirms that the biblical and traditional teaching on chastity and fidelity in personal relationships is a response to, and expression of, God's love for each one of us, and in particular affirms:

(1) that sexual intercourse is an act of total commitment which belongs properly within a permanent married relationship.,

(2) that fornication and adultery are sins against this ideal, and are to be met by a call to repentance and the exercise of compassion,

(3) that homosexual genital acts also fall short of this ideal, and are likewise to be met by a call to repentance and the exercise of compassion,

(4) that all Christians are called to be exemplary in all spheres of morality, including sexual morality, and that holiness of life is particularly required of Christian leaders.[13]

The outcome of this debate was a claim of victory by both sides. Tony Higton claimed in a post-debate revision of his booklet *Sexuality and the Church* that the Synod voted by a ninety-eight per cent majority that fornication, adultery, and homosexual acts are wrong, and are to be met by a call to repentance, adding the rider that 'the call for repentance necessarily implies homosexual acts are sinful'. Some press and television reporting at the time gave a contrary impression, presumably because they rightly sensed that the main intention of the Bishop of Chester's motion had been to avoid the stark wording which brought together all three offences as equally and in all circumstances sinful. It seemed that Chester's success left the Synod committed to a milder and gentler judgment – falling short of the ideal.

The use of the word 'ideal' in this motion was *prima facie* attractive, but in fact it has its difficulties. When Bishop Baughen gave his exegesis of '*planasthe*' and '*planais*' as a wandering away from God's truth it was clear that he supported the standard interpretation. St Paul, of course had used the words judgmentally. Those who succumbed to idolatry were deceived in their minds and dishonoured God in their bodies. To mitigate the severity of this, Baughen turned to Romans 3.23, where Paul condemns Jews and Gentiles alike for falling short of *the glory of God*. That prepares for the gospel of grace. But Baughen also said that homosexual acts fell short of God's 'ideal', and this was a conceptual shift. The word ideal does not appear in the Bible. It comes from Greek philosophy, where Plato and others use the concept to describe mankind's moral striving towards a perfection not to be achieved in this life.

Baughen talked about the ideal of heterosexual marriage, clearly enough, but in ordinary English speech, to say something falls short of an ideal suggests tolerance. In the circumstances, we say, it is not ideal, but the best that can be managed, and that probably is what many liberal people, including perhaps some Synod members think about homosexual behaviour in stable relationships. Obviously, Baughen's attempt at compassion was not meant to go that far, but the use of the word 'ideal' may have led some people to think it did, especially if they had not followed closely his exegesis of the Greek words in Romans 1 and I Corinthians 6. It is never easy to disentangle the final steps of amendment and re-amendment at the end of a Synod debate, and perhaps the effect of Forster's addition was not fully appreciated at the time. Taken as a whole, as it appears in the Official Report, the finally approved motion admits of Higton's interpretation. The tantalizing question remains whether or not most members of the Synod intended that meaning. It is possible that some did not. Tense debates before television cameras are an unsatisfactory way of sorting out complex moral questions.

Whatever differences in interpretation there may have been of the 1987 Synod Motion, it was clear that the result was a firm repudiation of homosexual genital acts. The 1979 Gloucester Report proposals appeared dead and buried, and it remains to be seen whether or not the issue can be raised again in Synod in the next few years. A strong argument that it should be is presented in the recent pamphlet *Homosexuality and a Pastoral Church* by Canon Eric James,[14] on the grounds that the 1987 debate was conducted without prior discussion in the church at large. This discussion, he argues, should have been based on the Gloucester Report, which has been allowed to go out of print. While it is true that by using the Private Members' motion procedure, Tony Higton was able to bypass the normal method of bringing controversial matters to the Synod based on carefully prepared reports, it seems unlikely at present that Synod will want to discuss this subject again in the near future. It may be that the House of Bishops will have more to say when they have mulled over the Osborne Report, but the Methodist Conference in England and the General Convention in America may tackle it earlier.

The Government View of Sex Education in Schools, 1987

In the early autumn of 1987, while the General Synod Business subcommittee were recognizing that the Higton motion would have to be debated at the November meeting, Her Majesty's Government Department of Education and Science, across the road so to speak, were putting the finishing touches to a new set of guidelines for sex education at school. When published in September 1987, they caused something of a stir by the recommendation that there should be no advocacy of homosexual behaviour in school teaching. The background to this guideline was the evident fact that some local authorities had felt it right to include the subject of homosexuality in the sex education syllabus, though how it was dealt with in the classroom remains largely a matter of hearsay. Obviously, children would encounter references to homosexual behaviour in the course of daily life, and some objective teaching about it was desirable, to help them place it in context and discourage unnecessary or excessive homophobia. But some people felt the wording of the DES paper was too negative, and ignored gay rights. The guidelines were followed by a clause (28) in the Local Government Act intended to discourage Local Authorities from spending rate payers' money on other programmes which appeared to promote Gay Lib convictions.

The Government guidelines stress the key role of parents in sex education, but recognize that schools also have a duty. Under the 1986 Act, sex education is the responsibility of the School Governing Body, and Local Education Authorities have a duty to ensure pupils give 'due regard to moral considerations and the value of family life'. Pupils need to know the law as it affects sexual relations. Schools cannot avoid controversial subjects such as contraception and abortion, and balanced information and the recognition of ethical questions are needed here. Schools founded on religious principles will want their beliefs to affect the way these subjects are presented in the classroom. The guidelines then turn to the subject of homosexuality:

> There is no place in any circumstances for teaching which advocates homosexual behaviour, which presents it as the 'norm', or which encourages homosexual experimentation by pupils. Indeed, encouraging or procuring homosexual acts by pupils who are under age of consent is a criminal offence. It must also be recognized that for many people including members of various religious faiths, homosexual practice is not morally acceptable and deep offence may be caused to them if the subject is not handled with sensitivity by teachers if discussed in the classroom.

Although these guidelines do not have the force of law they do have the power of the Secretary of State and the DES behind them. Clause 28 of the Local Government Act is firmly expressed:

> A local authority shall not promote the teaching in any maintained school of the acceptability of homosexuality as a pretended family relationship.

However, some have suggested that because school governors are responsible for school programmes the Act technically does not apply to them. It was clear, however, that HMG intended to prevent any effort by local authorities in school which might be understood as promoting homosexuality.

There was a good deal of discussion of the DES guidelines and Clause 28 of the Local Government Act in Parliament and the media and it would have all been much in the minds of the Synod members at the time of the Higton debate. The repudiation of any homosexual propaganda was not only a sign of the swing away from tolerance in public opinion of which the Government was properly aware; it was also a reminder that the Church of England was being frequently criticized by Members of Parliament, either for refusing to give a moral leadership to the nation, (cf. Higton's speech) or for becoming too closely involved in political matters. The smell of disestablishment was uneasily in the air, and it was no moment for Synod to pass any motion which would further strain church and state relations.

To help those responsible for church schools, in January 1988, the Synod's Board of Education produced a Memorandum of Guidelines for Church School Governors on Sex Education. The Memorandum is based on the belief that church schools will need to include positive provision for sex education. It notes that dioceses may produce their own guidelines. It makes two crucial points. The first is the need for a caring climate in the school. 'Regardless of background, behaviour, and sexual orientation pupils are to be caringly accepted within the "Church School".' The second is to emphasize the importance of the moral climate for such education. Governors must exercise their responsibilities so that sex education is given in the school within a 'moral, family oriented and Christian framework'. It concludes with a valuable checklist of questions for Governors.

Some Dioceses produced their own guides. The London Diocesan Board for Schools has produced a Memorandum for Teachers and Governors in Church Schools on Lifestyles and Sexual Orientations. This Memorandum begins by acknowledging the spectrum of sexual orientation in society and the position of homosexual people in the law and in our culture. It proceeds to note the historic rejection of homosexuality by the church and notes a more open attitude in recent times. The Memorandum believes that 'any good education programme must include some treatment of homosexual relationships alongside any treatment of heterosexual relationships'. Material needs to be accurate and objective. It seeks to strike a careful balance in style and approach. 'Since heterosexuality is the norm and the great majority of children will incline to it, attempts by extremists to persuade them that homosexuality is preferable should not be encouraged. On the other hand actions and attitudes that make homosexuals feel inferior, second class citizens, and attempts to persuade them to make an effort to be different are equally undesirable. The aim should be to 'help pupils accept themselves for who they are.' . . . But there is of course, a distinction to be made between describing equal value to all people as such, whatever their orientation or activities, and ascribing equal validity to the expression of different kinds of relationships.'

The Lambeth Conference, 1988

The Synod vote in favour of the Chester amendment in the 1987 debate was very large, and despite the later uncertainty that everyone intended quite what they had voted for, it was widely regarded at the time as the best possible resolution of a difficult situation, especially as the 'Osborne' group were already well into their work. However, the surrounding media interest in the debate itself, and the inevitable consequence of widely disseminated simplistic impressions of what was involved almost certainly influenced the somewhat hasty debate about homosexuality at the Lambeth Conference in August 1988. Those parts of the Official Report from the Section on Christianity and the Social Order, and the Resolutions of the Conference, which deal with homosexuality and AIDS are quoted verbatim below.

When the draft of the Report and Resolution were circulated to members of the Conference in preparation for the final approval stage in plenary session, Bishop Paul Moore of New York tried to add an extra clause which would press for the elimination in each Province of the Anglican Communion of discrimination against homosexual persons and to support their human rights. Those Lambeth bishops who were familiar with the present state of the civil law on this matter in some American States, and how it was affecting the teaching profession, as Clause 28 was in England, readily understood the point he was making. But it was soon clear that among Africans particularly, but also among others, it was thought the wording Moore suggested would be seriously misunderstood in their dioceses. Several attempts to amend the words were made, along the lines of the Chester motion in the English Synod, but time was too short for agreement to be found, and Moore's motion did not survive.

The Conference Report, *The Truth Shall Make you Free*,[15] discussed homosexuality in Section Four – 'Christianity and the Social Order', under the sub-heading 'Sexual Orientation':

> Despite its basic assertions about marriage and family, there is much confusion in the area of the Church's doctrine and teaching about sexuality. *Transforming Families and Communities* witnesses to this on the basis of extensive Communion-wide consultations. Thus, on the vexed question of sexuality, it reports:
>
>> The question of sexual orientation is a complex one which the Church is still grappling with: many Provinces have traditionally maintained that homosexuality is a sin whilst others are responding differently to the issue. As sexuality is an aspect of life which goes to the very heart of human identity and society it is a pastorally sensitive issue which requires further study and

reflection by Church leadership. (Note: This quotation is from a report about families prepared in 1987 for the Lambeth Conference, publ: ACC.)[16]

We recognize that this issue remains unresolved, and we welcome the fact that study is continuing. We believe that the Church should therefore give active encouragement to biological, genetic, and psychological research, and consider these scientific studies as they contribute to our understanding of the subject in the light of Scripture.

Further study is also needed of the socio-cultural factors which contribute to the differing attitudes towards homosexuality, mentioned above, in the various Provinces of our Church. We continue to encourage dialogue with, and pastoral concern for persons of homosexual orientation within the Family of Christ.[17]

The Report also deals with sexual abuse, noting:

In some African and Asian countries represented among us, the traditional cultures have been more supportive of families, and fewer problems of both heterosexual and homosexual abuse have appeared. The Church everywhere can approach these problems positively by acting to strengthen family structures and the bonds of marriage. Each diocese should have a commission on family life that would initiate appropriate preventative programmes.[18]

The problem of AIDS is discussed next in the Report at some length as A MAJOR THREAT, and the church is advised not to wait until different theological presuppositions and different interpretations of scripture are settled before bringing the compassion of Christ and the renewal of the Holy Spirit to those in need and distress:

It is important to distinguish between the theological arguments about the way in which the disease is acquired and those which relate to pastoral response. To confuse the two may well identify the spread of AIDS with homosexual practices (despite the fact that in many countries the virus is spread in heterosexual relations) and with drug abuse. In this way, important factors affecting the spread of the disease – such as poverty, war and deprivation – are ignored. AIDS exposes the vulnerable places and people in our society, and our negligence towards our neighbours. AIDS is a challenge to the Church and the whole of society.

Disease of any kind poses difficult theological questions. Christians believe that God created a world that is good. It is too simple to suggest that all disease is the result of sin, although some patterns of behaviour can be identified as likely to lead to sickness of mind or body, or both. AIDS has been especially associated by some with the 'judgement of God', but there is no more reason to think of it in these terms than any other disease, though the social factors which have encouraged its spread point to specific problems in all societies. It requires a special sensitivity in pastoral care to exhibit God's love to persons living with AIDS who need not only the assurance of God's love and close identification with them in their suffering, but the immediacy and reassurance of physical human contact in their inevitable fear. The ministry of God's healing will need to be intense, accepting, and full of hope for the ultimate future of the individual. The Church needs to develop specific forms of prayer and liturgical rites to assist in the ministry to those living with AIDS. Examples are available in the Dioceses of New York, California and Los Angeles.

AIDS has reinforced the need for human beings to observe faithfulness and permanence in sexual relationships, as the Christian Church has always taught. Nevertheless, such an approach to human relationships is by no means universal. In the present state of emergency the Church should support those governments and medical agencies seeking to prevent the spread of AIDS by making clean needles available to certain drug users and encouraging the use of condoms in both heterosexual and homosexual activities. Such support should be given in a way which makes it clear that the Church is not condoning the practices involved.

People with AIDS, their families and friends, will experience a wide range of emotional response to the circumstances in which they find themselves. Among these emotions, anger, outrage, guilt, remorse, recrimination and a sense of injustice are likely to be dominant. In its supportive ministry the Church will need to offer the good news of God's loving acceptance and forgiveness of every human being and encourage the same loving response in others. In particular, church members will need to be trained to understand and express this love in word and action.[19]

The Conference passed the following resolution:

Human Rights for Those of Homosexual Orientation

1. Reaffirms the statement of the Lambeth Conference of 1978 on homosexuality, recognising the continuing need in the next decade for 'deep and dispassionate study of the question of homosexuality, which would take seriously both the teaching of Scripture and the results of scientific and medical research'.

2. Urges such study and reflection to take account of biological, genetic and psychological research being undertaken by other

agencies, and the socio-cultural factors that lead to the different attitudes in the Provinces of our Communion.

3. Calls each Province to reassess, in the light of such study and because of our concern for human rights, its care for and attitude towards persons of homosexual orientation.[20]

In the second clause of this resolution, reference is made to the 'socio-political factors that lead to the different attitudes', and this difference was clearly evident in the discussion. As its number reveals, this Resolution was a late addition, the main resolutions from Section Four being grouped together between twenty-four, concerning Palestine and Israel and forty concerning militarism etc. Resolution twenty-nine concerns AIDS, and this includes an affirmation of the biblical teaching that sexual intercourse is an act of total commitment which belongs properly within a permanent married relationship (2D. Rep. p. 222). This is the same wording as appeared in the English General Synod motion of 1987, and at one stage in the Lambeth Conference it seemed likely that the subject of homosexual behaviour would not be included in a separate resolution, being adequately dealt with in the Report of Section Four, and by implication in this affirmation of Resolution twenty-nine. In the event, the conviction held by some Bishops that the Conference should say something positive about Homosexual Rights (and there was a LGCM lobby asking for that) was matched by the anxiety of others, notably from Africa and Australia that the traditional attitude should be re-asserted. It was clear that reports suggesting the Church of England was permissive about this had spread far abroad, so Resolution sixty-four accurately reflected the Bishops' reluctance to be embroiled in anything more divisive than their agreement to further study of 1978.

The American Episcopal Church: General Convention Resolutions

The General Convention has had a series of reports to consider and pass resolutions which show some similarity to those of the English Anglican Synod and the Lambeth Conference, reflecting the same shifts of opinion. As a brief guide, the official texts of the resolutions of 1976, 1979 and 1989 are given, and it will be noted that further work is in progress.

1976: Human sexuality – homosexuals are children of God

The House of Deputies 'Resolved, the House of Bishops concurring, that it is the sense of this General Convention that homosexual persons are children of God who have a full and equal claim with all other persons upon the love, acceptance, and pastoral concern and care of the Church.'

1979

The House of Bishops resolved as follows:

Whereas, we are conscious of the mystery of human sexuality and how deeply personal matters related to human sexuality are, making it most difficult to arrive at comprehensive and agreed-upon statements in these matters; and

Whereas, we are aware that under the guidance of the Holy Spirit the Church must continue to study these matters in relationship to Holy Scripture, Christian faith and tradition, and growing insights; and

Whereas, the Sixty-fifth General Convention recognized '. . . that homosexual persons are children of God who have a full and equal claim with all other persons upon the love, acceptance, and pastoral concern and care of the Church . . .'; and

Whereas, all the clergy and laity of the Church are expected to render compassionate and understanding pastoral care to one another and to all persons; therefore be it

Resolved, the House of Deputies concurring, That the Sixty-sixth General Convention receive with gratitude and appreciation the Report and Recommendations of its Standing Commission on Human Affairs and Health with special reference to the requested study of the matter of ordination of homosexual persons; and be it further

Resolved, the House of Deputies concurring, That this General Convention recommend to Bishops, Pastors, Vestries, Commissions on Ministry and Standing Committees, the following considerations as they continue to exercise their proper canonical functions in the selection and approval of persons for ordination:

1. There are many human conditions, some of them in the area of sexuality, which bear upon a person's suitability for ordination;

2. Every ordinand is expected to lead a life which is 'a wholesome example to all people' (*Book of Common Prayer*, pp. 517, 532, 544). There should be no barrier to the ordination of qualified persons of either heterosexual or homosexual orientation whose behaviour the Church considers wholesome;

3. We re-affirm the traditional teaching of the Church on marriage, marital fidelity and sexual chastity as the standard of Christian sexual morality. Candidates for ordination are expected to conform to this standard. Therefore, we believe it is not appropriate for this Church to ordain a practicing homosexual, or any person who is engaged in heterosexual relations outside of marriage.

The motion carried by a vote of ninety-nine to thirty-four.

General Convention 1989

Resolution on Human Sexuality:

> *Resolved*, The House of Bishops concurring, that this Sixty-ninth General Convention affirms that the Biblical and traditional teaching on chastity and fidelity in personal relationships is a response to, and an expression of, God's love for each one of us; and that all Christians are called to be exemplary in all spheres of morality, including sexual morality; and that holiness in life is particularly required of Christian leaders. In this context, be it further,

> *Resolved*, that this Convention, responsive to the call of the Standing Commission on Human Affairs and Health, 'to find a non-judgmental occasion to listen and talk,' and in the spirit of the Presiding Bishop's statement that 'there will be no outcasts in this church,' strongly urges each diocese and congregation to provide opportunities for open dialogue on human sexuality, in which we as members of this Church, both heterosexual and homosexual, may study, pray, listen to and share our convictions and concerns, our search for stable, loving and committed relationships, and our journey toward wholeness and holiness; and be it further

> *Resolved*, that the accepted sources of authority for Christians, namely Scripture, tradition, reason and experience, supplemented by the 1976, 1979, 1982 and 1985 statements from the General Convention on human sexuality, the resolution adopted by the General Synod of the Church of England in November 1987, the 1988 Report of the Standing Commission on Human Affairs and Health, and ongoing scientific research be commended for use in this dialogue; and be it further

> *Resolved*, that each diocese report its findings and experiences to the Standing Commission on Human Affairs and Health no later than December 1990 and that the Standing Commission evaluate the reports and produce a composite report for presentation to the Seventieth General Convention.

Postscript

At the end of this very long history one can say that the 'eighties' has proved a disappointing decade to those who hoped at the beginning of it that the Gloucester Report and similar pleas would inaugurate a more courteous era for gay Christians. The Pastoral Letter from the Vatican, the outcome of the General Synod debate on the 'Higton' motion debate, the anxious reaction to Bishop Paul Moore's private motion at the 1988 Lambeth Conference, the banishment of the Gay Christian Movement from their office in St Botolph's Church, and the hesitation in the House of Bishops (and in the Board of Social Responsibility) that the Osborne Report should be published, all show that it has not yet arrived. The situation outside the church is also threatening a shift towards intolerance. With the passing of Clause twenty-eight, and the regulations for the Civil Service recruitment to the Diplomatic Service stating firmly 'Homosexuality, even if acknowledged, is a bar to employment in the Diplomatic Service', we seem to be back where the Wolfenden Committee started.

The prospect for gay men and women in the nineties is not all gloom. Some Christian organizations follow the pattern of the British Council of Churches in making it clear that sexual orientation is not a relevant matter for recruiting staff. For the ministry, that may also be true, but not if the prospective minister admits to having a permanent relationship with a partner. At least we can say that the institution of pederasty is not now the problem it was for St Paul and the early church Fathers. But there are frequent reports of the revival of child homosexual prostitution in some parts of the world, and the work of Josephine Butler may need to be done again, though this time without, please, hasty and clumsy legislation. By education, especially at local level, the Christian congregations need to recover their confidence that the church has no outcasts.

PART FIVE

9

The Church with a Human Face

Introduction

Suppose we forget for a moment all that has gone before and start again. Suppose we know little of church history, have forgotten where we last put our Bibles, find Synods a bit of a bore, and never read the church newspapers, but are thinking about our friend Mike, who is gay. Mike works with us in the office, and when he first came we noticed quite quickly that he was a bit different. The girls in the typing pool were naturally far faster, in their intuitive way, and knew at once he was of no interest to them. There was nothing objectionable about him of course, indeed he was above average in many ways that count in an office, but they just knew he could never be their 'Mr Right'.

But Mike became a friend, dropped in to supper occasionally, and eventually earned our family's highest mark of approval, he came to Sunday lunch. And then, with the omnibus edition of 'Neighbours' on the telly, and Match of the Day, well, he stayed to tea. The question came to mind – dare we ask him to come to the evening service at our local church. No, he says, he has nothing fixed for the evening, but he'd rather not. It's a long story, he says sadly, but I'm waiting to find a church with a human face.

This little parable tries to say what I'm after in this chapter. I borrow the title from the English translation of a book about ministry by the Dutch Catholic theologian, Edward Schillebeeckx,[1] not because he says anything much about morality in it, but because I share his view about ministry in the sense of my parable. A gay person, like Mike, asks that the church minister to him, that is serve him in his needs as well as proclaim to him the imperishable riches of the gospel and lift him up to God in worship. If he is ministered to, Mike may come to the point of offering himself as a minister of that same church and gospel, a development we come to later. We cannot linger with this simple parable, to explain what exactly might have put Mike off church in the past, but if you have read so far, it is easy to guess. To

Mike, and so many gay men and women past and present, the church has not turned a human face.

Perhaps that begs the question, for we have seen all along that the problem is less with humanity, more with religious morality. Do you remember Sydney Carter's bitter protest song of the sixties?

It is God they ought to crucify instead of you and me

cries the thief from the cross to Jesus, misunderstanding Good Friday. When the church burnt homosexuals in the Middle Ages could they not cry the same. It is necessary, before we start analysing our morality to get this cry into our guts. We don't burn gay people anymore, but even in 1989 we turn them out of our churches, and Mike is not prepared to take that risk. Not, of course, that we actually say 'don't come with us into the building', but if he wants to be a member in good standing, there will be conditions implied for him as a homosexual which we as heterosexuals do not have to face. To avoid those special conditions, he will have to conceal part of the truth about himself, a strange situation in a community which claims to be open to all.

Marshalling the Arguments

At the end of the previous chapter it had become clear that after a decade of indecision, the Church of England has through its General Synod refused to endorse any significant departure from the traditional Christian teaching that homosexual behaviour is sinful. The Vatican statement of 1986 takes the same position, and no other major Christian church has officially departed from it. To the majority of Christians, the outcome has been probably welcome; amidst much moral uncertainty, on one issue at least, the church has remained faithful to scripture and its own teaching through the ages. To a minority, including but extending far beyond those who are responsible gay Christians, the integrity of the church has been again compromised by clinging to an outmoded and legalistic ethic, when the demand of the Spirit is to present to the world a church with a human face.

If that is a correct description of the way the issue divides Christians, before analysing the arguments on both sides in some detail, it may be helpful to set out the case against change and the case for change in a brief systematic way.

(a) Against change

(i) Scripture. A careful analysis of the relevant scriptural texts has not produced any weighty support for the exegesis that the texts were

about hospitality or perversion by heterosexual people. The obvious truth that they were, as all scripture is, set down with the information then available about sexuality and in the conceptual models of their times, not ours, has not provided persuasive enough arguments to disregard these texts.

(ii) The continual teaching of the church. Again, despite the strong advocacy of Boswell and others, the evidence that the Christian hostility to homosexual acts was a later development, not part of the churches' original teaching has not been convincingly proved. It is claimed that the evidence from scripture and of the continual teaching of the churches, Catholic and Reformed, are inter-dependent, and consistent, based on the premise that human sexuality finds its only proper genital expression in heterosexual marriage.

(iii) Reason. Although reason might suggest that modern empirical knowledge demands a change of attitude, in fact the standard pattern of thought has been retained to confirm that the obvious biological purpose of intercourse is the procreation of children. It is agreed that human sexuality is correctly understood to be about relationships as well as about children but there is a difference of opinion about the relative importance of these two purposes. Catholics stress that the intention to form a permanent relationship and to procreate (where that is medically possible) both need to be present, while Protestants give greater stress to the intention of a permanent relationship, seeing child-making as a desirable fulfilment of married love, but not essential to a valid commitment, even for fertile couples.

(iv) Medical and psychological research. Most of the research suggests that the homosexual orientation is not deliberately chosen, and cannot readily be changed by treatment or therapy. But because there is a distinction between orientation and action, it is not accepted that a homosexual person *has* to be physically active with his own sex. The long Christian tradition of celibacy or abstinence among hetero-sexual people provides a familiar model for commending a similar restraint on homosexual people. It may be more than mere coin-cidence that the Roman Catholic Church, which has the strongest tradition of unmarried clergy, and of chastity in pursuit of a religious vocation, has been most confident among the churches in keeping the old rule.

These four answers to the question why the churches have not changed their attitude are familiar enough, and may be seen as little more than the old arguments re-iterated, but that is not quite fair. The debate has been serious and prolonged. But the arguments *for* a change in attitude are also serious and cover much the same ground with different conclusions:

(b) For change

(v) The fundamental witness of scripture to the meaning of human sexuality is positive, stressing the basic need for human persons to relate in love, mirroring the caring relationship between God and his creation, between Christ and the church. The dominance of the pro-creative model belongs to early Judaism, and is culturally conditioned by their need to increase population and stabilize family life. The situation is changed by the threat of over-population, and by the fact that heterosexual marriage is highly popular and needs no special protection.

(vi) The consistent tradition of the church's moral teaching is best seen in its development and preservation of certain basic duties of man to man. These basic duties are universal and remain unchanged, and can properly be called natural laws, though in our day the language of Human Rights is more commonly used. Particular appli-cations of these duties emerge as rules or axioms which serve to guide Christians from day to day, but throughout Christian history these rules have been understood as provisional. Basic duties are fixed, rules can be changed if and when they no longer adequately serve the duty that gave rise to their original formulation.

For example, the basic rule of caring for the poor in their com-munity led to the condemnation of usury in Old Testament times, but that condemnation cannot be applied to responsible forms of capitalism. (It may be that the present forms of too easily available credit require a new axiom to protect the poor?) The rule that worship should be decently ordered in Corinth led St Paul to ask the women of Corinth to be silent and wear hats, but this is not of universal application. More important than that trivial example is the changing and in some respects still disputed role of women in a Christian community. The duty of peace making led to the rules of just war as a means of defeating aggression, but the development of nuclear weapons makes these no longer adequate. In the history of the church, therefore, many rules prove to be temporary applications of abiding principles, and the prohibition of homosexual behaviour is a rule of this kind, needing to be changed in the new situation.

(vii) Reason and conscience. Reason is the capacity God gives to human beings to discover and interpret experience. Human reason is essential to the notion of conscience, and orthodox Christian teaching has always been that the dictates of conscience must be followed. The

continuation of the old hostility to homosexual behaviour is contrary to the conscience of many Christians because it ignores the complexity and range of human sexuality as this is now understood. It obviously includes much more than the biological function of continuing the species, and it is unreasonable and inhuman to deny this.

(viii) The distinction between orientation and action is as true for homosexual people as it is for heterosexual people, but the virtues of abstinence and chastity can never be ordered, they are vocations which some heterosexual and some homosexual people are given to enable them to fulfil special callings within the church and for the service of mankind. The creation ordinance is that it is not good for man to be alone, and for the majority obedience to that command is found within marriage. For the homosexual that is not an option, so the nearest alternative, the only way they can obey the command is through a permanent and caring same gender commitment. While the Catholic view in *(iv)* above, requiring a procreative intention, prohibits this, the Protestant test of a morally acceptable relationship as loving permanent commitment could be met by homosexual men or women.

(c) Prejudiced attitudes

In addition to these four replies to the 'against change' arguments, gay Christians allege there are three extra factors in the debate which prejudice attitudes against them. These are:

(ix) Instinctive aversion to homosexual acts. The instinctive heterosexual reaction is to dislike homosexual behaviour, for reasons explained in chapter 2. Even when the homosexual case is put in a calm way, there is an almost intuitive homophobic reaction to it. The dice, one might say, are loaded, and the presumption that homosexual behaviour is mostly in the form of anal intercourse is not easily rebutted, even though it is not approved by many gay couples. Gay Christians suffer from a mistaken identification with other forms of Gay Lib advocacy which are more strident, and often advocate life styles which are promiscuous, and produce publications which Christians find pornographic. Committed gay relationships could witness to the Christian ethic for homosexual people as marriage does among heterosexual couples.

(x) Dislike of the gay scene. Not only because of its difference but because of its supposed and in fact sometimes actual association with political and cultural radicalism, Gay Lib has proved an affront to conventional conservative public opinion, and this has become more

marked in recent years. It is not just a prejudice, it is a symbol of an underlying unease in society about its cohesion and future security. Other special interest groups, such as the Campaign for Nuclear Disarmament, provision for unmarried mothers, etc. all challenge confidence about the stable ordering of society and its government. What was once seen as a mark of a society improving the quality of life among its members by a broader toleration of difference has become inverted. Tolerance, it is supposed, has contributed to the breakdown of order; it has become an agent of instability, a threat to be held at bay. The policy of the Government is inevitably affected by such signs of public unease. An anxious society cannot afford too much liberality.

(xi) Heterosexual guilt. Failure to live up to Christian standards is not confined to homosexual people. The present instability of hetero- sexual marriage is one sign that human relationships are not easy for anyone now that the traditional supports are eroded. Statistics suggest not much difference in the divorce rate between church goers and unbelievers. All fail, and all need mercy. Although officially, mastur- bation is still declared sinful, it is extremely common among hetero- sexual people, and is tolerated even though it is clearly contrary to the procreational ideal. It is illogical, gay people say, to accept this among straight people without much demur, and then damn it among gays. A factor in homophobia, it is argued, is the transference of guilt and sense of failure, using homosexual people as scapegoats.

The cumulative interacting effect of these prejudices make it difficult for a tolerant attitude to gay people to be maintained in the churches at the present time, when there is a set of the tide against 'radicalism', understood as the demand for change. A better meaning of the word is 'back to the roots', and this reflects the intangible but nevertheless strong urge Christians have at the moment to repossess and re-state their central convictions. The world picture is one in which the strong religions are gaining adherents by being distinctive from failing secularism. That distinctiveness cannot, however, be effectively communicated without fresh thought, of a genuinely radical 'back to the roots' kind. As with doctrine, so with morality. One cannot speak now of creation without taking account of modern astronomy and one cannot speak now of Christian sexual morality without taking account of contemporary understandings of relation- ships. Since that seems difficult for some Christians, it is easily assumed that the safer course is to reaffirm the traditional rules, re- iterating them in the old familiar language. To proclaim afresh in each generation the abiding truths of Christian morality in a way that communicates effectively is a different and harder task than just shouting the old slogans loudly. We need to speak clearly, of course, but we need to speak out of our present situation, not from a past one.

Moral Principles and Pastoral Care

Mike's determination to stay out in the cold is the result of what he regards as the church's failure to understand his position, and adjust its rules accordingly. He knows that the Christian churches are unable to resolve the moral problem of homosexual behaviour. Early in this book, I suggested that the main reason for the lack of decision is a clash of loyalties. Loyalty to scripture and the long tradition of the Christian church that homosexual genital acts are sinful, clashes with the recognition in our day that sexuality is about relationships. If homosexual people are to develop an intimate relationship with another person and express love physically, they will have to do that with someone of their own gender. They think the gospel demands more from the Christian churches than an offer of sympathy accompanied by the requirement that homosexual people must practice abstinence.

As any pastor knows, discussing a problem with an already settled solution in mind tends to stultify the interview. To avoid that artificiality, the pastor finds himself listening with a more open mind, and the consequence is an inability to pass judgment. The interview may end with some such agreement as 'While what you are doing is contrary to the Christian ethic, and is not ideal, in the circumstances, it seems to be the best you can manage.' In other words an unhappy compromise is struck between what ought to be done in obedience to the Christian ethic, and what is going to be done in the actual situation. To caricature the outcome, the enquirer goes away saying 'Father said I ought not to, but I may.' In other words, the pastoral advice is logically inconsistent with the moral principle in the sense that permission is being given to break the rule.

Inconsistency of that kind is not unusual in the church, and is seen most obviously in other pastoral problems to do with human relationships. Many people plan marriage after a period of living together, and the minister preparing them for the sacramental union knows that it is pastorally pointless to suggest they separate until they are joined together again in church. Faced with marriage breakdown, similarly, a pastor will quickly sense whether or not there is any real chance of the relationship being revived. If not, he can only say 'marriage is meant to be a life-long commitment, but in the circumstances ...' As a slightly different example, we might take the wartime resistance leader. It is wrong to lie, he may be counselled by the priest, but in the circumstances, you are not obliged to tell the Gestapo all the truth.

Although this seems a similar permission, another and perhaps more sophisticated analysis of it suggests that the clash of loyalties apparent here can be resolved by reckoning that opposing the Gestapo in pursuit of, say, a just war, and saving the life of one's compatriots by refusing to confess is in fact to obey a higher principle than truth telling. In other words, the demands of a secondary principle can be rightly disobeyed in obedience to a higher one.

It is important, of course, and sometimes very difficult, to tease out which principle is actually the higher one in moral puzzles of this kind. At risk of over-simplifying a complex subject, one can say that in most such cases, the fundamental command to love one's neighbour is correctly expressed in the standard commandments. Thus to love is not to murder, not to steal, not to commit adultery. But the whole history of moral philosophy is littered with problems not easily solved in this way. One might say that slavery is unloving, but for most of Christian history it was thought adequate to command masters to be just and gentle with their slaves, not free them. Perhaps that is really an example of obeying an interim rule until the overriding principle of freedom was established. Another example, much debated in mediaeval times was whether it was right to steal in order to escape dying from starvation. The answer was yes, provided that once the thief found work, he must repay the owner, presumably secretly. Even if circumstances demand the breaking of a secondary rule, in pursuit of a higher one, the secondary rule is not thereby made totally redundant. Thus the resistance leader may lie to the Gestapo but not to the Inland Revenue.

Some people see this distinction between primary and secondary principles to be true of the homosexual problem also. The rule that you should abstain from sex outside marriage is secondary to the rule you shall be loving, or put another way, to encourage the basic principle of love is a higher loyalty than to insist on obeying traditional rules concerning homosexual behaviour. As a guide to pastoral practice, this has much to commend it. Permission to break the rules can be pastorally sensitive, and indeed realistic, but it leaves a certain uneasiness in the conscience, and a feeling that something is wrong somewhere. One way out of the difficulty is to regard the permission as temporary. You cannot obey now, but your vocation is to alter the circumstances so that you can, e.g. heterosexual people living together do not break up, they get married. They are not obeying the rule of chastity at the moment, but by marriage they can alter the circumstances and then they will be chaste.

But the analogy is not precise, for the gay person is not asking for forgiveness, nor a temporary turning a blind eye. He or she asks the church for permanent permission to live sexually in the only way open to people like him. Unless there are to be two different rules, one for straights, one for gays, the moral unease persists, and while the churches continue to derive their sexual morality solely from the primary principles of procreation or heterosexual marriage, no real possibility of changing the rules for homosexuals, exists. And Mike, if he happens to have a same sex partner, stays outside the church.

Changing the Rules

The situation is that no major church has found a way of changing the rules without apparently abandoning some essential principle that has to be maintained. In addition to the prejudicial factors listed above, it has to be recognized that the churches' official bodies have not been faced with decisions about the morality of homosexual behaviour in a vacuum. In particular, while the need to be seen as pastorally accepting to homosexual people is not denied, the wholehearted shift from a procreational model of definition for the purpose of human sexuality to one in which the relational model is given predominance or even equal weight has to face the objection that such a shift would be taken to apply not only to homosexual behaviour, but to all aspects of heterosexual behaviour as well.

Obviously, to introduce the 'quality of relationship' test for gay people would open the way to an expectation that heterosexual people could use the same test for their own relationships, and the consequence might be a further loosening of the moral imperatives towards expressing sexuality in terms of chastity and marriage. In fact, of course, the debates about sexual morality in the churches in the fifties and sixties started with an attempt to find a relational model which could accommodate better the mood of the times. This was that the old Christian prohibitions of sex outside marriage, and easy divorce were outmoded, not merely by a change in public attitudes, but by a new and valuable understanding of human nature and sexuality, for which the old restrictive rules were inappropriate.

That attempt did not mean that situationist Christians ceased to be strongly in favour of the virtues of chastity and marriage; it did mean that these virtues were to be seen as expressions of God's love, and not just as traditional rules of the church. The new morality was not merely a surrender to laxity masquerading as permissiveness, it was understood by its most intelligent proponents at the time as a genuine step forward in describing Christian rules as God's way of enhancing the dignity of human life. It was, one might say with hindsight, not the fault of the authors of the 1963 Quaker Report, Bishop John Robinson and Professor Joseph Fletcher etc., that their attempts to raise the standards of sexual morality were popularly misinterpreted as a licence which said 'Love God and do as you like.'

The origin of that slogan was Augustine's maxim *'dilige et quod vis fac'*, best translated as *'love God, and then what you will, do'*, and this was no charter for moral laxity. Coming from him, we should not expect it to be, for the essential meaning of it is that those who choose a life of loving attention to God will be guided by him what they ought to do. To be sure, what they do will always be loving, and that is the first principle, but nothing antinomian is implied. Love leads to the formulation of commandments as axioms or rules which guide a person to see what love usually does in a situation like this, breathing new life into the constraints of a rule-bound morality.

Four Options for the Moral Rule

So far in this discussion, the impression may sometimes have been given that there were only two options open to the churches. Either they must cling tenaciously to the old prohibition of all forms of homosexual behaviour, or they must give permission to those who cannot act heterosexually to follow the consequences of their own orientation and have same gender experiences without qualification. In fact, these two options are at the extreme ends of the spectrum of possible moral attitudes the churches can take. In the public Synodical and similar debates, proponents of one extreme or the other have often succeeded in suggesting that the only alternative to their own view is either total licence or total restriction, while the largely silent majority have wanted to escape from such limited choice, but have found it difficult to express other views with sufficient clarity. It seems to me there are four genuine options, and that only by taking all of them seriously can the churches now make genuine progress. All the options have, of course, been mentioned earlier – it is time to set them out schematically.

The essential difference between the four options set out below lies in the choice made about how to describe the fundamental meaning given to human sexuality. For this fundamental meaning I use the expression 'primary purpose' (a different one in each option) to indicate something stronger than a purely personal preference.

All these four primary purposes have been claimed by Christians to describe the real character or significance of human sexuality as God intends it to be. Further, a primary purpose indicates an 'ought', that is a moral imperative it would be wrong or sinful to ignore, unless after careful reflection conscience dictates otherwise. It follows that the options are in a genuine sense real alternatives which have to be debated, accepted or rejected, but, since they have the character of moral rules or axioms they need not always be mutually exclusive. The difficulty of the debate in the past has so often been that those who hold, for example, Option A, feel obliged to reject all the others, and similarly, those who choose Option D tend to have little respect for Option A. Those holding Options B and C tend to think that their attitudes are broad enough to include the positive aspects of Options A and D.

In fact, of course, in actual human life and experience, we do not find ourselves thinking in such logically tidy ways, and our own perceptions inside a relationship probably include more than one option, or a shift from one to another as circumstances change and develop, hence the tension between moral principle and pastoral care already discussed. Thus, for example, heterosexual people who both have jobs and both expect to continue working after marriage may be well aware of the value of a permanent committed relationship, but be uncertain whether or not they should start a family. Then, two same sex people of middle age who had long hoped to enter a heterosexual marriage and have children may find a permanent companionship which meets their present needs most happily, though it was not what they hoped for earlier on in life. Others again, who have lived together for a while, eventually marry because they wish to become parents, while for some strongly fixed in homosexual identity, the idea of any deep heterosexual commitment is deeply repugnant. Faced with these and other perceptions, a moral theologian will try to find some ordered pattern for the questions to be decided, hence these four options seem to cover the possible alternatives open to us.

Option A: Procreation is the primary purpose of sexuality, to be expressed exclusively in marriage, and children if medically possible.

Option B: Heterosexual relationships are the primary purpose of sexuality, to be expressed in love within marriage, and children if responsibly wanted.

Option C: A loving and sustaining relationship with another human person is the primary purpose of sexuality, and that relationship should be ideally with a person of the opposite gender and grow into a commitment to permanent marriage, and children if wanted.

Option D: A loving and sustaining relationship with another human person is the primary purpose of sexuality. Either same gender or different gender relationships may be entered depending on basic orientation, which should be followed.

It may be helpful to examine these options in two stages, with a preliminary comment about how they differ from each other, followed by a brief analysis of the theology of human sexuality each is based on, to connect up with what has been said previously in this chapter about arguments for and against changing the rules.

(a) The differences between the options

Option A, by making procreation the primary purpose, thereby clearly excludes all possibility of morally acceptable homosexual relationships, and also of course excludes the use of contraception to prevent procreation. This is standard Vatican teaching.

Option B, replaces 'procreation' with 'heterosexual relationship' as the primary purpose and therefore allows a fertile couple to choose not to have children. This is the orthodox Protestant view and equally excludes homosexual relationships.

Option C takes loving and sustaining relationships as the primary purpose of human sexuality, as the basic premise, and differs from Option B in understanding heterosexual marriage as an ideal expression of this purpose, but not as the *only* possible kind of relationship that could be morally acceptable. This option allows for a permission to act differently in special circumstances, while maintaining a commendation of permanent heterosexual marriage. The Gloucester Report recommendation of 1979 reflects this option, in that it was firmly committed to the understanding of human sexuality as primarily a heterosexual relationship, but allowed that there were circumstances in which homosexual relationships were justified. By changing the initial premise from heterosexuality to sustaining love, Option C widens the scope of possibilities for moral human relationships, but does not ignore the importance of marriage and children.

Option D has the widest scope for individual choice and circumstance and regards love and commitment as the primary purpose, irrespective of gender. In view of what is said above about the intention of the new morality to commend the virtues of chastity and marriage, it should be clear that Option D is in no necessary sense a weakening of the approval of permanent heterosexual relationships, family life and children. But, because it depends solely on a theology of relationships, it leaves the choice of gender for any partnership open to be decided by the direction of the sexual drive of the persons in the loving relationship. Christianly understood, this option requires the same depth of commitment as the other options though it would be thought inappropriate to use the word 'marriage' in the context of same gender relationships.

(b) The theological bases of the options

In *Option A*, the principle of 'procreation' as the primary purpose of human sexuality is being used not merely to describe an act of fertilization, but a continuum in which the male and female partners enter a commitment to each other and to the nurture of their children, and to mutual help, society and comfort in marriage. This is in fact the standard teaching the Christian church continued from the Bible and Judaism that mankind should be fruitful and multiply, and has often been described as part of the natural law. In our day, it corresponds to biological reality and social common sense. Every child should be a wanted child, and placed from its conception in a caring and perm-anent environment. Where a pregnancy occurs between unmarried people, marriage is to be commended unless there are factors which suggest that no satisfactory relationship can be established, or proper care for the child is unlikely. In fact, as every clergyman and registrar knows, a significant proportion of those women who get married are already pregnant by the man they marry. To encourage 'natural' parents to own their child, the law provides for the subsequent legitimization of the child if they marry after the child is born.

Option B takes the other biblical principle for human sexuality as primary. It is not good for man (or woman) to be alone, so marriage is understood as creating a permanent committed relationship within which the procreation of children and their nurture is a chief but not essential element. The key feature in the relationship is loving fidelity, a reflection of God's faithfulness to his people (e.g. Hosea) and Christ's bond with his church, for which 'bride' language is used in the New Testament, and in popular hymns. Children cannot be essential, partly because not all who marry are fertile, and partly because not all fertile couples wish to have children. It was once thought immoral to refuse if the capacity was there; the threat of over-population and such factors as inherited genetic defects have modified that view. The change is reflected for example in the new (ASB) order of service for marriage compared with the *Book of Common Prayer* and the 1928 revision by shifting the mention of children as a purpose of marriage from its original first position. Marriage is no longer described as a remedy against sin and to avoid fornication (1662), nor that the natural instincts and affections implanted by God should be directed aright (1928), but that with delight and tenderness they may know each other in love and through the joy of their bodily union may strengthen the union of their hearts and lives (ASB).

Option C suggests breaking the link between sexuality and pro-creation. The arguments for that link have stood the test of time, in many places and many cultures but they were in fact empirically based. The old morality was not as it was claimed strictly *'given'* by God as the sole proper expression of sexuality, but chosen to fit in with the other recognized aims of society. It suited a world where life was short, poverty threatened, childbirth was hazardous and abortion dangerous, but these considerations have now lost some of their prudential force. Since contraception has become readily available and usually effective, the choice whether or not to make love is disassociated from the requirement of a secure commitment within which sexual intercourse may lead to children. Abortion is the easy remedy for those who conceive accidentally. There need be no unwanted children. Since fornication and adultery no longer lead to pregnancy, once the all too visible sign of these irregularities, and the cause of distress and marriage break-up in the past, sex has become a private matter, decided by personal choice. In this option, hetero-sexual marriage is regarded as the ideal, and 'living together' without that permanent commitment is not, but this option seeks to come to terms with contemporary life styles.

Faced with these social changes therefore, Option C recognizes that the procreational principle has lost its force and has to be replaced. And, therefore, outside the Roman Catholic Church, a theology of sexuality has to be based on a different ground, as the ASB shows. Sex belongs to permanent relationships and commitment, the one flesh relationship of which the Bible speaks is separated from the procreational vocation, and stands on its own feet so to speak. Quite often Christian moralists will argue that it is better so. A morality deriving from relationship in fidelity is a stronger morality than one deriving from fear of pregnancy. Prudence is a weak virtue.

When the primary purpose of human sexuality was described in terms linking it with marriage and procreation, as in Options A and B, it followed that homosexual behaviour must be a sinful deviation from the norm. Recognizing that gay people are exceptions to the standard pattern, different gender coupling, they can be accepted as a special case within Option C. This seems to be what the Bishop of Chester originally intended in the 1987 General Synod debate. But his amendment 'homosexual genital behaviour falls short of the ideal', was altered by the inclusion of the requirement of repentance, moving the final decision of Synod firmly back towards Option B. There was virtually no voice expressed in that 1988 debate in favour of Option A.

Option D goes further than Option C by suggesting that it is not necessary to move from sexuality to either marriage or procreation. It shares with Option C the argument that those links were made not from the essential nature of sexuality in itself, but from an empirical assessment of how to control the always powerful instincts of human sexuality in a world less sophisticated than ours.

Those who advocate Option D concentrate on the quality of human relationships. They do not deny the empirical values needed by society in the past, but they see them as prudential rules, and negative in tone. Their effect has been, both in Judaism, from where they originally developed, and in the Christian era (notably influenced by St Augustine), to tie down Christian sexual morality in restrictive forms, and this is an ill-service of the God whose character is best declared as loving and liberating of the human predicament. With respect to homosexual people, in particular, this option suggests, restriction of their capacity to make loving and sustaining relationships with people of their own gender must be contrary to the Christian ideal.

Christian Morality versus Secular Morality

Implicit in much of the recent debate has been an assumption that there is a sharp distinction between the moral rules for Christians and the rules for everyone else. It has not always been so, but as the ways of the church and of the world have seemed to grow more and more separate, it seems an obvious conclusion to reach. We need to be clear about the status of Christian moral rules in a pluralist world where Christian belief is optional, and by no means universally accepted.

Earlier in this book, in the historical part, I paid a good deal of attention to the legal prohibitions and their modification, because that history tells us something of how society expressed its attitude to homosexual behaviour, both in the Christendom period, when Christian morality was dominant, at least officially, and through the Englightenment period when state law was slow to change traditional rules. Only in our own post-war period of liberal tolerance have there been major alterations in the law reflecting a society mixed in its faiths and agnosticisms, and with no universally agreed system of moral precepts.

The distinction between sins and crimes was made in mediaeval moral theology to allow for the fact that the Christian virtues, gentleness, kindness, self-control and similar internal dispositions of the Christian spirit were outside the ambit of legal control or enforcement. You cannot have a legal duty to be loving. But the old understanding was that social life was governed by Christian principles, or ought to be; the good Christian went a second mile in his spiritual obedience. That view of things has now been virtually lost.

This lack of a sense of universal rules has led Christians to concentrate on their own systems, but one still has to ask in what sense is Christian morality different from secular morality? There is a popular view that in a secular world Christian rules declare the will of God in contrast and often in conflict with the way of the world. This sometimes appears to be the view taken by New Testament writers, but on close examination the contrast is being drawn between particular facets of Christian and pagan morality. Clearly pagan sexual vice is one example of such sharp conflict, but we saw how Plato in his later writings set down a prohibition of homosexual behaviour as severe and in the same terms as that of St Paul.

The degree of opposition between Christian and Pagan morality is not fully or consistently worked out in the early church. Or to put that more positively, while the Jerusalem church continued to honour the basic precepts of the Decalogue, St Paul and others also respected the classical system of Greek and Roman authority and law. In his Epistle to the Romans, chapter 13, Paul commends obedience to the governing authorities because there is no authority except from God and those that exist have been instituted by God. There is seen to be a natural order which pagans can by reason and conscience discover without being Christians. As the Jews had a notion of the Noachic principles, that part of the Torah which applied to Gentiles, so the church eventually developed a doctrine of natural order and law which derives from God, but is not part of his special revelation to the church.

This doctrine of Natural Law, as worked out by mediaeval theologians like St Thomas Aquinas depended a good deal on his positive attitude to Greek thought, and in particular to Plato. It was in some ways an optimistic view of human nature and reason, and was sharply criticized by the Reformation theologians as not taking seriously enough the corruption of the Fall. Karl Barth made it a central theme of his theology that God's word and not human reason was to be the only reliable guide for Christian morality. But this doctrine does not in practice enable the Christian church to read off a solution to each and every moral problem from scripture *simpliciter*. It is a misuse and disrespect for scripture to use it as a moral code of practice. The church has always known the proper use of scripture in moral dilemmas is to establish from it the basic ground rules and then to work from them to particular precepts.

These biblically based ground rules, since they come from God and are part of his creative will, can never be unreasonable, and so can be formulated as Natural Law. The danger of Natural Law system is, however, that it can be misused, if its precepts are never subject to modification. The standard criticism of a fossilized Natural Law is that it dies the death of a thousand qualifications. New data, like new wine, cannot be put into old wineskins. That warning heeded, the tradition of Natural Law as that which is good for all people, religious and irreligious alike remains important, not only as a guide to basic principles, but also as a corrective to Christian people when they are tempted to resolve moral dilemmas by withdrawing into a private morality of their own. Moral theology's agenda is what is universally good, not merely what is good for Christians, and the prophetic task of the church is to declare God's will for the nations – *et urbe et orbe*. More philosophically expressed, this becomes the proposition that, since God is good, what he creates is good, and that is not completely destroyed by the Fall. Disobedience to the natural order does not make that order redundant. Ultimately, the rules Christians offer for managing human sexuality are not just for themselves, they are to be offered to every person in the world, straight and gay. Not every one will accept them of course, but that does not allow us an excuse for not formulating our morality in a reasonable and intellectually respectable way available for every human conscience.

The expression 'Natural Law' is generally used in the Catholic Church to maintain the position that Christian morality has this universal character, at least potentially, but since the Enlightenment it has to some extent been replaced in other churches by appeal to a system of human rights. These rights are set down in such documents as the United Nations Declaration, and various Conventions that flow from them, and Gay Lib has often claimed such rights as the moral basis of their own appeal. When one asks how Human Rights are to be identified, the answer has to be from reason and conscience, which amounts to much the same as the traditional argument for Natural Law. The secular claim to universal human rights therefore points to the same truth as the Christian natural law, that God's good order is available to every person.

The Way Forward: Some Personal Conclusions

Readers who have reached this point will, I hope, feel that although for a short book on a complex subject, there has had to be much compression and selection, the various views have been recorded without too much bias or polemic. My own position at present, and it is possibly typical of many *via media* Anglicans, is to feel most sympathy with a solution that includes the perspectives of Option C, but recognizes that the churches are at the moment more comfortable with Option B.

Stating my own view in this way does not mean I want to deny any value to either the traditional procreational view of Option A, nor find the arguments of Option D totally false. In a church attentive to the leading of the Spirit which comes to us also by honest reflection on the data given in and by God's world, what Gay Lib, and personalist ethics about human sexuality have to say to us has to be taken seriously. The only way forward, it seems to me, is to recognize that all four options are witnessing to some element of truth the Christians must hear and assess in this polyphonic world.

It is not possible in Christian thought to dismiss the procreational argument altogether. Any serious theological appraisal of the facts of human life and sexuality must include a statement about the opportunity human beings have to pass on their life to the next generation, and affirm that as part of God's creative order. The population explosion and limitation of resources arguments demand that the freedom to procreate is no longer absolute, it has to be qualified by these realities, as it does by the willingness of parents to take responsibility for any children they plan to conceive. But the witness to the positive value of procreation must not be tied to any outdated claim to what is natural. The content of the word 'nature' changes as human understanding of it moves on. The complexities of modern science about for example sub-atomic particles and the basic 'stuff' from which the universe is built up warns us that all descriptions of what is natural are only models, temporary explanations which serve until modified or replaced. It is said by modern scientists that Einstein's theory of relativity is outdated, but adequate enough for reaching the moon. Similarly, the theory that all homosexual behaviour was a wilfully chosen perversion of nature can no longer be sustained.

The relational argument equally bears witness to a fundamental truth about humanity, that we are two genders who live side by side on this planet, and have to acknowledge each other as equal persons. The mystery of the Christian sacrament by which 'the twain become one flesh' places this complementarity into a new dimension, allowing humans the opportunity not just to come together for breeding. In marriage, we incorporate the biological function into a deeper and wider entity of loving and permanent association. Jack Dominian has described modern marriage as a 'sustaining' relationship in which friendship and the whole range of being a person, male or female, physically and psychologically can be discovered, explored and developed, and sometimes changed, by a life long commitment. It is more than a contract 'for better for worse', it is an opportunity for dynamic growth as persons.[2]

The homosexual minority cannot belong with integrity to a community which declares sexuality to be concerned solely with procreation, except perhaps in the minimal sense of fostering a child, or more obliquely by following vocations which include the care or education of other people's children. But their condition does allow them to enjoy many aspects of relational sexuality, its complementarity, its friendship and emotional security, and for those who judge that right, physically. A gay couple deeply committed to each other can undoubtedly have a sustaining and developing relationship which helps them to grow dynamically as persons, and, they would say, to grow as Christians by sharing together something of the generosity of love. A positive rule for them has to be based on some recognition that their circumstances do not allow them to follow the procreational principle, but in other respects fulfils the relational criterion.

To allow homosexual people to make their own choice between abstinence and sustaining same gender relationships is not to be entirely personalist, but it can not be made to fit within the old kind of 'against nature' and procreational arguments. It seems to me that the cause of Gay Lib has been seriously damaged by the assumption that personalist or situationalist ethics is ruleless. As I have tried to show above, divine love leads to commandments which set the patterns for its expression. In John Robinson's phrase, 'conventions and laws are the dykes of love in a wayward and loveless world'.[3] A dyke has two forms; it can be a ditch or trench through which water can usefully flow, or it can be a wall to hold back the water from doing damage. A moral rule therefore can be the means by which God's love flows usefully into the world. It can also be a wall by which God protects human beings from actions which would harm them. And most often a godly rule serves both purposes at once. The Christian rule that sexuality is to be expressed within marriage, channels love into fulfilment and also protects love against its trivialization in temporary affairs. A Christian rule about love between same-sex people could channel their love into permanent relationships, and protect them from the degradation of one night stands as a false solution to the condition of being loved by no one. I do not see that radical step being taken by any of the churches at the moment, but it fits with the pastoral concern expressed in the 1979 Gloucester Report.

Perhaps that suggestion failed to win broader acceptance because it was expressed in somewhat hesitant language. It did not spell out what circumstances would justify the choice of a homosexual relationship which included physical expression. No one can prescribe in advance exactly what intimate actions a pair of people in love may feel suits their condition, so it may have been better to speak of a pastoral permission to choose what is right for them, with no further definition than that used for example for married love in the ASB. They must find their own equivalent of the opportunity to comfort and help each other, living faithfully together in need and in plenty, in sorrow and in joy.[4]

NOTES AND BIBLIOGRAPHY

Detailed notes to individual chapters are in some instances followed by a list of titles for general reference

2. Understanding Homosexuality

1. Alan P. Bell and Martin S. Weinberg, *Homosexuality: A Study of Diversity among Men and Women*, Mitchell Beazley 1978, p. 231.

2. June M. Reinisch, *The Study of Sexual Behaviour in Relation to HIV*, The Kinsey Institute, Indiana University, and the American Psychologist Magazine, Nov. 1988, pp. 921–7.

3. Elizabeth R. Moberly, *Psychogenesis: The Early Development of Gender Identity*, Routledge & Kegan Paul 1983, and *Homosexuality: A New Christian Ethic*, James Clarke 1983, particularly chs 1 and 2.

4. Sigmund Freud, The Pelican Freud Library, ed. Angela Richards, Vol. 7, *On Sexuality*, Penguin Books 1977, p. 46.

5. Plato, *The Symposium*, trans. W. Hamilton, Penguin Books 1978, Speech of Aristophanes, pp. 59–65.

6. Plato, *The Laws*, trans. T. J. Saunders, Penguin Books 1975, p. 340.

7. Montgomery Hyde, *The Trials of Oscar Wilde*, William Hodge 1948, p. 236.

8. Jack Babuscio, *We Speak for Ourselves: The Experiences of Gay Men and Lesbians*, SPCK 1976, new edition 1988, p. 5, reproduced by permission.

9. Ibid., p. 6.

10. Ibid., p. 8.

11. Donald Eadie (ed.), *Dear God I'm Gay*, GIG Publications 1989.

12. Ibid., pp. 44–46.

13. Ibid., pp. 33–37.

14. David P. McWhirter and Andrew M. Mattison, *The Male Couple*, Prentice-Hall 1987.

15. Ibid., pp. 81ff.

Wainwright Churchill, *Homosexual Behaviour among Males*, Hawthorn 1967
G. Parrinder, *Sex in the World's Religions*, Sheldon Press 1980
John Bancroft and W. A. Frank, in *Sex and Gender*, ed. M. S. Schwarz and A. S. Moreczewski, Pope John XXIII Centre, St. Louis, Miss. 1983, chs 4 and 5
John Bancroft, *Human Sexuality and Its Problems*, second edition, Churchill Livingstone 1989, especially chs 3 and 6

Chris Glaser, *Uncommon Calling – A Gay Man's Struggle to Serve the Church*, Harper & Row 1988

3. The Old Testament

1. Gerhard von Rad, *Genesis*, SCM Press and Westminster Press 1981, pp. 215–22.
2. D. Sherwin Bailey, *Homosexuality and the Western Christian Tradition*, Longmans 1955, pp. 1–28; and see for comparison, John Boswell, *Christianity, Social Tolerance and Homosexuality*, University of Chicago Press 1980, pp. 90–97.
3. J. Alberto Soggin, *Judges*, SCM Press and Westminster Press 1981, pp. 283–89.
4. Martin Noth, *Leviticus*, SCM Press and Westminster Press 1977, pp. 127ff. and *The Laws in the Pentateuch*, SCM Press 1984, pp. 20–28.
5. Dale Patrick, *Old Testament Law*, SCM Press and John Knox Press 1986, pp. 145–62.
6. D. J. Atkinson, *Homosexuals in the Christian Fellowship*, Latimer House, Oxford 1979, pp. 82–86.

John Barton, *People of the Book? – the Authority of the Bible in Christianity*, SPCK and Westminster Press 1988

4. The Inter-testamental Period

1. James H. Charlesworth (ed.), *The Old Testament Pseudepigrapha, Vol. 1: Apocalyptic Literature and Testaments*, Doubleday and Darton, Longman and Todd 1983.
2. II Enoch 10.4, in Charlesworth, op. cit., p. 118.
3. Sibylline Oracles Book 3: 183–87, Charlesworth, op. cit., p. 366.
4. Sibylline Oracles, Book 3: 590–600, Charlesworth, op. cit., p. 375.
5. Mishnah, Sanhedrin 7.4, trans H. Danby, Oxford University Press 1933, p. 391.
6. Josephus, *The Jewish War*, Penguin edition 1981, p. 273.
7. *Philo*, Loeb Classical Library Vol. 7, Heinemann and Harvard University Press, p. 499.

5. The New Testament

1. Robin Lane Fox, *Pagans and Christians*, Viking 1986, pp. 340–51.
2. Everett Ferguson, *Backgrounds of Early Christianity*, Eerdmans 1987, pp. 75–6.
3. Ibid., pp. 53–8, and Jane F. Gardner, *Women in Roman Law and Society*, Croom Helm 1986, chs 2 and 4.
4. Robin Scroggs, *The New Testament and Homosexuality*, Fortress Press 1983, chs 3 and 4.
5. Walter Burkert, *Greek Religion*, trans. John Raffan, Blackwell 1985, p. 292.
6. TACITUS, *Annals*, Penguin edition 1956, p. 351.
7. Lane Fox, op. cit., pp. 351ff.
8. This text has been scrutinized by many authors, e.g., Bailey, op. cit., pp.

38–40, Atkinson, op. cit., pp. 86–90, Scroggs, op. cit., pp. 14–16, and Boswell, op. cit., pp. 107ff.

9. Karl Barth, *Church Dogmatics*, III.4, T. & T. Clark 1961, pp. 164–66, quoted in Edward Batchelor Jr (ed.), *Homosexuality and Ethics*, Pilgrim Press 1980, pp. 48–51.

10. See above p. 65. *Midrash Rabbah Genesis*, ed. Freedman and Simon, Soncino Press 1939, p. 338.

11. See below ch. 8, p. 169.

12. Scroggs, op. cit., Appendix A, pp. 130–39.

John Stambaugh and David Balch, *The Social World of the First Christians*, SPCK and Westminster Press 1986

Wayne Meeks, *The Moral World of the First Christians*, SPCK and Westminster Press 1986

C. K. Barrett, *The Epistle to the Romans*, A. & C. Black 1962

C. K. Barrett, *The First Epistle to the Corinthians*, A & C. Black 1967

C. H. Dodd, *The Epistle of Paul to the Romans*, Collins Fontana 1959

6. From St Paul to Sir John Wolfenden 1957

1. D. Sherwin Bailey, *Homosexuality and the Western Christian Tradition*, Longmans 1955.

2. John Boswell, *Christianity, Social Tolerance and Homosexuality*, University of Chicago Press 1980.

3. Peter Brown, *The Body and Society*, Faber & Faber and University of Chicago Press 1988.

4. John A. T. Robinson, *Honest to God*, SCM Press 1963, and Alastair Heron, *Towards a Quaker View of Sex*, Friends Home Service Committee 1963.

5. The Didache, *Early Christian Fathers*, Library of Christian Classics, SCM Press and Westminster Press 1953, p. 172.

6. Aline Rousselle, *Porneia: On Desire and the Body in Antiquity*, Blackwell 1988, pp. 128–40.

7. Brown, op. cit., p. 383.

8. St Augustine, *Confessions*, trans. E. B. Pusey, Everyman edition, Dent 1939, p. 43.

9. Epp. 211.14, trans. W. K. L. Clarke.

10. Brown, op. cit., pp. 420ff.

11. Boswell, op. cit., p. 153.

12. *Cleanness*, Oxford University Press 1974, pp. 32–3.

13. G. K. A. Bell, *Randal Davidson*, Oxford University Press, third edition 1952, pp. 786–89.

14. For the Commons Debate, see *Hansard*, vol. 526, cols 1745–56.

15. For the Lords Debate, see *Hansard*, vol. 187, cols 737–45.

H. Montgomery Hyde, *The Other Love*, Heinemann 1970

Peter Wildeblood, *Against the Law*, Penguin Books 1957

T. Rees and H. Usill, *They Stand Alone*, Heinemann 1955

D. J. West, *Homosexuality Re-examined*, fourth edition, Duckworth 1977

Jeffrey Weeks, Coming Out, Quartet Books 1977

7. The Limits of Tolerance Shift – 1957–1979

1. Home Office, *Report of the Committee on Homosexual Offences and Prostitution*, Cmnd. 247, HMSO 1957, para. 52, p. 21.
2. John Robinson, *Honest to God*, SCM Press 1963.
3. Published by the Church Information Board and edited by D. S. Bailey. Appendix 1 had appeared in Rees and Usill, *They Stand Alone*.
4. Church Assembly, *Report of Proceedings*, vol. 37, pp. 441–79.
5. Methodist Church Citizenship Department, Report 1958.
6. *Towards a Quaker View of Sex*, p. 36.
7. Norman Pittinger, *Time for Consent*, SCM Press 1976, pp. 97–8.
8. *Honest to God*, pp. 105ff.
9. LGCM is listed in the 1989 Year Book, no address, but they have in fact moved to Oxford House, Derbyshire Street, London E2 6HG, telephone 01–739 1249.
10. Vatican Declaration 1975. Text in *L'Osservatore Romano*, 22, Jan. 1976, sec. 8, and Catholic Truth Society, p. 10.
11. *Human Sexuality – New Directions in Catholic Thought*, ed. A. Kosnik, The Catholic Theological Society of America and Search Press 1977.
12. *Dei Verbum*, Catholic Truth Society 1987.
13. Cf. Wolfenden Report, pp. 66–7.
14. *Homosexuality*, Confidential Report, Board of Social Responsibility 1970.
15. *A Christian Understanding of Human Sexuality*, Division of Social Responsibility, Methodist Church 1979.
16. *Homosexual Relationships: A Contribution to Discussion*, Board for Social Responsibility, Church Information Office 1979, reproduced by permission.

Rachel Moss (ed.), *God's Yes to Sexuality*, The Report of the British Council of Churches, Collins Fount 1981
Jim Cotter, *Good Fruits: Same-sex Relationships and Christian Faith*, Cairns Publications 1988
Michael Ruse, *Homosexuality: A Philosophical Enquiry*, Blackwell 1988

8. A Decade of Indecision – 1979–89

1. The Lambeth Conference Report, CIO Publishing 1978, pp. 63–65.
2. General Synod, February Group of Sessions 1981, Report of Proceedings, Vol. 12, no. 1, CIO Publishing 1981, reproduced by permission.
3. Ibid., p. 411.
4. Ibid., p. 414.
5. Atkinson, *Homosexuals in the Christian Fellowship*, Latimer House 1979.
6. Synod Report, Vol. 12, no. 1, 1981, pp. 434–5.
7. General Synod, November Group of Sessions 1987, Report of Proceedings, Vol. 18, no. 3, Church House Publishing 1987, p. 913, reproduced by permission.
8. Tony Higton (ed.), *Sexuality and the Church*, Action for Biblical Witness to Our Nation 1987.
9. Synod Report, Vol. 18, no. 3, 1987, p. 919.
10. Ibid., pp. 291–3.

11. Ibid., pp. 923–5.

12. Ibid., pp. 930–32.

13. Ibid., pp. 955–6.

14. Eric James, 'Homosexuality and a Pastoral Church: A Plea for Study and Discussion', Christian Action and Modern Churchpeople's Union 1988.

15. *The Truth Shall Make You Free*, The Lambeth Conference 1988, Reports, Resolutions and Pastoral Letters from the Bishops, for Anglican Consultative Council, Church House Publishing 1988, reproduced by permission.

16. Alan Nichols, Joan Clarke and Trevor Hogan, *Transforming Families and Communities: Christian Hope in a World of Change*, for Anglican Consultative Council, AIO Press 1987.

17. *The Truth Shall Make You Free*, p. 187; see Resolution 64.

18. Ibid., p. 188.

19. Ibid., pp. 189–91.

20. Ibid., p. 237, Resolution 64.

9. *The Church with a Human Face*

1. Edward Schillebeeckx, *The Church with a Human Face*, SCM Press 1985.

2. Jack Dominian, *Marriage, Faith and Love*, Darton, Longman and Todd 1981, ch. 4.

3. *Honest to God*, p. 118.

4. The *Alternative Service Book* 1980, p. 288.

INDEX